To Dave + Pat Williams
all the best! Donna

the reasons I have always th~
luckiest one—to have you a
often tell stories about "what ~ght
me" and "what my father did w..n us growing
up" . . . and "how my father influenced me."
Your influence goes on and on, Dad.
I realize more and more as I grow older that
I had no ordinary childhood. We were lucky
to have parents who were fully involved and
always there, who cared about all the things
we were doing and actively participated in all
aspects. Other people are amazed when I tell
them my childhood experiences and about all
the things we did together.
So I cherish the memories of Stratton Mt
skiing, football and running races in Mr.
Clark's field, Yankee Stadium, the flat tire
on the way to Fenway Park, foul-shooting
contests, playing catch, Madastone camping,
cross-country family trips, skijoring and hot-
dog roasting, tomato soup and grilled cheese
sandwiches, Ho Chi... Trail . . .

EVERY Sunday

A Father and Daughter's Enduring Connection

Donna W. Dearborn

DONNA W. DEARBORN

WW PUBLISHING
CHESTER, VERMONT

WW PUBLISHING
CHESTER, VERMONT

EverySundayMemoir@gmail.com
www.EverySunday.net

ISBN: 978-0-9912053-0-1

Cover and text design by John Reinhardt Book Design

Printed in the United States of America

PHOTO CREDITS / PERMISSIONS

All photographs by the author and her family, except for the following:
Pool dedication, page 164, *Brattleboro Reformer*
Senior Center, page 165, *Brattleboro Reformer*
Retirement article, page 205, *Brattleboro Reformer*
Presentation to George Aiken, page 205, *Brattleboro Reformer*
With Theresa Brungardt, page 207, Vermont Recreation and Parks Association
With George Plumb, page 207, Vermont Recreation and Parks Association
Washington's Birthday Cross-Country Ski Race, page 242, Lewis R. Brown, Inc.
Recreation Department office, page 324, *Brattleboro Reformer*

Grateful acknowledgment for permission of the Springfield College Archives and Special Collections to reproduce a column from The *Student* (April 13, 1951), page 318.

To Dad,
with Love

ACKNOWLEDGMENTS

I WOULD LIKE TO THANK Jeff Monseau at Springfield College Archives for piling my desk high with Springfield *Student* newspapers and helping me reconnect with my dad through the sports columns he wrote years ago.

Thank you to Jan Frazier for the inspiring and safe atmosphere of her writing groups and my fellow writers for their feedback and encouragement in the early stages of this book. I greatly appreciate Susan Hunt and Nancy Stiller reading initial drafts and giving me their valuable insights. Thank you to Margaret O'Connell for her keen eye, willingness, and generosity.

Profound gratitude to my editor, Kate Gleason, for her invaluable guidance and vision and the great pleasure of working with her.

Special thanks to John Reinhardt who provided extraordinary support, just when I needed it, and for his design expertise, unwavering enthusiasm, and heartfelt embrace of this project.

Above all, I am indebted to my family—to my dad who showed the way—with grace—and to my mother for her support and living life with exuberance. Thanks and love to my husband, Wally, for his unending patience and belief and forever appreciating the importance of this endeavor. He is my rock and I am indeed blessed to share my life with him.

"My father gave me the greatest gift anyone could give another person, he believed in me."

JIM VALVANO

ONE

ON A DRIZZLY SEPTEMBER SUNDAY, I sat in the nursing home with a man who looked exactly like my father but had to be an impostor, this silent man with far-off eyes. I looked deep into them for signs of a response, answers to my questions, something, anything. It seemed like he'd been sitting in a wheelchair forever, two years feeling like an eternity. Could this be the same man who had counseled and mentored me, the charismatic leader and expert communicator who had a special touch with people?

My weekly Sunday visits brought to mind our letter writing tradition that we'd started when I went away to college and continued for more than thirty years—every Sunday—no matter where we were or what we were doing. I always looked forward to Dad's Sunday epistles. *I write your letter*, he penned, *as a matter of priority instead of waiting until I have time, for I don't usually have much time and you—yes, you—are prime priority, like the State of the Union message*. Or: *Just a few thoughts this morning for our talented, creative, energetic daughter. We love you and are proud of you. If you weren't our daughter we'd adopt you.*

I took his right hand, the one that wasn't paralyzed, and squeezed it. "Dad," I said again. "I brought you two clippings from one of your old letters to me."

He turned his eyes to meet mine and squeezed my hand back. After a few long minutes, he said my name which he seemed to retrieve from somewhere deep inside. Even though he didn't talk much these days, he never failed to know who I was.

Could this be the same Frank Dearborn who'd co-written the sports columns for his college newspaper that he'd sent me long ago and I'd brought to show him? I looked down at the two yellowed pages in my lap. The column was titled "To Be Frank and Earnest," named after himself and his co-writer Ernie Hoffman.

"Do you remember writing this one, Dad?" I began to read aloud:

> A whole week has gone by since the birth of our column, and as yet there hasn't been any burning in effigy, nor any throwing of rotten eggs and tomatoes. As neophytes to this game of sports writing, we hope these signs mean somewhat the same as the old saying, "No news is good news." And so we feel brave enough to warm up the typewriter for a second trip. We do welcome and encourage comments, material, and suggestions you fellows may have to offer. And if you are one of the few Massasoit tribe members who can afford to buy rotten eggs and tomatoes, we even welcome those too if they're legitimately aimed (Springfield College *Student*, April 13, 1951).

No response. His brown eyes darted from side to side as he fidgeted with the edge of his sweatshirt.

"Here's part of the final column you wrote a year later:"

> It doesn't seem possible that just a year ago the Good Ship "To Be Frank and Earnest" was launched on the crest of a new wave

> of sports writing in "The Student." After a year of at times bumpy nautical sailing, it's hard to fathom that the two coal stokers who provided the coal to keep the ship going, after a short year, must now put down their shovels, stop the engines, and scuttle the ship…
>
> We were looking at the ship's log the other day and were struck with the realization that the sea of sports we were privileged to navigate on certainly had its beautiful and thrilling aspects…
>
> And now we two coal stokers have received word that a new ship, fresh with new designs and inventions, is about to be launched this Spring. Yes, from the cradle to the grave in one year—but what wonderful sailing! In all sincerity, it was great to have all you readers on board. The engines stop, the coal stokers jump overboard to safety, and the Good Ship sinks to its grave with a final sighing…GLUB! (The *Student*, March 7, 1952).

I looked back at the man across from me who couldn't possibly be my father. But his plastic wrist bracelet confirmed—"Frank Dearborn 107-1 Shafer," like a statistic, a prisoner.

Approaching the summit of Mount Washington.

Leaving Lakes of the Clouds Hut, we inch east from cairn to cairn in the pea soup fog and clouds.

TWO

I SAW DAD sitting next to the piano in the nursing home dining room. At first glance, he looked like my dear, old dad, with a fresh shave, recent haircut, and wearing his favorite blue plaid shirt.

I stooped down and gave him a hearty bear hug. As he kissed my cheek, he squeezed me with his strong right arm, his paralyzed left arm and wrist contorted in permanent flexion. With his muscles long ago atrophied in his motionless left leg, he was unable to walk, even stand. Alive, but not living, at least not his idea of living. As a recreation director and in retirement, he'd been always on the go: walking, hiking, exploring, playing, traveling, loving life and all it had to offer. Was this what life had to offer?

Was this truly the vigorous man who skied with me through snowy Vermont woods, hit scorching forehands on the tennis court, and threw long bombs for touchdowns on the football field? Was this my adventurous father who hiked the highest mountain in the northeast and braved white-out conditions with Mom and me?

I THOUGHT BACK to that day when Dad, Mom, and I hauled ourselves up yet another steep section of the Lion's Head Trail in the White Mountains, using sturdy roots for handholds. Cooler air and breezes refreshed us. Stopping to catch our breath, we peered over at treacherous snow- and ice-filled Tuckerman Ravine.

"Sorry, Dad," I said, "we can't take the Tuckerman Ravine Trail. I know that's the route you had your heart set on."

"That's okay. I can see why it's still closed. I wouldn't want to attempt it with all that ice!"

"It's the middle of July!" Mom said. "I can't believe there's that much snow and ice here."

"Well, this is Mount Washington, Mom—it's another world up here."

At least we were within sight of the impressive ravine. My ruddy-complexioned dad sat there in awe of our surroundings, a model of pure contentedness. In his royal blue shirt, navy blue Milford Track baseball cap with matching navy socks, he was a strikingly handsome man of the mountains, even at age sixty-nine.

"Mom, over here, hang on to this knob," I suggested to my diminutive mother.

"I need longer legs for this!" she lamented.

She always wished she had longer legs and here is where it would have helped being taller than five feet two inches. Yet my feisty mother didn't let her short stature keep her from scaling the rock slabs and scampering up steep, slippery gullies. Rugged calf muscles set off her well-toned legs which propelled her steadily up any incline. I looked down the slope to see her bobbing head of gray, perfectly-permed hair, red bandanna in one hand, two-water-bottle fanny pack around her waist. She thrived in the mountains, free of worries and easy to be with.

We had over four thousand feet of elevation to gain from Pinkham Notch where we had spent the previous night at the Joe Dodge Lodge and enjoyed a sumptuous family-style dinner feast. Dad happily swapped stories with six enthusiastic hikers from Georgia and North Carolina.

At 6:30 we had loaded up with pancakes and eggs at the Pinkham Notch all-you-can-eat breakfast buffet and started up the mountain to reach the 6288-foot-high summit of Mount Washington. We had reservations at Lakes of the Clouds Hut, a ninety-bunk Appalachian Mountain Club facility situated on a five thousand foot shelf near the foot of Mount Monroe. We had overnighted at Galehead, Zealand, Carter Notch, and Mizpah, but this one had eluded us.

"This is exciting!" Dad said. "How many times have we walked past there and wished we were staying?"

"I wouldn't be doing this if you weren't with us, Donna," Mom added, revealing confidence in her Outward Bound instructor daughter, on board if I was their planner and guide. Besides, Mom and I had had an understanding for a long time—I would carry her sleeping bag and extra clothes if she would continue to go on overnight outings.

"I'm glad we can do this!" I added. I had the perfect window of opportunity between Outward Bound courses and the chance to have an adventure with my most faithful hiking partners.

"This is a good spot to put on another layer," I suggested, as we reached the Alpine Garden, winds whipping and temperature dropping. We donned our windbreakers.

Respecting the unforgiving nature of this mountain, we had filled our packs with extra clothes, food, and emergency gear—whistles, headlamps, matches, a lighter, Swiss army knife, an ensolite pad, space blanket, and a first aid kit easily accessible—just in case.

"Did you notice what they were wearing, Dad?" I whispered, after we passed a couple in cotton T-shirts and sandals.

"Yes, can you believe it?"

Not surprisingly, we passed many hikers who were not prepared with proper clothing and footwear, as many people flock to the White

Mountains with the solitary goal of climbing the prestigious highest peak, vastly underestimating the strenuous nature of the climb.

Later, a father hunched over his shivering daughter, whose hiking boot had broken apart. My roll of tape enabled him to cinch her boot together so she could resume the climb and get warm.

Straight ahead loomed the ominous sign, a reminder that many hikers have died on Mount Washington, perhaps victim of the unpredictable changes in temperature, wind, or precipitation that are commonplace on this mountain. "STOP," the sign warns. "The area ahead has the worst weather in America. Many have died there from exposure, even in the summer. TURN BACK NOW if the weather is bad."

We didn't have to turn back, for we could see for miles on this unusually clear day, enabling us to identify some of the other peaks of the Presidential Range: Madison, Adams, Jefferson, and one of our favorites, Eisenhower. Dad and Mom devoured handfuls of deluxe GORP, a tasty mixture of peanuts, raisins, cashews, almonds, M&Ms, and dried fruit that energized us.

"We're almost there!" I shouted.

We carefully made our way over false summits and loose rocks until we reached the summit.

"Five hours—that's not too bad," Dad said.

Even though we had been to the summit numerous times, it remained a thrill to climb the tallest peak in the Northeast where the highest wind speed in the world, 231 miles per hour, was recorded in 1934. Dad and Mom had first hiked Mount Washington forty-four years earlier, a few months after I was born. At age sixty-nine and sixty-eight, they stayed strong and lean, even fitter than in their earliest hiking days. We stepped from the rugged rocky trail and peered out from under our windbreaker hoods to see a sharp contrast to our world of the previous five hours.

The summit held buildings, cars, kids in strollers, women in high heels, and license plates from all over the country.

"It's crazy, isn't it?" Dad said. "We sweated and climbed for five hours and these people just drove up."

"Most of them couldn't do what you just did, Dad. Good job, Mom, Dad. How about some soup? Might as well take advantage of the amenities."

On board immediately, Dad never turned down an offer of food. Mom readily agreed.

After our soup break, Dad said, "Which is our trail? There are so many."

"Right here, the Crawford Path," I said. "Follow these cairns and white blazes. We're on the Appalachian Trail for the rest of the day. Only 1.4 miles to Lakes of the Clouds Hut," I said.

Leaving the summit pandemonium behind, we followed giant rock cairns south on the renowned Crawford Path, passing hikers going in all directions on the extensive network of trails on the flank of Mount Washington. Thick, gray clouds suddenly filled the sky, just as we reached the hut. We gladly set down our packs as we gained protection from the imminent storm.

"I'll go check us in," I said.

After I confirmed our reservation, I hurried into one of the bunkrooms to claim the coveted, easy-access bottom bunks for both Mom and Dad. Triple bunks reached to the ceiling.

Heavy rain and high winds soon battered the hut. Hikers continued to burst through the doorway until the hut's capacity of ninety was reached. Consistent with the unpredictability of Mount Washington weather, the storm dissipated and we were able to go back outside and explore the alpine environment of lakes, fragile plants, and rock outcrops.

Dad enjoyed conversing with many fascinating people, especially a friendly, older man from Rhode Island. This brave minister had taken thirteen teenage kids for a week-long trip in the White Mountains. A shy mother, there with her young daughter and a friend, had never looked out upon such a spectacular scene. Experienced and well-equipped hikers shared the bunkrooms with novices on their very first hut trip.

Even with so many people in such a small space, the hut crew flawlessly served a top rate lasagna dinner to ninety hungry hikers in no time—fresh-baked bread, tossed salad, lasagna, and cake for dessert, served in a family-style atmosphere conducive to sharing the day's adventures with others. The skies cleared, enabling us to see a hundred miles west into Vermont and New York, especially the distinctive profile of Camel's Hump. Dad, Mom, and I lingered outside the hut, captivated by the views and brilliant setting sun.

In the morning we awoke to yet another weather change, winds of more than fifty miles per hour pummeling the hut. Completely socked in with clouds, visibility was five feet at best. It was the exact opposite of the clear skies we observed when we went to bed.

"Wow, look outside, Dad," I said, surprised at this unexpected change in the weather.

"What are we going to do?"

We decided to wait for the eight o'clock weather report from the summit observatory and carefully consider our options. Unfortunately, the report only confirmed what we already knew, plus the dismal forecast that no immediate improvement in the weather was predicted.

We talked over our options, my parents a stark contrast in personality and style. Deliberate and patient, Dad wanted to understand all the options and information and consider all angles. On the other hand, Mom favored quick decisions. Impulsive and always on-the-go, she preferred to act—immediately. Dad was ready to sit at the table, sip hot chocolate, observe the weather a bit longer and go through our options one more time. Mom paced nervously, anxious about the harsh conditions awaiting us. I felt immense responsibility.

"Are you comfortable heading down?" I asked them.

"We're ready—whatever you think is best," Dad confirmed their complete faith in me.

"Let's go," said Mom, halfway to the door already and glad to finally be underway.

Game to head down the mountain, my parents felt secure under the leadership of their daughter who had taught navigation to Outward Bound students and came equipped with map and compass.

Even though it was the middle of the summer, we dressed for winter in our warm hats and gloves with a rugged windproof shell covering two layers beneath it. Inching east from cairn to cairn into the pea soup fog and clouds, within seconds we could no longer see the hut, visibility two to three feet at best. The severity of the situation hit me. We were three little bundled up, huddled souls in a sea of uniform gray, surrounded by clouds, fog, and gray orthoclase granite. I relied solely on compass and map to navigate us to The Camel, ledges that resemble a kneeling camel. We walked hunched over, closer to the ground so we could brace ourselves against the wind gusts and hang on to a cairn or rock outcrop for balance.

I turned around and couldn't see my mother who was last in line behind my father. I felt a chill race down my spine. She liked to be last in line, so she could feel comfortable walking her own pace. This day I wanted us in a compact column, close enough to be able to reach out and touch one another at any time.

"Mom!" I shouted. It was difficult to hear words amidst the deafening wind blasts.

"I'm here," came the faint reply.

"Mom, I'm putting this whistle around your neck. Blow it immediately, loudly if you can't see Dad."

I took frequent bearings using the map and compass to ensure that we were heading the right direction. They could see that even I was challenged to the utmost. Another gust of wind nearly blew us flat. Mom was silent. My usually talkative dad was subdued.

I knew my mother was still there when I heard her say, "This feels like an Outward Bound course!"

Mom had declared that she did not want to take an Outward Bound course, at least how she envisioned a course. I took Mom's words as a signal that she felt out of her comfort zone, that place we encourage Outward Bound students to venture into, just beyond the familiar and comfortable in order to be challenged and grow. Mom's idea of fun was to avoid survival mode.

Dad tended to get cold easily, so I kept a close eye on him and made sure he wasn't shivering. It was imperative that we stay together, look after each other, and quickly navigate to lower elevations. This was beyond an Outward Bound challenge, for there was much more at stake—these were my parents, my treasured parents who put their complete trust in me.

Three fuzzy forms appeared in the distance, like apparitions moving toward us. Three young kids garbed in skimpy, cotton street clothes made their way to the summit, without packs, extra clothes, or food. Disappearing before we could even say a word, they seemed determined, foolhardy, and oblivious to the dangerous and potentially life-threatening conditions ahead.

We immediately focused back on our own task, plodding steadily down Mount Washington, which was certainly living up to its reputation.

"Here's the Davis Path! We're doing well!" I said. "Are you warm enough Mom, Dad? Are you OK?"

Our threesome rejoiced at each junction with a trail sign, relieved we were on our way to lower elevations. Eventually the Davis Path led us to the prominent rock outcrop, Boott Spur. Careful to avoid the edge of Hanging Cliff, we steadily dropped to the Boott Spur Link. Not until we had descended to an elevation of nearly 4300 feet at Split Rock did we finally dip below the ferocious cloud cap and extricate ourselves from the scary windblown environment.

"Can you believe it's this clear and sunny down here?" I asked, ecstatic in relief.

What a sharp contrast as we crossed over the dividing line between the stormy summit above and the green valleys of Shangri-La below. Smiles replaced solemn, serious looks.

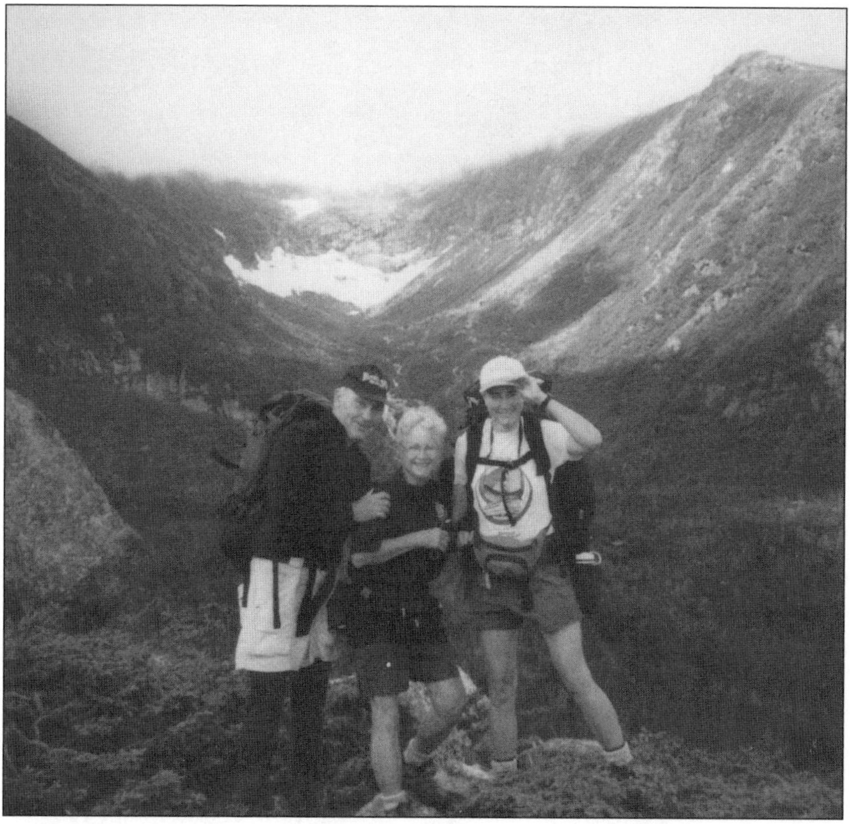

Tuckerman Ravine comes into view while hiking down Mount Washington on the Boott Spur Trail.

"That was really something. It's good to finally sit down and take a break," Dad said, in his typical understated way, starting to relax, yet still shaken by the intensity of our ordeal.

"Well, you always wanted to stay at Lakes of the Clouds Hut. We did it," I said. "That's not quite how you envisioned it. You never know what will happen in the White Mountains."

For the previous two hours we had not been able to stop or relax, so we sat on the Split Rock promontory and let the built-up tension flow out of our muscles. The three of us drank water, snacked, and savored distant views for the first time that day, relieved and grateful.

Always on the go—hiking, biking, running, and skiing.

THREE

WHO WOULD HAVE EVER thought this vigorous man would suffer a stroke? Not Frank Dearborn—no! Not the vibrant recreation director and community's role model for health and fitness.

On August 31st, Dad and I had written our Sunday letters as usual. We had celebrated Dad and Mom's anniversary at our house and played tennis, only three days before my husband, Wally, and I drove to northern Ontario to start our wilderness canoe trip.

I MADE ONE last phone call home—eleven days until the next one. Early the next morning a floatplane would deposit Wally, our Labrador, Gerda, and me in remote Scarecrow Lake in northwestern Temagami. I called Dad and Mom to let them know we'd made it safely to Auld Reekie Lodge in Gowganda, Ontario—675 miles from home.

"Hi, Mom. We made it to the lodge—we're flying out first thing tomorrow morning," I said. "How are you doing?"

"David just took Dad to the hospital."

"No, Mom! What's wrong?"

"He thought Dad was slurring his words...the left side of his face drooped a little," she said in a subdued tone.

"Oh, no! I can't believe that, Mom. Had you noticed anything unusual today?"

"No, he played tennis with John this morning. We took a walk after that and then he just finished mowing the lawn. I didn't really notice anything." Mom was all matter-of-fact.

"Oh...Mom...I hope he's doing okay. I wish I wasn't so far away—it took us almost fifteen hours to drive here. I feel so helpless. I want to know everything you find out. Call me as soon as you know anything!"

I walked unsteadily back to our table where dinner had just been served.

"What's wrong?" Wally said, as soon as he saw my face.

"It's Dad. David is driving him to the hospital right now because he was slurring his words."

"Oh, no, honey."

"I don't have a good feeling about it—I'm really concerned. I hate to say it, but it sounds like a stroke. I can't believe it—not Dad—I hope I'm wrong."

My appetite vanished. All I could think about was how inconceivable it was that Dad was having a stroke. He prided himself on his healthy lifestyle and program of fulfilling activities—those he purposely chose and prioritized.

I thought of the events of the previous few days in search of any sign I'd missed.

We had talked with Dad the previous day—he sounded fine, happy to hear from us as we drove through the Adirondacks on our way to our Canadian canoe adventure. Their tennis match was cancelled due to rain, but he had walked twice.

Dad and Mom had stayed at our house over the weekend two days prior to that phone call. We'd had an active though relaxed time, a fun celebration of their 51st anniversary.

Nothing in Dad's letter of August 31st foreshadowed the events of three days later. In his weekly letter Dad was his usual upbeat and appreciative self, thanking us for the great weekend visit they just had at our home and excited about our upcoming wilderness canoe trip in Ontario.

AN HOUR LATER, the phone rang at Auld Reekie Lodge. Mom confirmed that Dad had suffered a mild stroke and was on his way to Dartmouth Hitchcock Medical Center.

My family needed me—I needed to be with them. There was no question we'd return home and abort our trip.

It was way too late to start the long drive, so we waited until morning and made it as far as St. Albans, Vermont, at 8:30 that night. Still two hours from the hospital, it was too late to see Dad that night anyway—at least he was stable.

The next morning at the hospital, Dad welcomed our warm hugs, surprised and glad to see us.

"You're supposed to be canoeing!" he said.

"We needed to be with you, Dad," I told him.

Dad seemed sad we'd cancelled our long-planned adventure and at the same time comforted that we were there.

Diagnosed with a right frontal lobe hemorrhage of uncertain cause, Dad walked unsteadily and appeared confused at times. We found it hard to believe—relieved it wasn't worse.

Three days later Mom and I visited with Dad in his hospital room.

A tall nurse walked in with her clipboard and said, "Frank is ready to go home this afternoon."

"No rehab?" I asked.

"No," she said.

The news came as a complete surprise. We assumed Dad would transfer to a rehabilitation facility near home for a short time, so we all could learn how to manage the effects of the stroke, since he obviously couldn't be left alone. With so many questions and few answers, we quickly realized how little we knew about strokes.

We thought we had more time. This was happening much sooner than expected and their home at Howard Street wasn't ready yet! Dad couldn't navigate stairs, their upstairs bedroom certainly out of the question. We didn't yet have the special low bed with a railing set up downstairs. And I worried that it would be too stressful for Mom, who'd had a heart attack six years earlier.

"Okay," I said, quickly formulating a plan. "We'll take him to our house. It's all on one level, only one stair. I'll pull out the couch—that bed is lower and easy to get into." If Dad could go home, we wanted him home! We'd work out the details.

OUR HOME PROVIDED the perfect intermediary spot as we waited for delivery of the hospital bed to Howard Street. Dad gladly settled into "his B&B," though the contrast from a mere eight days prior was dramatic. On August 31st, Dad had excelled at family tennis, walked our three-mile loop, and finished his daily crossword puzzle—fully enjoying all our normal routines. On September 8th, Dad walked unsteadily—noticeably weak on his left side—tennis, walks, or crossword puzzles unthinkable. I watched in disbelief as he shoveled in his food, a drastic change for this lifelong slow and deliberate eater.

Dad laughed when I gently reminded him that he had been brushing his teeth for a long time and the enamel would soon start to wear off. He maintained his sense of humor, though his judgment was severely impaired. Why did he shave the same part of his face over and over or leave the water faucet on after he was done?

Minute by minute, we all learned together. That first day home we just used common sense to keep Dad safe and it worked. We had so much to learn about full-time caregiving.

While we understood that Dad's left side was impaired because the stroke occurred in his brain's right side, we hadn't heard of something called "left side neglect." I researched this perplexing phenomenon to understand why Dad had no awareness of his entire left side. Classic left side neglect helped explain why Dad ignored the food on the left side of his plate and bumped into furniture and door jambs on his left. In Dad's view, his left arm and leg did not belong to him.

Luckily the hospital bed arrived at their home in Brattleboro the next day. When we arrived, we immediately noticed all the impressive alterations my brother, David, had made to the place—a grab bar to help Dad step up into the house, another one to step from the landing into the kitchen, plus railings and many other safety measures. Skilled carpenter as well as devoted son, David came quickly to the rescue.

Home health care and therapy quickly materialized. Visiting Nurse Association nurse, Amy, arrived to evaluate Dad as soon as he got home. She organized occupational, physical, and speech therapy to begin immediately. We welcomed professional guidance, hopeful that Dad would progress rapidly and soon return to his normal routine.

Occupational therapists (OTs), Dee and Kris, helped Dad reacquire skills lost or diminished due to his stroke such as buttoning his shirt, shaving, and dialing the telephone. Dad quickly mastered the hand exercises Kris assigned—raising and lowering fingers one by one with his palm flat on the table, picking up a coin, and others. Therapists wisely wanted family members involved, especially Mom, so she could give Dad the same cues when they weren't there—especially, to slow down.

Dad had to learn to use his body all over again! He'd mysteriously lost the ability to accomplish tasks he'd routinely performed for years without thinking.

Dee helped Dad with his first shower using a chair in the shower. It was a long time before Dad could manage independently and David assisted him on shower duty for weeks.

Since Dad had dysphagia, damage to the part of the brain that controls muscles for swallowing, he took a swallowing test to determine what he could safely eat and to find out if the texture of food should be modified. The speech pathologist gave him homework, including gargling exercises. The simplest tasks requiring his utmost concentration, Dad took smaller sips and bites, tried the re-swallowing technique and eventually stopped coughing while eating.

Dad had to deliberately think each step through. No wonder he was frustrated and impatient at times. Kris offered help with kitchen tasks but Dad just laughed—he didn't care for cooking and had no intention of learning at this point. Dad quickly outgrew OT.

Mom slept on the living room couch near Dad's hospital bed in the dining room. She didn't sleep well, as Dad often woke up in the middle of the night and wandered around. When I stayed overnight, I took over the couch and sent Mom upstairs. Even with all our help, Mom bore the heaviest burden of responsibility, the first few weeks a nightmare.

Physical therapists helped Dad strengthen leg and arm muscles, especially his stroke-damaged left leg. Every day he dutifully performed his exercises for balance, strength, and endurance.

As well as Dad progressed with his exercises, he cared most about walking normally again. A vigorous three-mile walk (or run) had been at the heart of his daily routine for years. For the first couple weeks, he needed one of us on each side when he walked. We drove to my brother's place, so my dad could be outside and practice in privacy. When he stumbled, we caught him. Soon he needed someone only on his left side and gripped a walking pole in his right hand for balance. I remember the first steps he took unaided outside, three weeks after his stroke. I felt like the proud mother of a toddler, quietly cheering the first solo steps and at the same time nervous about the quickened pace that signaled the imminent lack of complete control.

David stopped by frequently with coffee and newspapers, aided Dad on increasingly longer walks, and made more valuable improvements at their home to make life easier and safer for Dad.

Dad developed instant rapport with his speech therapist and particularly welcomed her guidance in organizing his thoughts and communicating. He thrived under Nancy's tutelage, an eager student conscientiously completing his homework. Initially she helped Dad strengthen his facial muscles by puckering his lips to a kiss, stretching his lips to a big smile and saying "hawk." He felt silly, but he realized the exercises helped him progress. Whether it was word search, scrambled sentences, ordering of events, or mini crosswords, he tackled each assignment with vigor.

I often observed Dad's therapy sessions to learn how I could help him make progress. I urged him to slow down in his writing, eating, and walking.

Friends frequently called and stopped by for visits—invaluable company, conversation, social interactions, a break from the structure of therapy. While Dad and Mom appreciated the gifts of food—muffins, corn chowder, chicken soup, whoopie pies, lemon meringue pie, chocolate cake, apple pie with ice cream—their friends' presence and support meant the most.

Mom's life had changed drastically in a moment, instantly thrust into the role of full-time caregiver of her previously self-reliant husband of 51 years. Friends provided respite, visiting with Dad so Mom could take walks, play tennis, or shop for groceries.

We put our lives on hold in order to support Dad and each other, never wavering in our commitment and maintaining our vision of Dad returning to his normal activities. We had no doubt he would regain what he had lost.

Through hard work and determination, Dad hurdled roadblocks and made steady progress, embracing his full-time job.

DAD WROTE SO FAST his writing was illegible. Even he couldn't read it. Sunday letters stopped. We made up for our lack of weekly written communiqués with in-person visits at least four times a week including regular overnight stays.

Slowing down in order to write legibly proved to be no small challenge. Dad diligently practiced writing every day on his yellow legal pad.

"Take your time, Dad. Slowly...slow down," I reminded him. "Try to write a little bigger."

He laughed at his first several attempts—he couldn't believe it. What happened? Though it was tremendously frustrating, Dad didn't despair and accepted the challenge with the same positive attitude he'd always had. He'd master it!

Meanwhile, anxious to send e-mails again, Dad wanted to type. Why not try? Two and a half weeks after his stroke I agreed to help him try to type an e-mail.

He turned on the computer and accessed his e-mail.

"Who do you want to send an e-mail to?"

"Josh. He e-mailed me about one of the blind students he's working with—sounds like a handful. Let's answer him."

Always a fast typist, Dad's fingers flew over the keys. When Dad finished one long paragraph, he started another.

"Wait, Dad," I said as I tried to slow him down. "Let's read it before you write any more."

He proudly rolled his chair back from the computer so I could lean over and read his e-mail. Groups of letters seemed to form words, but I didn't recognize the words. Even his grandson's name was spelled wrong. I couldn't read any of it and I strained to make sense of it.

"Dad, I can't read it. Can you?"

He scanned his e-mail and couldn't read it either. He could tell me what it said, since he'd written it.

"It looks like Chinese," I pointed out. "Or some foreign language!"

We laughed at the accuracy of that statement.

"I guess you're right," he concluded, with his usual good sense of humor.

"Maybe you're not quite ready to type. I think your left hand hit the wrong keys. Your right hand is okay. We'll work on it. I think the first thing is to slow down. That's challenging, isn't it?"

He sighed and shook his head.

"I know you can do it—it's just a matter of time."

He went back to handwriting on his legal pad.

A few days later, I received Dad's first letter in the mail—handwritten on his yellow legal pad—a landmark moment. Capital letters gave way to cursive in the second half. His message came through clearly despite uneven printing and misspellings. It didn't matter that Dad, usually proficient in spelling, spelled "weak" with 2 "k"s. Three weeks after his stroke, we gratefully resumed our weekly letter writing:

September 26, 2003
Hi Donna,
Doing it now before I get tired. Weakk from my busy day. It was a good one thanks to you. Fun talkiing with the OTs—you talk their language, thank goodness. Thanks for all the time and advice you had for me. I need the help. You're terrific and posiitiive attitude you have.

Things look a little better tonight. Hope the bed change works out. Mom seems pleased. The lady coming in to help is a big step—thankks for working it out—she seems fine and caring. Good job!

Have a good work party at Charlestown—get in some tennis.

See you Monday. Thanks for coming. Dave is happy we have help for Mom. Day by day and hope for the best. You're very special and appreciated.

Love, Dad

The next week, he sent me another letter:

Dear Donna,

Wanted to send my weekly msg, mail it this noon as we go to Dave's. Will practice typing on the computer this pm.

Thanks for all your time and effort in making Sunday such a marvelous, special day. Super—singing, walking, having fun, rooting for the Red Sox (winning), and visiting. Great memories. Slept like a rock last night 10–6. Ready to go this am. See Dave—walk. Have speech therapy tomorrow—Nancy at 9:00—that's a treat. Lovely day—cool and pretty out—saving up a lot of bike trips later. Still have the Northfield Loop on our agenda.

Looking ahead to the trip to Hanover—want to get it over with and go to the next step. Bleeding bothers me. Want to chart the future and forget the whole matter. I'm sure you understand zeal to get it over.

Your mom sure has been good about dealing with this whole event—as you and Dave have been super to step in and give great help and support . . . special for me to have such a great family. Amazing that it would happen like it did—out of the blue. Thanks a million for your good advice and support. I love you—you're precious.

Keep in touch—write and come see me. Will talk with you soon and see you Friday the 10th. Much love and thanks, Dad

When we drove to Dartmouth Medical Center for the much-anticipated CT scan, Dr. Simmons cleared Dad for more activity and gave us an uplifting report.

At least Dad could safely navigate the stairs by himself and have unlimited access to his computer. I made special trips to Brattleboro just to help my Dad relearn to type on a keyboard, to remind him to slow down, take his time, and orient his fingers on the correct keys.

Dear Donna,

It's 6:45 A.M. *Sunday and I just got up from sleeping 11–6:30 nonstop—soundly. What a good sleep—no alarm and no deadline. Mom is cooking bacon and eggs. I like this idea of no deadlines or worries about what I have to do or dealing with tasks that bother me. Make life simple and full with no frets or stresses. Mom was so pleased to sleep all night and mentioned it—so that is a gain.*

Great memories of the football game Sat. and good time thanks to you and Wally, your good care, and extra special accommodations.

I am writing slower to make it more legible. The words come but my printing is poor—need much work on that. Will see my speech therapist Tues. morning. Nancy does written activities that make me concentrate and scan, makes me think and plan which I need at this point. My stroke affected those areas and I have to program my thought process to relearn those functions. Hard to believe it is necessary as it is something I used to do so easily (complex, isn't it). My goal is to get back and do the other things I enjoyed so much. It is quite a task but worth the battle.

This is an experiment—to write early when my mind is fresh and full of ideas. I am happy at this time with my lifestyle—free and simple with improving health and very little frustration—plus rest and a good sound schedule. Do have questions in my mind about the future. Will continue to work on solutions!

Generally I am encouraged as I can walk, talk, eat, and do things so much better than Sept 3rd. Enjoy my walks on Dave's trails 40 minutes each time. Use the cane very little, which is good for my balance. Also went to Meetinghouse Cemetery and did a loop, very pretty and good footing, try to vary the site. Wish I could be independent and drive and work outside but hopefully that will come!

Always mindful and appreciative of your support and constant care of my health, Dr. Dearborn. I like the Sunday AM writing and giving you my thoughts. Hope you can read this fine print—any suggestions?

Much love and thoughts about how lucky I am to have such a talented daughter. Will try again next Sunday AM. Have a good week—enlighten us with your calls. Love, Dad

Great progress—Dad's first letter typed on the computer:

November 20, 2003

Dear Donna,

Doing word processing to write a note to Nancy for my lesson tomorrow. She is working with me Friday to help me with my computer skills, so here is hoping for a good result. I find I have to go painstakingly slow and review a lot. This is my belated Sunday letter.

Manning just drove into the yard to widen the driveway and hope we are still here to use it. With all the repairs to the house and yard we want to reap the benefits, in using it, and seeing it. Who would have predicted all these things would happen?

Feel so good when I get up, like I could take care of everything, but I do get tired as the day goes along. Wish there was a magic wand that could restore things to normalcy for other than memory I feel I can do anything and do it well.

Will finish this on snail mail and talk with you later. I feel good about typing even this little bit. I will practice more, for maybe I can do a little e-mail to my friends.

Must get back to church soon, even though I don't sing for I need that fellowship for my mind and being—no time to desert the

Lord, if you know what I mean. So much going on inside my head at this crucial time—can't help thinking about it!!

Will write often as thoughts occur. I need your help—much love, Dad.

Dear Dad and Mom,

Gerda and I had a great hike up Mt. Willey on Wed., first time ever on that summit. You would have loved the Crawford Notch and Mt. Washington views from there. The trail was very steep with several ladders. It took us 2 hrs. to hike up. Gerda had a blast! Next year I'll try to finish hiking the remaining 4000 footers I haven't hiked, 7 left out of 48.

Yesterday we did more trailwork on the Green Mt. Trail, this time with Wally's chainsaw so we could remove the rest of the blowdowns.

You're doing great with your typing. See you soon.

Love, Donna

Dad's first e-mail after his stroke:

Dear Donna,

My first attempt to send you an e-mail, so let me know if you get it. Many thanks for the good time at your house. We had a great time and very special to be able to hit a tennis ball after all the inactivity—a milestone. Thanks for your patience.

Have lost some of my computer skills and need a refresher from you, so come by in the near future . . . how to correct, etc.

Not easy to grow older . . . it boggles my mind . . . but hope to deal with it and live to be old enough to do many more new things. Much love always . . . look forward to your visit.

Hi Dad and Mom,

Dad, your e-mail came through just great. Good job! Keep up the good work. You can write me anytime for practice.

We're off to the Dartmouth Grant in the morning at about 2am or so, to stay in Johnson Brook Cabin for 3 nights. There's no cell phone service so we'll call when we're on the way home on Thursday. I plan to go to the Messiah Sing on Saturday with you, Dad. Let's sit together near the front and sing away. I have my score all set to bring.

Have a good week. Will miss talking with you a couple times a day.

Love, Donna

"*Comfort ye, comfort ye my people*," sang the tall, bearded tenor soloist to begin the 33rd Annual Community Messiah Sing at Centre Congregational Church in Brattleboro.

"Is it really you?" I asked. I squeezed Dad's arm, to confirm that he was actually there and acknowledge the miracle that he was sitting beside me at the *Messiah*. I could see the emotion in his eyes, his furrowed brow, and lips that were pursed tightly together in a way that says you're filled with joy, but at the same time you could almost cry and you're desperately trying not to. Luckily the first piece was sung by a soloist. Not ready to sing just yet, we contentedly sat there, surrounded by familiar notes from the massive pipe organ.

My dad and I had been to this annual holiday event the year before, regulars for many years at this sing that always fell on the first Saturday in December—one of our favorite days of the year and our way to begin the holiday season. We loved Handel's *Messiah*, especially at this community sing, which attracted people from all over and welcomed everyone regardless of musical experience or ability. The full church pulsated with energy and joy, filled with the notes of Handel's powerful music during this impromptu singing of the *Messiah*. We'd usually sit next to people we didn't know, though we knew that they, too, loved this occasion and poured everything into the two-hour sing. We couldn't wait to see who the soloists were each year. Little did they know Dad and I rated them and picked our favorite.

Typically in the days leading up to the annual Messiah Sing, Dad and I retreated to the basement of my parents' home with my musical score, old tape deck, and cassette tape to practice before the big event. We belted out the words, and when we didn't hit the right notes, as was often the case, we cracked up in laughter. No matter how much we practiced, some sections proved difficult. We had fun regardless of the quality of our singing.

Dad usually waved to me from the tenor section in the right balcony, and then I'd give a little wave back from my pew near the front of the church in the alto section. I loved peeking up at the balcony to see him singing lustily, a significant boost to the enthusiasm and volume from that often small section.

While still a tenor, Dad sat next to me in the alto section this year because of his stroke three months prior. On this day, he wanted the security of having me nearby, as the stroke left him uncomfortable in large groups, in sharp contrast to most of his life during which he organized, led, and addressed large groups with competence and ease. Likewise, I felt better having him next to me, having become protective of him ever since his stroke.

"Can you believe it, Donna?" he whispered, barely able to speak.

I nodded and gave him a hug.

"*Every valley shall be exalted*," sang the talented tenor soloist.

"We're here," Dad said reverently, as he looked around the church decked out with large, evergreen wreaths for the start of the holiday season, seeing in the fresh way that only someone who had so many things taken away can appreciate.

Chills ran down my spine. I had no words for that moment.

The previous three months flashed through my mind—the day my dad took a three-mile walk, played tennis, mowed the lawn, and then in a flash became incapacitated and reliant on us. I felt proud of the way he embraced rehabilitation as his full-time occupation and attacked his assignments with vigor and dedication, progressing quickly.

I wanted to help him resume his favorite activities, especially singing. Dad loved to sing! His robust voice rang out loud and true in his church choir and with the senior singers in his retirement. Reluctant to be back in public, Dad felt overwhelmed and uncomfortable with more than a few people at a time. I remembered his first foray back to his singing groups.

"Would you like to go to choir practice? I'll go with you, if you want," I had offered. Dad liked that idea, so I called Luella, the choir director for both his choirs.

"That's wonderful!" Luella said, the joy obvious in her voice.

She welcomed me wholeheartedly to practice and perform with them, side by side with my dad, whatever we wanted. I had sung in the youth choir at that same church over thirty years prior so I had a true homecoming.

The choir faithful cheered, cried, and hugged when we came the first time. It was obvious how much they missed Dad who had sung with this group for forty-six years. Some could barely walk, all except one older than Dad. They wondered why Dad—the most vigorous and active of the bunch—suffered a stroke. They had always looked to him to lead, to keep them laughing and positive, and now they rushed to his side. Their outgoing yet humble, hilarious, poised, never-lost-for-words leader returned to their ranks. Chronically short of men, the choir welcomed back his sweet tenor voice.

The entire church choir adopted me into their ranks, realizing that Dad wouldn't be there if I didn't accompany him, spot him on stairways, guide him to the proper seat in the choir loft, and drive him to choir practice and church. Though Dad knew he wasn't ready, he couldn't help yearn for the day he could drive again.

The many songs and hymns Dad knew by heart came rushing back and he often didn't need to read the music. At times when he relied on the hymnal and started leafing through the pages in the middle of a number, I'd gently remind him that we were on the correct page. Yet most important, my simple presence, just being there next to him, enabled him to trust that all was well.

Staying pretty close to home for most of the three months since his stroke, Dad had only recently taken forays downtown alone. We remained uneasy about his judgment in certain instances, such as crossing a street. And so, on this snowy day I gladly accompanied my dad step by step the half mile from his home to the church.

On the 6th day of December, I marveled at how far he had come since September 3rd.

"*Glory to God, glory to God in the highest, and peace on earth.*" My dad sang this magnificent chorus beautifully and gladly shared my score. The lively conductor waved his wand to direct us singing one of our favorites. We hit most of the notes correctly, two little grateful voices amongst hundreds of *Messiah*-lovers.

"*The trumpet shall sound.*" Trumpet notes resonated through the church, accompanying the liquidy smooth tenor soloist.

"*Hallelujah, Hallelujah, Hallelujah,*" my dad belted out the words as we all stood to sing Handel's "Hallelujah Chorus." "*For the Lord God omnipotent reigneth, King of Kings and Lord of Lords, and He shall reign for ever and ever.*" We knew this chorus well, the most well-known part of the *Messiah*. How joyous. How satisfying. Dad sang with confidence, as beautiful as ever.

"Maybe next year I'll feel comfortable back up in the balcony with the rest of the tenors," he hoped aloud, following our favorite chorus.

THREE DAYS LATER, I drove to Brattleboro for Dad's final speech therapy session with Nancy and to honor the occasion, Dad's graduation from rehabilitation. His final therapist signed off—an emotional goodbye. Much more than a speech therapist, Nancy had become a friend and an integral part of Dad's recovery.

We headed to David's for a late-morning snowshoe outing, followed by grinders for lunch. Dad, Mom, and I moved quickly for the first few minutes to get warm, then leisurely sauntered around the fireplace loop. Dad beamed with joy and the simple pleasure of snowshoeing in his familiar woods, his favorite all-season playground for more than ten years.

We climbed a gentle rise into an open hardwood grove of tall oaks, smooth-barked beech and stately maples. Decked in his royal, navy, and white ski sweater Mom knit, Dad soaked up the sun's rays and stopped to take it all in. He had made vast progress with balance and strength since his stroke three months prior and continued to regain endurance through longer and longer walks. We celebrated another landmark reached—thrilled and thankful.

Dad had enough and took a short cut at the very end, Mom and I not far behind.

Suddenly, as he reached David's driveway, I saw him fall.

"Help, I can't get up!" Dad cried out.

"I'm coming," I answered, as I sprinted to his side.

"Dad, are you okay? What happened?" I knelt by his side.

"I can't get my snowshoes off."

"I'll help you," I offered. "Okay, they're off." I helped him to a seated position.

He struggled to stand up and couldn't, so I helped him to his feet. He seemed unsteady, so I balanced him on one side.

He thanked me for my help, but something seemed very, very wrong.

Just then David drove in, home for lunch. We stood in his driveway—what timing.

"Hey, how was the snowshoeing?" David asked.

"It was good, but Dad fell at the end and couldn't get up. His left leg seems weak."

"Can you put any weight on it, Dad?" David asked.

"I'll get a chair," I offered.

David and I did a quick assessment, asked Dad questions which he answered accurately and quickly. He looked okay, but we soon realized his left arm and leg had no feeling, his left arm hanging lifeless by his side.

"Dad needs to get to the hospital—now," I urged.

"I'll call the ambulance." David dashed into his house to the phone.

We kept Dad warm and comfortable. While he continued to speak clearly and coherently, we worried when feeling didn't return on his left side.

We reassured him that help was on the way. Even so, he became increasingly alarmed. Why didn't he have feeling in his entire left side?

NO! It can't be! It felt so wrong and inexplicable that Dad was having another stroke, yet all his symptoms led to that assessment.

Why? After all his hard work—ninety days of unrelenting attention to full recovery!

Later at Brattleboro Memorial Hospital, we found Dad coherent, talking, and glad to see us. But the doctor confirmed what we already knew—another stroke. With the worry of continued bleeding, he arranged to have Dad transferred immediately to Dartmouth Medical Center on the DHART helicopter.

By the time we saw him two hours later, Dad seemed confused and had trouble speaking, his paralysis far more severe from this second stroke, due to widespread hemorrhage in the right parietal as well as right frontal lobe. We felt completely helpless as we witnessed Dad deteriorate even further, while ostensibly receiving the best care at the most highly-respected medical facility in our area.

Stop the bleeding! Please help my dad! This was a huge blow that left us despondent.

We visited Dad seven to eight hours a day in the hospital as the bleeding subsided and he stabilized.

Two days after his stroke, I sat with him in the intensive care unit. He didn't open his eyes much all day, but during our evening visit, he expressed himself lucidly. We talked candidly, as we always did.

"It's quite a Christmas present," I lamented.

"Life is what you make it," Dad replied, with his usual upbeat attitude.

Dad wondered—why did this happen—again—so soon—after trying to do all the right things? We all had those same questions and no answers. It didn't make any sense.

"I promised myself I'd do everything I could to lick this," he told me.

"You've worked so hard, Dad. You've done everything. This is a shock."

"It's traumatizing to your mother, David, and you."

"I wish I understood it. Tell me anything that's on your mind, Dad. I'm here for you."

"I don't want to fill an encyclopedia. No one wants to hear about problems." He paused. "I'm scared. I'm a walking zombie. I'm frustrated. They keep asking me to move my fingers and toes . . . and I can't."

"Of course you're scared and frustrated. Anyone would be."

"I want to thank you, while I still can," he said, "for being there for me, tonight and always."

Unsettling and chilling, his words revealed gratefulness, but even more so—uncertainty and apprehension. He sensed the tenuousness of life and the fragility of his brain's blood vessels. If this second stroke could happen, without warning and so soon after the first, what else might occur—a troubling insinuation.

We all faced an uncertain future.

Our family felt demoralized over the next five days, as Dad experienced a lot of vomiting and headaches. He felt tired and depressed, slept poorly, and lacked any appetite, all normal post-stroke side effects. I alerted the nurses when I observed facial spasms which progressed to seizures, necessitating anti-seizure medication.

During his hospital stay, I felt like Dad's protector as I watched over him, advocated for him, and ensured he received the best care. I willingly acted as an assistant nurse and helped with a multitude of tasks. We all supported Dad and assured him he wasn't alone.

After eight days at Dartmouth, Dad's doctors released him to enter the rehabilitation program at Grace Cottage Hospital, a half-hour drive from Brattleboro.

GLISTENING ICE-COATED BRANCHES and glazed deck railings greeted us on December 17th—the day Dad would be transported from Dartmouth to Grace Cottage to begin rehabilitation.

Freezing rain during the night had coated everything with ice, our driveway an ice rink. When I walked out onto Flamstead Road to check the road conditions, I could barely stand up.

"Will the ambulance still go today?" I asked the social worker at Dartmouth.

"Yes, the ambulance is leaving at nine o'clock and should be in Townshend by eleven. They'll go by way of Brattleboro," she informed me.

We needed to be there when Dad arrived—to welcome him and help him adjust to different surroundings and new people. Our dirt road probably had worse conditions than the paved roads, I justified.

Pulled irrepressibly, Mom and I set out from my home in Chester under conditions we normally wouldn't drive. Slowly creeping along the icy back roads into Chester, I reminded myself to breathe and relax my grip on the Passat's steering wheel. We averaged less than twenty miles per hour to Grafton on roads as treacherous as I'd ever experienced. At times we merely inched along, blinded by the bright glare off the ice. Finally Grace Cottage Hospital appeared after an hour and fifteen minutes to cover twenty-one miles.

Mom and I walked tentatively through the front door, still tense from the drive, into the unknown of a new place, already exhausted from hospital visits. Do we meet Dad here?

Carol warmly welcomed us. No—the ambulance hadn't arrived.

Within minutes it pulled up.

"Hi, Dad. We're here!" I called out, so he'd hear a familiar voice.

"Hi, Donna," he answered. He felt exhausted from the trip.

"How was your ride, Dad?"

"Bumpy!" he exclaimed.

"We'll settle him into his room. Why don't you join us for lunch! It's downstairs—follow me," Carol said.

Mom and I didn't argue—we needed sustenance! Stress had taken its toll and we hadn't eaten well for the previous eight days we supported Dad at Dartmouth.

Prime rib, potatoes, vegetables, salad, and decadent desserts! What luck! We landed smack dab in the middle of their staff Christmas dinner—a memorable, delicious meal that nourished our bodies as well as our souls. Mom and I smiled as we filled our plates and graciously accepted our gift, the timing perfect.

Dad settled into the routine of Grace Cottage for intensive rehabilitation. The small, homey, friendly hospital fit the bill, just the right place for Dad to try to regain use of his paralyzed left arm and left leg. The staff welcomed our whole family, including our dog, Gerda.

Mom and I each went there six days a week, staggering our four- to seven-hour visits. Wally, David and his family, and many friends and relatives visited Dad frequently. To our surprise and delight, they served unequivocally excellent food.

I worked side by side with physical and occupational therapists to help Dad try to walk again and maneuver his left hand and arm. The speech therapist aided him in organizing his thoughts and communicating effectively again. We had high hopes he would return home after undergoing rehabilitation.

I pasted photos of our family into a notebook for him, decorated it with stickers, photos, and positive thoughts: *Dad, we love you . . . we're always thinking about you. We're with you all the way!*

Our weekly letters stopped again but I looked forward to resuming our tradition as soon as possible after this temporary hiatus.

In the meantime, Sunday letters transitioned to daily encouragements in Dad's notebook. Every day we wrote in it and left it on Dad's bedside table.

> *Dad, it's good to be with you on Christmas Day. We had quite a crew here today, 8 of us for dinner—prime rib and cheddar potatoes. You look good with your haircut, manicure, and nice shirt on. WE LOVE YOU. Your pal and daughter, Donna*
>
> *. . . Wally, Donna, and Gerda for supper on New Year's Eve and watched a football game. We hope we'll all be playing ping pong next New Year's Eve.*
>
> *The wounded Gerda pup came to visit. She was attacked by a dog on New Year's Day and has a hole in the top of her head. She wanted to come visit her grandfather, her best buddy.*

Dad knew Gerda from the first day I had her, instantly loved her, and regularly asked when I was going away on my next Outward Bound trip so he could take care of her. Dad was a true dog lover, especially attuned to Gerda's needs, and had a strong bond with her for almost nine years by this time.

. . . we're working on your left hand and arm again today, trying to inspire it with massage and range of motion. It's sunny this morning but they say a storm is coming in. We think about you all the time. We're with you in spirit when we're not physically here. Love you.

. . . good strides standing today with Siobhan (physical therapist), also using a modified walker. Your left shoulder shows signs of movement, along with your left hand. Good work, Dad.

We talked with Dr. Geurts for a progress report and we are making progress, especially this week and last. One day at a time.

. . . you took 10 steps with left leg brace and hemi walker. That was exciting to witness. Then you did it again.

. . . when speech therapist Deb was here, you tried to stump her with your riddles and impress her with trivia. She says you're speaking clearer. You took more good steps today—3 times walking at least 10 steps. Good walking! Hope you sleep well tonight. We're all thinking about you and love you.

Dad "walked with assistance," they said. He termed it "staggering" which was accurate.

. . . Doris, Donna, and Gerda here for lunch. Lots of visitors today—Cy, Wilma, Brad, Bob, then Charlie from your Friday morning coffee group. Siobhan had you walking 3 long stretches across the PT room with the leg brace on.

. . . Gerda is visiting her grandfather for the day, plus Mom, David, Mia, Meka, Billie, and Doug. Billie brought lemon cake and coffee. I brought my piano music and we had a sing-a-long in the Activity Room. You sang well—some old hymns. Dad, we hope you have a peaceful night.

. . . you walked 2 long stretches down the hall. You get into the rhythm and want to keep going—I don't blame you. Love ya, Dad.

. . . we started the day off with a visit from Brian at 26 Howard St. to assess your home. He had lots of valuable insight.

What changes would we have to make so Dad could return home? Make an entrance from the back yard into the dining room? Install a downstairs bathroom? How could we make it wheelchair accessible?

Brian, the physical therapist, shared grim news during our home assessment at Howard Street. He told us that usually someone in my dad's condition would go directly to a nursing home from the rehab center—but they would help us sort out the details to try to care for him at home. The cold, hard facts were that he'd require twenty-four-hour close supervision and a lot of assistance. They didn't expect him to walk again. The bleak assessment didn't deter us from continuing to encourage Dad to try to walk or hoping he still could.

Dad dictated this report for me to write in his notebook word for word: "this is truly a relaxed day for all of us. We had good weather and practiced PT in the gym with Brian. He gave a thorough test on many skills we should have. It taxed our abilities but it was so much fun that we decided to do it again tomorrow." Then he laughed. "Supper was special and we ate quite a bit—shrimp salad sandwich which was very good and soup, mandarin oranges, juice, and milk. We had a good visit with David on the telephone and Josh earlier."

Dad made progress, yet he also suffered some seizures that robbed him of more of his abilities. After forty-five days of intensive therapy, he still needed a wheelchair, couldn't be left alone, and essentially required round-the-clock care. How could we care for Dad at home? We prepared for the nursing home but held out hope that Dad would continue to rehabilitate, Vernon Green Nursing Home hopefully a temporary abode. After all, recovery can be expected to continue up to six months after a stroke.

We said goodbye and thanked all our good friends and caregivers at Grace Cottage who had been wonderful to us.

I SETTLED DAD into the passenger seat of my Volkswagen Passat and turned the heated seats on high. January 30th dawned a cold day. No wonder Dad was bundled up in a heavy jacket, wool hat, and mittens.

"We're off to Vernon, Dad," I said, trying to sound cheery.

Dad and I both knew it was far from just an outing. Physical therapists had done all they could and his therapy at Grace Cottage Hospital was finished.

Our everyday presence and support at Grace Cottage helped Dad derive maximum benefit from his rehabilitation. Yet despite assisting, encouraging, and inspiring our highly-motivated Dad, we fell short of our goals—for Dad to walk, care for himself, and—above all—to return home.

Dad was moving to Vernon Green Nursing Home in Vernon where Mom and David awaited our arrival.

"Hi, Dad," said David, as he helped maneuver Dad out of my car and into the wheelchair.

"Hi, David. Good to see you!"

Staff at Vernon Green greeted us warmly and settled Dad into room 115. We shared the noon meal with him, filled out lots of paperwork, and started to learn the ropes at the nursing home. Therapists evaluated Dad.

"Mom, why don't you go now," I suggested. We all dreaded the moment of leaving Dad the first day. At least she wouldn't have to leave last.

I tried to remain stoic when it came time for me to leave, yet dread dominated. How could I leave Dad in this foreign place with strangers—all new faces—and entrust the staff we had just met to care for him night and day?

"Bye, Dad. See you soon. We love you. We love you so much," I said as I gave Dad a hug and walked quickly down the hall.

I managed not to cry until I reached my car, then the floodgates opened. Saying goodbye that first day in the nursing home was devastating—one of the saddest moments of my life. The cold, stark reality hit—we were leaving him there—alone—to stay. I cried all the way home, haunted by the image of Dad sitting there in his wheelchair—apart from his family.

Dad had a new "home" at the age of seventy-five. How drastically his life had changed in a few short months. Home was no longer 26 Howard Street with Mom, his wife of fifty-one years.

We missed him tremendously in our daily lives and did everything we could think of to support him and keep him part of our lives. At first we brought Dad home to Howard Street or David's place for meals and visits.

"The highlight of the day is just being here," Dad said with his trademark optimism and appreciation, when Wally and I picked Dad up and brought him to David's house for his birthday. We dined on lasagna, salad, and Mom's luscious three-layer chocolate birthday cake. Dad had a great time and loved the change of scenery and celebration in his honor.

We continued to write in Dad's notebook that we'd started at Grace Cottage—to encourage and shower him with love. Loads of wonderful friends visited—delivering hugs, ice cream, support, and conversation. They, too, left messages of support in Dad's book.

Long walks outside, pushing Dad in the wheelchair, rejuvenated us all—fresh air, different scenery, and a break from the nursing home. It was a rare day that we didn't venture outdoors for at least an hour and reap the many benefits of being in nature.

Vernon Green staff celebrated all holidays in grand style—with decorations, costumes, special snacks, different drinks, and dancing. Frequent music programs particularly appealed to Dad—keyboard, piano, singing, accordion, and guitar. The staff poured energy into bringing joy to the residents of the nursing home, not only entertaining them, but involving them in beach parties, a Halloween haunted house, Father's Day antique cars, Christmas in July, and a Mardi Gras celebration complete with masks.

WHAT ELSE COULD WE DO to help Dad? We hadn't given up hope that Dad would walk again, improve with further rehabilitation, and return home. At the very least how could we help him regain some use of his paralyzed left arm and left leg? Nursing home physical and occupational therapists worked with him but achieved minimal improvement.

Acupuncture has been used as a supplemental therapy for stroke patients to promote the body's natural healing ability. We hired Dr. Xu to give Dad sessions at the nursing home, hoping it would help increase blood flow and decrease inflammation. David and I met Dr. Xu two evenings a week, as he used acupuncture needles to try to stimulate Dad's paralyzed muscles.

Sometimes Meka helped her grandpa through acupuncture by singing songs from school and showing him her latest arabesque dance moves. Dad sang songs, counted to make the time go faster, and loved our evening visits which meant additional time together. Initial results indicated improvements, but unfortunately swelling and water retention in Dad's legs hindered further progress, so we stopped treatments after ten weeks.

Mom felt the biggest void, forced to live alone without Dad. Even though she visited him in the nursing home regularly and faithfully, she suffered tremendously.

In an attempt to lift Mom's spirits, Wally and I whisked her away for two nights on a Mother's Day excursion to the historic Mount Washington Hotel, a place she and Dad had always wanted to stay. We hiked Mount Willard, a moderate hike with a grand view overlooking Crawford Notch, but a blizzard roared in early the next day so we didn't play tennis on the famous red clay tennis courts covered in four inches of snow. Donning our fancy duds for exquisite meals in the large, regal dining room, we missed Dad and couldn't help feel how much he would have loved it. Our enjoyment was tempered by Dad suffering another seizure in our absence.

Three weeks later, Wally and I picked Dad up at Vernon Green.

"Hi, Dad! I said. He looked handsome in his best blue plaid shirt.

"Hi, Donna!" His face brightened.

"Dad, we're taking you to 'your B&B' overnight!"

"That sounds good," he replied.

We gathered medications, chuck pads, and extra clothes, loaded Dad's wheelchair into the Passat, and drove north to Chester at eleven o'clock, right on schedule. Just to get to our home required a substantial endeavor—a full hour-long drive from the nursing home. Mom, Josh, and his girlfriend, Katie, drove up from Brattleboro and met us there at noon. We whisked Dad into the hallway on Wally's expertly-built wheelchair ramp.

Josh was essential to my plan, indispensable with helping me with transfers of all kinds—into and out of the car, wheelchair, toilet, and bed. As time went on, Dad needed much more help standing and transitioning.

We sat down to lunch in the dining room, the best room in our house—a wall of almost pure windows, with an Atrium door which opens onto the back deck.

"The view looks different than last time I was here," Dad said.

He had the best view in the house, looking out onto the lush green lawn with maple, birch, and apple trees fully leafed out.

"You're right, Frank," Wally said. "Last time it was late November and most of the leaves were off. It looked a lot different then."

We dined on quiche, turkey grinders, broccoli salad, and cream soda. Mom made chocolate éclair cake for the perfect dessert.

Dad relaxed completely—funny, sharp and appreciative. We never knew what his status would be from one day to the next—alert or sleepy, talkative or nearly speechless. He watched some of the Red Sox game, then rested.

By far our biggest undertaking in the four months Dad had been at the nursing home, every aspect of this overnight stay required significant consideration and planning, to ensure his safety, comfort, and happiness. With Dad requiring so much care, getting ready for bed was quite a production, though we made each step fun—teeth-brushing, washing up, changing clothes... and finally into bed.

My parents' usual bed in the blue-carpeted "Dearborn Room" was too high. Fortunately, the pullout couch in the living room was appropriately low enough for Dad. With Dad and Mom on the pullout bed, I arranged my sleeping pad on the floor next to Dad's side of the bed, so I could keep a close eye on him during the night and be there if he needed anything.

"It's so quiet," Dad whispered.

Not interested in sleep, Dad wanted to talk, so talk we did.

The peacefulness of our home in the country fostered a relaxed atmosphere, in sharp contrast to the beeping, buzzing nursing home.

Dad lay in bed wide-eyed, taking in the whole scene around and above him—antlers, deer mounts, batiks, a grandfather clock, photos in frames, hemlock beams, and Wally's Artist Conch carvings.

"This is something!" he declared. "Are any of those animals alive?"

I laughed, relieved to have his old humor back.

The three of us sleeping like sardines all in a row brought back memories, times when we shared close quarters—in various Long Trail shelters, White Mountain huts, Milford Track huts, and Oregon lodgings.

"Remember the Overleaf Lodge, looking out at the Pacific and walking the beach?" I asked.

"I loved that place," he said. "I'm glad we stayed two nights there. I enjoyed that whole trip, every day was unique."

"What was your favorite hut in the White Mountains?"

"Lakes of the Clouds was an experience!"

"It sure was—with three bunks high, then the white-out and high winds."

"Zealand Hut was memorable."

"I think that was my favorite night, as we were the only guests and we put our mattresses all in a row in front of the woodstove."

"And the Northern Lights—what a show that was." He grinned. "This is fun. Just like a slumber party."

"This is amazing—to have you here, Dad. All of us together."

"Thank you," he said.

For a while I forgot that so many things had changed—that Dad was paralyzed on his left side, couldn't walk, and needed so much help.

Dad was himself— humorous and astute, laughing and in good spirits—like old times. I forgot I was on duty, that he had had a seizure just three weeks prior.

As Mom and Dad finally fell asleep, I fought against sleep and remained vigilant, to make sure Dad was safe. I felt a huge responsibility, my head filled with all my duties as head nurse and caregiver, but it was well worth it. I slept very little, changing the wet bed in the middle of the night and keeping watch over my dad with the awareness that seizures were always a possibility.

I had asked myself—what can I do that Dad would love? This is the result—a twenty-four-hour whirlwind tour, an overnight visit to his favorite Bed and Breakfast, a glorious slumber party with unexpected nighttime sharing.

After all our energy, time, and effort poured into helping Dad recover from his strokes, I needed a healthy goal and resolved to climb my remaining White Mountain four thousand footers—only eleven left—rather than revisit the familiar ones. I brought Dad with me in spirit, knowing he would want me back in the mountains doing what I love.

The entire mass of Owl's Head loomed before Gerda and me, bathed in late afternoon sunlight. On this mid-October day the line of demarcation between light and dark swiftly advanced up the ridge. Just as the sun's last few rays glimmered on the highest knob of Owl's Head, clouds yielded to blue sky—at almost six o'clock.

Devoid of the sun's warming rays, no more psychological warmth, I inched inside my sleeping bag on Gerda's pad just outside our tarp. Even covered with my old down parka, Gerda eyed my sleeping bag until she could no longer resist and snuggled in as close as she could get.

By 6:30 it was pitch black, our world narrowed to our tiny tunnel, winds blowing fiercely, noisily in the middle of the vast Pemigewassett Wilderness eight miles from the nearest road. Winds hadn't let up at all since Gerda and I were nearly blown off the Owl's Head slide earlier in the day as winds of forty to eighty miles per hour whipped the high peaks when I summited my 48th and final White Mountain four thousand footer.

After reaching the tops of Passaconaway, Monroe, Wildcat D, the Tripyramids, and the Bonds, only Owl's Head remained, an eighteen-mile roundtrip from the Kancamagus Highway. I needed my best buddy, nine-year-old yellow Labrador Gerda, with me on my final peak. Was eighteen miles too much? The conservative choice won out—for Gerda's sake—to camp overnight and make it a two-day trip. We had a fleeting celebration at the treed-in summit, trees beneficial that day in providing much-appreciated protection from the cold wind. I felt relieved to make it down the steep, treacherous slide to our little makeshift campsite. Most importantly—I shared it with Gerda, and felt Dad along in spirit.

MORE THAN ANYONE, Mom needed some mountain time too. Leave it to her to set a mighty goal, to hike the Northeast's highest peak to mark her 75th birthday—"to see if I can still do it." She and Dad had first climbed Mount Washington in 1953 when I was six months old and they had summited several times since. On the 2nd of September, 2004, we were blessed with ideal conditions for our Mount Washington summit bid. We eased into the climb over the first two miles of the Ammonoosuc Ravine Trail to Gem Pool, a striking emerald pool at the base of a cascade. Then the real climb began, as the trail became noticeably rougher, but Mom deliberately, steadily ascended the steep boulder-strewn pitches. I grabbed Mom's hand at times to help her scale a tricky spot or cross one of the many brooks. We missed Dad so much and mentioned him frequently. It felt like a miracle to be away for a whole day.

We stopped at Lakes of the Clouds Hut to reflect, replenish, and reminisce about our night at the overflowing hut with Dad seven years prior and our socked-in weather conditions. Never for a moment did I doubt Mom would reach the 6288-foot-high peak, this slight woman with enormous grit and determination. Our reality of Dad confined to a wheelchair fostered our tremendous gratitude for simply being able to walk, let alone hike, scale rocky ridges, and gaze out at spectacular vistas from the highest promontory... furthermore, on a day with no wind and clear skies. We rode the Cog Railway down the mountain that day on a crowded train with standing room only. A nice fellow generously gave his seat to Mom. This day in the mountains was enormously therapeutic—symbolic of trying to carry on with life, despite our immense sorrow.

I WONDERED HOW we could bring joy to Dad, how to enliven his world and brighten his days.

Wally hauled out the tennis rackets and we tried a grass version on the lawn. Dad, sitting in his wheelchair, gripping his own Wilson racket, improved rapidly in this modified game and replicated his reliable forehand. We tossed and Dad connected, sending the ball over Wally's head. Dad howled with laughter—he loved that. We loved it—some of our best times and longest laughs.

We played catch with the tennis balls, re-enacting familiar games with good memories attached. Dad said if I didn't throw so many wild pitches, he would have done better.

"Dad, let's go to the tennis courts," I suggested one midweek day.

"Okay, sounds like fun."

Sue generously transported us in the wheelchair van to the local tennis courts where I tossed tennis balls to Dad as he sat in his wheelchair. I cheered when the ball arced perfectly over the net and into the court. Even though the wind played havoc with the ball, Dad did well with the challenging task of playing tennis from a wheelchair. We found ourselves in the middle of the action having fun alongside little kids swimming and older boys playing tennis and baseball in this vibrant park at the start of summer vacation.

"Everyone wants to have a 'Donna,' but I'm not giving you up to anyone," Dad said.

Not long after, on the Fourth of July, Wally, Gerda, and I arrived at eleven o'clock for our usual Sunday visit—so we thought. Dad looked sharp and was especially alert. To our surprise, he was enthused about the annual parade and couldn't stop talking about it. He really wanted to go! He never missed it and oftentimes ran in the "Four on the Fourth" four-mile road race that finished at the town Common. We hadn't planned to go, but when we sensed his excitement, we scrambled to find a way on the spur of the moment. Could we pull it off?

Times had changed. We struggled to transfer Dad into our car and relied on a wheelchair van when we went somewhere, and not surprisingly a van was not available at the last minute.

Taking note of Dad's yearning, the kitchen staff helped us by serving Dad's lunch a little early. Maybe we could do it. After quickly finishing lunch, a strong team carefully maneuvered Dad into the front seat of our Passat and we sped off to Brattleboro to catch the parade, Dad thrilled to be in the middle of this hastily-conceived adventure.

Miraculously we found a parking space in a supermarket parking lot right on the parade route, perfect front-row viewing for Dad. For a full hour Dad sat right in the middle of the festivities and celebrations, listening to drums and piccolos, watching Shriner's go-carts, and commenting on the floats. He waved to numerous people in the parade he knew, delighted when they waved back. I called Mom and she met us there.

Watermelon topped off our true Fourth of July celebration. It was a good change of pace from our usual Sunday visits—for Dad and for us. In a setting that out of necessity was highly structured and planned, this spontaneous action was refreshing.

Pool time! On another hot, sunny July day, Sue transported us to the Vernon town pool. Josh and Katie joined us for a Saturday pool session, helping Sue and me ease Dad into the water from his wheelchair. The buoyancy of water enabled Dad to stand and walk again, truly a miracle. We cradled him ever so slightly for balance. He laughed and bobbed as we guided him across the pool several times. Dad stood tall and stretched, liberated from his wheelchair and soothed by the water—like his old self—however fleeting. I savored these beautiful minutes.

"It's good to be together," Dad said. The smile on Dad's face revealed volumes.

"Right on, Dad," I agreed.

We picnicked in the park with turkey sandwiches, grinders, chips, cookies, and watermelon, to prolong our magical outing.

IT WAS A GOOD THING we pursued tennis, went swimming, and raced off to the parade... while we still could.

Another seizure in late July set him back significantly. Dad wanted to know what was happening to him, talked less, and no longer sang. I tried everything to encourage him to sing and felt extremely disheartened to see another one of his favorite things vanish.

With trouble swallowing and chewing, Dad needed more help with meals, pureed food, and thickened drinks.

He was often sleepy, quiet, and at times uneasy. He tried to talk. He'd point at me as if trying to tell me something and just couldn't find the words. Yet out of the blue—he gave us definitions of words—"resplendent" and "inertia."

A month later another seizure led to an increased dose of seizure medication. His voice became weaker, his left hand and arm didn't move as well. The lift became necessary to transfer him. I had no choice but to abort my plan to bring him to our home for another overnight visit.

We held onto moments of lucidity, fleeting though they were, and offered him the one thing that mattered most—our presence.

FOUR

I TOOK DAD for a walk outside on a perfect September afternoon after he finished his lunch of baked cod, potatoes, and beets. Swamp maples flashed crimson across the street, the first hint of early fall color. Another resident, Vivian, was being pushed in her wheelchair by Spring, an activities assistant, and we challenged them to a race to the cedar tree at the corner. Those wheelchairs weren't built for speed, but our little competition sure put smiles on Dad's and Vivian's faces.

Revived by the crisp fall air, we settled in a quiet corner of the dining room and looked at the latest booklet I'd made Dad, filled with photos, stories, poems, and sayings.

"Dad, remember your camo poncho?" I asked, pointing to the picture of Dad standing in three inches of fresh snow on Tillotson Peak on the Long Trail in northern Vermont.

"Yes."

"It was just about this time of year. I'll read you the story I wrote about that day. Here goes:"

CAMO PONCHO WINS FASHION CONTEST

"Dad, looks like it could rain any second," I said.

"The weather forecast sounded a lot better than that," he replied.

"Well, we'll just go prepared for anything. Let's check our packs—warm layer, hat, gloves, rain coat..." I reviewed our usual day hiking list with my enthused parents.

"Darn it all, I can't believe I didn't bring my raincoat," murmured Dad.

That lonely raincoat was 160 miles away at home in Brattleboro. We weren't optimistic about a replacement, for we were in the remote Northeast Kingdom of Vermont in tiny Irasburg, population eight hundred, a town lucky to have one store.

We chose the Brick House B&B as our base for day-hiking a rugged 10.4-mile section of the Long Trail in northern Vermont. The friendly proprietors, French-Canadian sisters Rita and Madeline, had just served us their specialty crepes for a hearty pre-hike breakfast. Responding to our raincoat alert, Madeline and her witty husband, Omer, whisked us off to their only store, the Irasburg General Store.

"They'll have something," Madeline said confidently.

They had a little bit of everything, but not much choice in the raingear category. "Dad, here's a beautiful, plastic, camouflage poncho, one size fits all. And it's cheap," I added with a smirk. That was the best we could do.

We drove south in two cars, left our Honda Accord at the trailhead on Route 118, and then all piled into Madeline and Omer's small car for the drive north to Hazen's Notch. Up and up and up we climbed, slowly gaining elevation into the notch.

Windshield wipers started slowly, then high speed to try to keep up with the changing mixture as the temperature plummeted.

"It's snowing!" I shouted, with mixed emotions. As pretty as the white scene was, we were not prepared for hiking in the snow on this mid-fall day. It was September 28th and we were there to admire the brilliant colors of peak foliage from the Belvidere fire tower.

Our hosts delivered us to the Hazen's Notch trailhead on schedule. We all sat there for a quiet moment in the warm car, looking out at the intensifying storm. I think they expected us to come to our senses, call off our hike, and wisely return to the B&B with them. However, that wasn't the Dearborn way! We didn't drive all the way from Brattleboro to sit in a car or relax at a B&B.

The unexpected wintry conditions made life a lot more interesting and played right into our innate yearning for adventure, our curiosity piqued. What will it be like higher up? How cold the air, how deep the snow, how beautiful the scene? Will we stay warm enough? With our packs always chock full of extra layers, we stepped into the snowy world of Hazen's Notch to find out. We had each other, a strong, capable team of three that had traveled and hiked together on countless occasions.

My dad extricated his new poncho from its case, which released a strong, new-plastic smell. He struggled to put it on when the layers stuck to each other. How long had it been collecting dust on that general store shelf? Madeline raced to the rescue, peeling and unsticking tenacious layers of plastic, being careful not to make a hole in the much-needed garment. Finally Dad modeled his new look—completely draped in camouflage—and we all had a good laugh. Though not his style, Dad gave in to the new look, caring less for the alternative.

"We'll pray for you," promised Madeline and Omer, shaking their heads as they waved goodbye to us from the warmth of their car.

We were committed—our hosts gone and our car over ten miles to the south. The uphill trudge toward Haystack Mountain served to keep us plenty warm and spirits were high. Mom and I sported matching navy blue, sleek rain jackets, in contrast to Dad's billowy, multi-green poncho. I looked at him and smiled.

"You be careful what you say about my outfit," he admonished.

We appreciated the novelty of it, snow decorating every branch. The maple, beech, and oak trees didn't; they were taken by surprise. Still holding on to all their leaves, their branches drooped at strained angles under the burden of wet, heavy snow.

After two miles of hiking, we reached the top of Haystack, which was blanketed in four inches of untracked snow, such a cozy and intimate haven. Heavily-laden spruce and fir boughs enveloped us, dampening our clothing but not our spirits. We were able to stay just warm enough in the stimulating Arctic air to properly document this early winter scene with plenty of photos.

"Mom, your curls are all matted down." I laughed at her as we resumed our steady pace toward Tillotson Peak.

"I must be quite a sight." She smiled good-naturedly. We all were soggy, not just Mom.

An hour later we arrived at the next peak, where Dad regaled us with the history of the old Tillotson Camp: "This camp, built in 1939..." The brisk air cut his lecture short. He grabbed an extra-large handful of GORP as we headed to our highest point of the day, Belvidere Mountain, three more miles to the south.

Luckily we found a fire tower at the treed-in, 3200-foot-high summit.

"Let's go check out the view," I suggested, as we donned warm hats and gloves before ascending the slippery fire tower steps.

"Look, there's Jay Peak," Dad declared, pointing to the north. He seemed ecstatic that the snow had stopped and the clouds had lifted just in time.

"Over there, isn't that Camel's Hump?" said Mom as she pointed south. We scanned the brilliant 360-degree view revealed beneath us, the vibrant reds dominating the traditional peak foliage scene we'd hoped to see. Chilled by our dampness, we didn't stay long at the windy, exposed top.

We descended steadily downhill from Belvidere, finding it harder to stay warm, no longer the heat-producing factories we had been on the uphills.

"That heater will feel soooo good," Mom said.

I, too, was dreaming of our car's heater three miles away on Route 118.

We steadily dropped that final two thousand feet with no breaks, completing our 10.4 invigorating miles in style, with gratitude. Heater on high. We called our Brick House B&B friends to let them know we were safe and thank them for their prayers.

The camouflage poncho survived with just a few tears, serving its purpose this one time. No, Dad never forgot his raincoat again, nor have I ever stopped smiling at the memory of Dad's fashionable poncho.

(top) At her home, Deb always the gracious host.

(right) Deb and Dad relishing a family walk to Asylum Pond in Brattleboro.

(below) With Josh and Deb, after family ping pong.

FIVE

DAD GAVE ME a strong one-armed hug when I knelt down to greet him. Wally and I found Dad amazingly perky. It had been months since we'd had a visit like this. Gerda sidled up close to her grandfather and he reached down to pet her.

He drank his peach smoothie with barely a breath and seemed to pay attention to every word as we talked about our Canadian canoe trip. Wally asked him what it's called when you carry to the next lake.

"Portage," Dad said, without delay.

It astounded me that Dad said so many words and gave us accurate answers. Why was he more talkative and interactive this time? Our search for correlations or reasons yielded no answers. While we couldn't necessarily explain Dad's alertness, I was happy that we were with him to share the day. I had woken thinking about my younger sister, Deb, who'd died at twenty-seven, and realized that it was the day before her birthday.

"Dad, Deb would be turning fifty tomorrow," I said. "I think of her every day."

"I do, too," Dad said. "So often when I hear laughter I think it's Deb... you know her laugh? I couldn't get over that, when she died."

"You and Deb recited the 23rd Psalm together when she was in the hospital. Let's say it now for her."

And we did. Dad always said it by heart, but I held the laminated copy I made for him, just in case.

"She loved life," Dad said. "She died so suddenly. It's good to talk about her."

It had been more than twenty years...

DEB HAD BEEN FEELING POORLY for a few months, and her liver enzyme counts were up and down. Hospitalized in January, she had pain in her side, tenderness around her liver, fever, and diarrhea. Her doctors wondered if it was gallstones. Tests showed nothing abnormal, but her SGPT liver enzyme count remained unusually elevated with no apparent explanation.

She and I stayed in close touch by phone and letter, corresponding even more frequently than ever. She was increasingly anxious—rightly so—about the chronic hepatitis she had been diagnosed with ten years prior and the long term effects of the prednisone she'd been on. Doctors seemed to be doing little to help her.

I already planned to move back to New England—now it felt urgent. I couldn't wait to see everyone—especially Deb!

April 10, 1983, I drove all the way from Montana and sped across the Vermont border—ready to teach tennis at my old job in Brattleboro for the spring and summer and then begin graduate studies in biochemistry at Dartmouth College, only an hour's drive away. My brother, David, had just moved back to Vermont from Arizona. It seemed fitting to have us all together again.

Deb's health deteriorated rapidly, the cause not immediately attributed to her liver disease. Hospitalized in Brattleboro for a week, she eventually transferred to Burlington where her liver specialist told her bluntly—"You need a liver transplant or else you'll die." Unbeknownst to us, over a ten-year period, Deb's chronic hepatitis had silently progressed to this life-threatening status.

I AWOKE TO CRIES and the softly spoken words of my sister Deb.

"Are you done yet?" she asked, on the third attempt to draw one tube of blood.

I couldn't look at her bruised and swollen arms.

From my cot squeezed in between the window and her bed at Medical Center Hospital in Burlington, I reached over with my left hand to comfort her.

I had done the only thing I knew I could do for my little sister—be with her—so I'd spent the night with her in the hospital.

The day before, in between transfusions, Regina the nurse set us up to wash Deb's hair. Deb sat there with a big smile on her face while I shampooed and her husband, Brian, rinsed. Her seven-year-old son, Josh, was staying with our parents. Water all over the bed and floor, we made a mess that only added to our fun. Clean hair revitalized Deb.

We pretended we were on an afternoon picnic and tried new hairdos. How about braids? But the five hours without transfusions passed quickly. Soon Deb needed more blood. Jerked back to reality, we were still in the hospital room, not picnicking on the grassy hilltop. Deb's liver function had plummeted. How could things have gone downhill so fast? Why didn't they do something sooner? We needed answers—soon.

The night had started out quietly—almost like old times when we shared a childhood bedroom—but twelve years had passed since we'd been regular roommates.

Our relaxed night quickly turned into a nightmare, with transfusion after transfusion to counteract the internal bleeding. Platelets, followed by plasma, then red blood cells—on top of medications. Worst of all—the phlebotomist. How many more holes, how many more needles? Deb's vessels were constricted and beaten to hell. Please! You must be able to do better than that for my sister!

How could we sleep amidst the incessant traffic and transfusions? We talked and talked—about our fears, our family's love, the Bible, Deb's son, Josh, Dad, Mom, David, about everything that came to our minds. I'm grateful I stayed there that night—to listen to my sister, to talk and listen some more, to be with her.

The hint of dawn made us feel better. We had made it through the horrors of the night, only to face more during the morning hours—truly the longest morning ever. The decision to put in a central line came as a great relief for Deb's beaten veins, only it meant more trauma—an incision and X-rays to verify its accuracy.

Later that day I said a reluctant goodbye to Deb, not imagining that it might be the last time we would ever talk . . . that her liver was failing rapidly and she teetered on the brink of hepatic coma.

THE FOLLOWING DAY Deb was flown by air ambulance to Memphis, to the awaiting pioneers of liver transplant surgery—in desperate need of a new liver. Deemed "experimental surgery" at the time, liver transplant approval took time. After many frustrating phone calls, Deb's health insurance company finally agreed to pay the initial $80,000 needed to proceed.

Brian flew to Memphis that night and I followed a day later, praying for a liver to become available—immediately. Mom stayed home to help take care of Josh, and Dad would fly down in a few days.

I hailed a taxi at Memphis Airport and a burly black man whisked me to the center of the hot, noisy city late at night. On the way, a torrent of facts and fears gushed forth when the driver asked why I was heading to the University of Tennessee Medical Center. When he listened reverently and asked more questions, I shared even more.

"Deb's a wonderful mother—the best you'd ever find. She's scared—I can't wait to get there. They said they'd let me in no matter how late I arrived."

When we pulled up in front of the hospital, he handed me a small slip of paper with his name and taxi number on it. "If you need a ride, anything."

"Thank you, Tyrone. Thank you, so much," I said, as I hurried up the steps of the hospital.

It was midnight by the time I walked into intensive care at William F. Bowld Hospital, in anticipation of embracing and talking with my sister. I was unprepared for what I saw and grabbed the railing of her bed to steady myself.

She had drastically changed in the short time I was en route. Her hands were tied to the bed and blood gushed from her mouth as she moaned. Extreme liver failure had robbed her of blood clotting factors—she bled from everywhere. Ammonia from protein breakdown had traveled to her brain, causing disorientation at first, then coma. I assured myself this could not possibly be the same hepatic coma I had just studied in nutrition class, caused by an accumulation of toxic substances normally removed by the liver—but it was.

"Deb???" I called out softly, voice quivering. "I'm here. It's Donna. I'm here with you." But she was unresponsive.

I grabbed a couple of fitful hours of sleep in a small room right at the hospital.

The next day, a doctor told Brian and me, "A liver is available." Our hopes soared.

But an hour later, he said, "No, sorry, something's just not right with it."

Deb's condition deteriorated further. She needed a respirator to breathe.

More hope—a second liver.

No—the donor's family rescinded.

At 2 P.M. we received news of a third possible donor, though we knew not to get our hopes up. A thirty-two-year-old woman had died of a ruptured brain aneurysm in Texas. Yes—they confirmed—this will be Deb's new liver.

The transplant team began their marathon at 4 P.M. Friday the 13th of May with a three-hour flight to Midland, Texas, to remove the donor's liver. Well after midnight, the team started back to Memphis—another three-hour plane trip. Time was of the essence, as the liver needed to be transplanted within twelve hours of removal from the donor.

All afternoon and evening Brian and I paced and waited, helpless and worried, braced for the long haul.

The donor's liver arrived. At 3:30 A.M. Deb's surgery commenced.

When I asked to see Deb's liver, they brought it out in a plastic Playmate cooler—shockingly one-fourth normal size. No wonder she had experienced complete liver failure.

Reports from the operating room came every hour. Each time we leaped up and held our breath until we heard the update.

Three hours to go! We welcomed that 8 A.M. report. The long-awaited moment when we could see Deb felt even better. After the eight long hours of surgery, we made tentative steps back to the intensive care cubicle with anticipation, breathed a sigh of relief for making it through this crucial step, and at the same time realized we weren't likely to sleep well for a long time. It was only the beginning.

Relieved to be with Deb, I held her hand and whispered close to her ear.

"Debbie, we're here. We love you. Everyone sends their love—Mom, Dad, David, and your Joshua... We're with you all the way. All of us... We love you, Deb."

She seemed far away, but touching her and seeing her chest rise and fall gave me some assurance.

When Dad arrived the next day, he was floored. He'd taken two weeks off to be by Deb's side. It was one thing to hear reports over the phone and quite another to be there in person. Dad was devastated to see his middle child unresponsive, breathing aided by a respirator, tubes everywhere, a far cry from the moment a mere five days prior when he hugged Deb goodbye in Burlington.

I flew home to finish teaching my session of tennis lessons and cancel the next round so I could return to Memphis as soon as possible. I needed to get back to Deb.

While back in Brattleboro, I found Dad's frank reports difficult to hear. We all felt sick hearing the news that Deb's new liver wasn't performing well and she might need another transplant. Could she endure a second surgery? None of us could bear the thought of her going through another operation, with the inherent risk and further complications.

A story entitled "Precision Marks Donor-Liver Drama" graced the pages of the Memphis Sunday paper. We cringed when we read the surgeon's words quoted at the time of removal in Texas: "This is one of the most adverse livers I have ever seen in my life" (The *Commercial Appeal*, May 15, 1983). Evidently the donor's liver had been damaged during removal and surgeons sewed up the leak they had created. Confidence in Deb's new liver dwindled.

Anxious to join Dad in Memphis, Mom and I drove from Brattleboro to Memphis in two days. Having our car there helped, especially staying in the outskirts of the city at the welcoming home of Bob and Jean Amy who had offered us a place to stay.

On Saturday night, May 28th, our hopes plummeted further when Deb's temperature reached 104 degrees, indicating a new worry—infection. Deb could have picked up serious infections like peritonitis and pancreatitis during surgery. A new incision to look at her liver and surrounding areas revealed the infection had spread into her bloodstream and entire body—a devastating blow.

I willed her new liver to function as it should in clearing toxic substances in her bloodstream and for the antibiotics to silence the microbes in her lungs and stomach lining.

I held Deb's hand and focused every ounce of energy on my sister, trying to infuse her with love, positive thoughts, healing energy, and strength. Though the situation felt dire—breathing on a respirator, seizures, infections—I knew Deb would recover. She desperately wanted to live! She had so much to live for—especially her son. Sometimes she opened her eyes when I squeezed her hand and talked to her. Not for a moment did I think Deb would lose her battle.

The machines dwarfed me. Whirring, rattling, beeping, buzzing machines breathed for her, measured her heart rate, oxygen content, and blood pressure, infused her with powerful antibiotics to fight the mounting infection, and sucked out excess fluid. I prayed, breathed, massaged, and urged my sister to stay strong and keep fighting.

Dad reluctantly flew home to return to work on May 31st.

Two days later I told Deb about the record-breaking blood drive in Brattleboro. The blood she needed for her operation had to be repaid either in cash or in an equal amount of donated blood. Over three hundred people turned out to give blood in her name after we made a special appeal. On Thursday, from noon to five, so many donors showed up that the organizers had to tell some of them to come back and donate in Deb's name at the next scheduled drawing. At times, people had to wait in line two or three hours to give blood. I read their cards to Deb, reminding her how many people she had rooting and praying for her.

On Friday, June 3rd, at the 1:00 P.M. visiting hours Deb didn't open her eyes. We held her hand and talked to her as usual, but things had turned grave during the night. I didn't give up hope. I squeezed her hand and told her we loved her, that we were there and to keep fighting hard.

I know she heard me. I reminded her again—of the hundreds of cards with words of support and love and that everyone was praying for her.

Mom hadn't joined me at the one o'clock visit, but knew the report didn't sound good.

"She didn't open her eyes, did she?" Mom said when I saw her shortly after in the waiting room. Mom knew.

But Deb had pulled through before. Even if she had days, weeks, or months ahead to make the recovery—it didn't matter—I still felt nothing could stand in the way of Deb's complete recovery. I pictured the girl I'd known in childhood: such a tough kid, a passionate fighter, so unrelenting when she wanted something. Furthermore, she had us by her side; she had the whole town behind her.

In truth, Deb's body had weakened, years of prednisone nearly robbing her of her ability to fight infections. The side effect of that horrible medicine, which may not have helped her in all of those ten years, suddenly became one of the critical factors with regard to life or death.

At 1:30 P.M. the doctor gave us a bleak report, "We don't expect her to live beyond twenty-four hours... we could be wrong..."

Still I couldn't imagine death or believe it possible. I kept trying to keep a positive and hopeful attitude, focus on recovery, trust in God, and ultimately believe in miracles. I would have felt I'd betrayed her to think anything else.

Shortly after, the doctor gave Brian and me the cold and shocking news, "Debra has just expired."

It had to be a dream, I thought. We still felt prepared to fight long and hard. It's over? How could Deb be taken from us?

Despite enormous outpourings of love and prayers, emergency liver transplant surgery, a record-breaking blood drawing, and our unfailing positive energy, Deb lost her battle with liver disease at 1:50 P.M. on June 3, 1983.

In the confusion of emotions and thoughts, my disbelief, my tears, my shaking, numb body... the cold reality came first—I had to tell my mother. She read my face as soon as I walked toward her in the waiting room.

Then someone had to phone Dad back in Brattleboro.

My hands trembled as I dialed his work number. I braced myself to tell him the saddest news he would ever hear in his entire life, words that no parent should ever have to hear.

"Dad!" I squeaked out in a high, shrill voice, calling from a pay phone in the first floor lobby.

"Hi, Donna."

Chills ran up my spine, my knees caved in.

"Dad..." I tried again, my voice cracking.

How could I speak the words? How could I tell my dad that his twenty-seven-year-old daughter had lost her battle with liver disease?

"Dad...Deb's gone." I barely got those few words out.

"No...oh, no..."

Being 1300 miles apart at a time we most needed to be together made it that much harder.

A TALL, YOUNG, red-haired clergyman with a white collar walked toward me.

"Hi, I'm Charlie Grigsby," he said, with a warm handshake. "I'm here for you—if there's anything I can do."

"I'm going in..." I started to say, but couldn't finish, so I pointed to the door into intensive care.

"I'll go in with you, if you want," he offered.

"Okay," I agreed, barely able to talk, feeling weak and fragile.

He said a prayer, took my hand, and held me up, as I said goodbye to Deb. All her tubes and monitors unhooked and cleared away, she appeared to be sleeping—nothing wrong at all—resting. The peaceful scene contrasted sharply to the prior three weeks of life-saving frenzy dominated by procedures, tests, measurements, results, reports, and updates.

I felt relieved to see her peaceful and unencumbered, her normal self, even though she was gone from her body. Knowing she no longer suffered helped me accept that the battle had ended—no more waiting, hoping, or praying. Deb was gone from the earth—gone from the family she loved so deeply.

Deb—our family organizer and caregiver, our most generous, caring one. Our Deb who wanted to be a nurse and would have made an outstanding one . . . our Deb who wanted everyone to be okay.

Mom and I drove for two days from Memphis to Brattleboro, crying nearly the whole way, the trip a complete blur. How could we even drive?

We paid tribute to our dear Deb at a well-attended memorial service at First Baptist Church in Brattleboro. At the reception I had no appetite. How can people eat, I wondered. My sister is gone!

That night I lay in bed sobbing. I wanted to talk to Deb so bad. When I could stop crying for a minute I focused as hard as I could on communicating with her.

"Talk to me, Deb, are you okay?" I repeated many times.

I saw her at the end of a long, narrow tunnel, waving her hands.

"I'm okay, I'm okay," she said. Smiling, radiant, just like Deb. True to form, she wanted us to know she was okay.

"Everything's okay," she repeated.

Time felt all mixed up for weeks, for months. It didn't seem possible that Deb had been taken from us.

The passage of time made it more real. Her little red Mazda no longer pulled into the driveway at 6 Howard Street. Her bubbly laughter no longer filled the house. No more phone calls from her—especially that last one of the evening—as "bed-check Charlie" (one of Deb's nicknames) called our parents to say goodnight.

We felt so empty without her—our daughter, sister, and mother.

OUR WORLD WAS SHATTERED and we walked around completely numb. Life would never be the same for Dad, Mom, David, and me. The unimaginable had happened—Josh had lost his devoted mother just before turning eight years old.

We hurt to the core and went through the motions of living. Dad and I continued to write letters to each other every Sunday.

June 19, 1983
Dear Dad,

Much love to you on Father's Day. You're the best.

Here's a good picture of Deb from last fall when she and Josh drove out to Arizona with David and we had such a wonderful visit. I'm so glad she did that. David, Deb, Josh, and I had the greatest time together. Oh, how we all miss our Deb and we will never forget her.

It is a comfort to know you are by our side. We must all help each other to make it through this terrible time. Love, Donna

Dear Donna,

I like to think I will wake up and find it only a dream, a nightmare. But each day that passes makes me realize that our Deb is gone. It is beyond comprehension. My faith gives me the reassurance that we will be with her someday and I take solace in that. We will keep Deb alive in our hearts and memories and always remember Deb and the wonderful person she was.

We'll see you on the 4th for the Firecracker 4-miler. Looking forward to running in the race down Main Street with you. I am grateful you live nearby.

Love, Dad and Mom

Our Sunday letters helped, but our get-togethers were even more vital. I felt even more thankful that I lived within an hour's drive of my family so we could see each other often and share our feelings with the only ones who could truly comprehend the depth of our loss. We hugged, walked, talked, ran, hiked, and biked.

We felt ripped apart—off balance and reeling, disoriented and depressed.

Children are not supposed to die before their parents! Dad and Mom felt that a part of them had vanished. It didn't seem right for them to live when their child had died. They had lost a part of their future and experienced an unfathomable void and justifiable anger at the loss of their middle child.

Dad's faith, church family, and choir were vital to him—a lifeline. An invitation to become part of the Advisory Group with the Ministry of the Laity Program in Valatie, New York, came at an opportune time. Someone had recommended him as a person supportive of the concept that all Christians are ministers, yet not all called to the same ministry. Dad believed we are called to minister where we live and work every day and was honored to be a part of this group.

Dear Donna,

Back home tonight after driving from Kansas. Good to be with everyone and especially *great for your mother to be with her sisters for a week.*

I enjoyed reconnecting with all my colleagues at the national convention in Kansas City. I drove down to the meetings from Leavenworth each day for four days.

Thought of Deb a lot, as we spent two days on the way out at Green Lake Conference Center in Wisconsin, where she had gone for a week. She really enjoyed it there, even though she was homesick. Deb never liked to be away from home overnight—ever. We miss her every day—pulling into our driveway with Josh, calling us, our visiting her in Guilford. It's still so hard to believe she's gone. Let's get together soon. Love, Dad and Mom

I began graduate work in biochemistry at Dartmouth, pouring myself into my coursework, research, running, and racing—glad for tasks to focus on as a respite from my grief.

I needed to be strong and brave for my family which suddenly felt torn asunder and small. I felt shaky and vulnerable, acutely aware of death, with the feeling that everyone around me was going to die. Grief etched itself into my being. It seemed sacrilegious, wrong, and "artificial" to laugh or have fun. I felt I had let Deb down. Couldn't we have done more? How could this have happened to such a loving, generous person who had so much of life ahead?

Running helped me considerably to cope with the heartache and sorrow. I ran every day, usually on the Hanover golf course and adjoining pine paths—four to twenty miles at a time. I entered races throughout New England—local ones and popular events, races with a hundred runners or sometimes over four thousand people, flat and hilly courses... it didn't matter. I needed to run, to focus on a single task, concentrate on only my body's rhythmic, efficient movements—to gain clarity, relax, and maybe reach an endorphin-enabled meditative state. Worries and distractions typically vanished during runs. Running served as a lifesaver—my therapy, a way to manage my feelings, and eventually come to terms with the loss of my sister.

I raced ten kilometer races, half-marathons, and one final marathon. Halfway through the marathon, I rounded a corner and looked ahead. I saw Deb and Josh standing with Dad—so real—looking exactly like them. What a blow to realize as I ran closer that it wasn't Deb, and I was jolted back into reality. She would have been there cheering me on. It didn't seem possible that she was gone.

Holidays felt particularly tough, at first Deb's birthday when she would have turned twenty-eight and then at our traditional Thanksgiving with our extended family.

Christmas was the worst, since Deb passionately loved Christmas and everything about it—decorating, baking cookies, shopping, surprises, wrapping presents, finding the perfect gift for each person, and doing things for others. We missed her contagious spirit and joyfulness. Christmas carols made us cry, especially Mom.

Even though I'd just spent Christmas with my parents, a letter from Dad arrived a few days later:

December 25, 1983
Dear Donna,

We are so proud of you for your achievements at Dartmouth. You are always reaching another goal and we never fail to wonder what you'll do next. It's been fun and we love to share with you as you have allowed us to do.

We have such a fine family—all that we could ever ask for. We have faith that dear Deb is better off and that we will be united eventually. That makes Christmas what it really is, a time of the miracle of birth and rebirth, with the promise of John 3:16. I know you and I share this.

Much love, Dad & Mom

I felt grateful that Deb and I had become close as adults, leaving behind the sisterly spats we had while growing up. Our natural competitiveness from being two and a half years apart in age and always sharing a bedroom had vaporized.

I was glad I had been thoughtful in small ways. Once, knowing she loved my tan Birkenstock sandals and that she would never get any for herself, I biked to Main Street and bought some Birkenstocks, just like mine (we wore the same size, so I knew they'd fit), then bicycled the five miles to her house in Guilford—no special occasion—and handed her the box. Deb couldn't believe it, but tried them on—a perfect fit…the year before she died.

Our family talked about Deb a lot. It helped to remember—how she treasured family gatherings and made her sinful chocolate Wowie Cake…how,

Canoeing in Ricker Pond in Groton, Vermont.

On family vacation—tennis in Erie, Pennsylvania.

as a child, she loved to dress up Buster the cat in doll's dresses and hats, or how she feigned injury to wear splints and slings and use Dad's first aid supplies, bandages, and crutches. She always had a flair for interior decorating and relished rearranging the furniture once a week. One weekend I returned home from college to find our bedroom painted and wallpapered in red, white, and blue, beads dangling from the doorway, and my bed replaced by a trundle bed that could be slid back under her bed on rollers.

Deb adored Davy Jones of the Monkees and sang along with me to our favorite tunes by the Cowsills, Herman's Hermits, and the Mamas and the Papas. She experimented with distinctive hairdos and dressed up in her fanciest clothes and high heels to dance to the music on our records. "There's a Kind of Hush" played over and over.

If Deb and I finished our homework we often schussed our local ski slope under the lights. Sometimes we rode to Hogback on the Saturday ski bus and bombed down the Ripperoo, Sugar, and Rim Run. We'd take some runs on the Great White Way and Molly Stark Trail, looking for side trails or cut-offs through the woods. We loved the Glade for maneuvering in and out of the trees and the Meadow for sunbathing on sunny spring afternoons. We'd stop, take off our skis, bask in the sun, and go home with a tan. Deb became the best downhill skier in the family, captain of her high school team her senior year and a member of the Brattleboro Ski Patrol.

We remembered her generosity, spunkiness, and spirit. She could be a devil and occasionally rebellious. She knew what she wanted and would allow nothing to stand in her way—resolute and determined. Most of all—she loved. She cherished her son and always put others' needs before her own.

As THE WEEKS PASSED in my master's program, my dedication to a career as a biochemist waned. Could I really spend my time peering into a microscope ten or more hours each day? The death of my sister profoundly affected me, reminding me of the fragility of life, and inspiring me with an urgency to act and not delay if something wasn't right. I no longer took life, or anything, for granted. As I'd been so blatantly reminded, my own longevity was not guaranteed. I could not waste any more precious time pursuing a PhD that felt irrelevant.

With guidance from my advisor I wrote my thesis on research I'd already completed. I presented Dad with an autographed copy of my thesis entitled: *The Mechanism of Toxoplasma gondii Growth Inhibition by Gamma-Interferon and the Biochemical Basis of Borrelidin Resistance in a Toxoplasma gondii Mutant*, glad the late nights of writing, typing, and revising were over. I defended my thesis and graduated with a Master's Degree (instead of a PhD) in Biochemistry. Utilizing my original Master's Degree in Exercise Physiology, I became Director of the Human Performance Lab at Dartmouth where we assessed conditioning levels of about three hundred athletes on more than twenty teams and helped them achieve peak conditioning for their sports.

Dad's letters continued to arrive:

Dear Donna,

Took a short drive to Putney last night and thought of Deb as we passed the Pepsi place where she worked. Think of her often and miss her so much. We all miss her . . . hard to believe it's been 2 years. Dave has been to the cemetery a lot lately—and he says he's not afraid to die now. Can't help but feel so sad some days.

We have had many rich experiences that we can recall with laughter, sadness, and with joy. It is so important that we love and support each other and make our lives joyful in the memory of Debra, as she would want us to do. When we see her again someday we can tell her that we lived our lives fully and completely as she did when she was with us.

Our love, appreciation, and devotion to you as we look forward to the future. Much love always- Dad and Mom

SIX

ON A SUNNY SUNDAY in October, Dad sat patiently waiting near the front door of the nursing home. I loved finding him there in the peaceful hallway decorated with sconces, in a little buffer zone apart from the usual flurry of activity. He looked sharp in his new plaid shirt that snapped in the back. The aide said that when she told him "Donna's coming, Frank," he replied "My Donna," which were some of his rare words spoken that day.

I bundled Dad in his thick, blue fleece jacket with an afghan over his legs and we wandered down to the Birches, senior apartments affiliated with the nursing home, for some fresh air. Dad waved to John who lived across the street from the Birches in an immaculately-kept home. John walked to the roadside for friendly conversation when we wheeled by and reached out to shake Dad's hand. They knew each other from years ago.

"Good to see you, Frank."

"Thank you." It was good for Dad to see other people and to see life going on around us, something other than what happened in the nursing home.

Maple leaves glowed golden at peak foliage and purple asters held their own in the heart of autumn, one of Dad's and my favorite times of year. Dad seemed soothed by the smell of crisp, cool air and the sound of leaves crackling beneath the narrow wheels. A feeling of vibrancy and excitement in the air delayed us going back inside.

I set the brake on the wheelchair, pulled out our little blue and white foam football from my bag, and tossed it to Dad. He threw a strong pass back and caught my return throw. Then he reached back and heaved a long one that I barely caught on my fingertips.

"Wow! That brings back memories, Dad."

He shook his head in agreement. I felt certain that passing the football in the nippy fall air awakened memories in Dad, too, reminiscent of times that were an important part of his identity.

"DONNA, you go out for the long bomb," instructed Dad, our team's quarterback in a pickup game on our neighbor's field.

Crisp, fallen leaves swirled and blew across Mr. Clark's field as we huddled up.

I nodded to Dad. He received the snap and eluded the oncoming players. Then he lofted the football high and deep in a perfect spiral that fell gently into my outstretched arms as I sprinted beyond all defenders. I cradled the ball and crossed the goal line—touchdown.

A motley assortment of neighborhood kids gathered regularly at Mr. Clark's field, a grassy, rectangular expanse of land next to our large, gray two-story house at 198 Western Avenue in West Brattleboro where we lived on the top floor for nearly eight years. The Clark's immaculate white house sat on the other side of the field. Though there was a playground the size of a battlefield at Academy School, we called Mr. Clark's field our home turf and relished our private play area for roughhousing, running races, and jumping in the leaves, or playing games of tag, baseball, and especially football.

Jimmy, Alan, Ricky, Timmy, and others often rendezvoused for fall touch football games. I was eleven and usually the only girl, though occasionally Gretchen showed up. A tomboy like me, she loved football almost as much as I did. Dad joined us when he could—after work and on weekends. Even though Dad was thirty-six years old, he played with the exuberance of a kid and could still beat me in sprints across Mr. Clark's field.

I always hoped that I would be on my dad's team, to receive a pass from my favorite quarterback. Dad dreamed up intricate plays in the huddle, complex moves that were intended to befuddle the other team. They often did, though they sometimes confused us first. We had success with the buttonhook, double reverse, the out-and-back, and the razzle dazzle. I loved the simple long bomb most of all, the chance to run at top speed and the challenge of catching one of Dad's long, high passes while on the dead run.

Some fall afternoons Dad and I just passed the football back and forth. He helped me with my hand placement to improve my spiral and taught me how to punt.

He showed me how to run pass patterns he learned when he played *end* on the Franklin High football team. More than forty years later, Dad still clearly visualized the total elation of his teammates jumping around, congratulating him after he caught a pass in the end zone to tie their important game against Laconia.

When I was almost twelve, we moved to a small house at 6 Howard Street much closer to town. As a 6th grader, the move was traumatic for me—not only changing schools, leaving my friends, and giving up my shield as captain of the school crossing guards—but saying goodbye to football games on Mr. Clark's field. Our new backyard seemed tiny, only big enough for croquet, not football. I missed my old school, my friends, and especially my football buddies.

Soon the street became our new football field, the pavement not as forgiving as our old grass field. Not only did we have sidewalks, power lines, and an occasional passing car as obstacles, but the street sloped and a healthy patch of poison ivy flourished in one of the end zones. New neighborhood kids gathered for pickup games and our older, next-door neighbor, Peter, quarterbacked the opposing team.

Thanksgiving signaled the end of fall football, but not before one last hurrah—our annual Thanksgiving Day football game. The day before, we'd drive to Franklin, New Hampshire, to join our relatives on Dad's side of the family. Uncle Ernest wiggled his ears and Gramp gave his three Vermont grandchildren giant bear hugs. Nana bossily ordered her daughters, Margie, Lois, and Glenice, around her kitchen, efficiently organizing a Thanksgiving feast for at least twenty.

After our noon-time meal, we traipsed up the hill to Lois and Ernest's nearby house with the large, flat field. Dad split us into fair teams. Dave, Deb, and Brenda joined in the fun; sometimes Butch, Joe, and Daryl played. No mothers or aunts dared set foot on our makeshift field. To compensate for lack of speed and practice, our uncles held on to opposing players' jerseys, cracked jokes, and specialized in distractions. Illegal maneuvers, whooping, and cheering all played a part in high-scoring Thanksgiving Day family football which was, above all, hilarious and fun. We played till dark and retired to Nana and Gramp's house for pie and card games.

Thanksgiving remains my favorite holiday, with lasting memories of our legendary football games when I was oftentimes on the receiving end of a long bomb from my favorite quarterback for a game-winning touchdown.

SEVEN

AT THE NURSING HOME, I looked deep into Dad's brown eyes which focused on me. He inhaled a tremendous breath which seemed to take an eternity—almost frightening. Would he ever exhale again?

Bubbling through the exhaled torrent of breath came the simple words, "Hi, Donna," his only words that day, yet it was something. I knew he heard me; he knew me, wanted me there, and loved having me visit. Yet there was even more I didn't know.

As Dad became quieter, one by one, friends stopped going to visit. We understood—there wasn't much interaction with Dad anymore. No conversations, a few words now and then was the most we had. He'd answer yes and no questions, though sometimes he said no when we knew he meant yes. We tried talking to Dad in shorter sentences, using simple words, slowly and clearly.

We sat in our little corner of the Rose Room surrounded by comfy chairs and listened to my CD of classic church hymns, most of them familiar and some of Dad's favorites—"Faith of our Fathers" and "Holy, Holy, Holy!"

"Dad, sing the next one with me—it's beautiful." I sang solo:

This is my Father's world, and to my listening ears
all nature sings, and round me rings the music of the spheres.
This is my Father's world: I rest me in the thought
of rocks and trees, of skies and seas; his hand the wonders wrought.

I knew that Dad appreciated the music even though he didn't sing.

I opened a small photo album I brought. "Dad, here you are at Kid Gore Shelter," I said as I pointed to one picture. "You look good!"

He leafed through the pages and tapped on some photos, as if he were going to tell me something, but words did not come.

"What a day that was, Dad." Yes, what a day...

"THIS IS EXCITING!" Dad said to me one day as we hiked a 16.4-mile section of the Long Trail in southern Vermont. "Here's to a good day on the trail!" He seemed jubilant, his broad smile radiating joy.

Dad couldn't imagine a better way to spend a day than out on a trail with a small pack, water, snacks, and a good companion. I cherished the opportunity to hike with my favorite hiking partner. Dad sported blue shorts, a white T-shirt with a dark blue Nike swoosh, and matching blue and white hat, living up to his important standard of being *color-coded*, as he would say.

Retired less than one month at age sixty-two from his thirty-eight-year career as a recreation director, my father relished his newfound midweek freedom—more time for adventures of all kinds, especially on the Long Trail. He remained a few miles shy of becoming an "End-to-Ender."

We quickly hiked from the Arlington-West Wardsboro Road trailhead where my mother had left us at 7 A.M. She would pick us up at five o'clock sharp on Route 9 east of Bennington.

For a long time Dad had hinted to me about hiking this remote stretch of trail. No one else cared to tackle the marathon with him over Glastenbury Mountain. Finally, I had time to do it.

Dad loved our plan—no backtracking, the only downside to our point-to-point itinerary being the deadline. But we felt confident we'd reach the finish at the appointed time. After a few minutes of leisurely hiking on this mild, overcast day, I took Dad's photo next to the first sign.

"Dad, look at the mileage on that sign: 3.5 miles to Story Spring Shelter and 12.1 miles to Glastenbury Mountain. Something's not right." I did a double-take and studied the sign intently the second time. According to Dad's *Long Trail Guide*, Glastenbury should have been nine miles from where we were, not 12.1 miles. Had this section grown by three miles?

"What's the date on that guidebook?" I asked.

Dad opened the book to the copyright page and gave me a sheepish grin, embarrassed to find it out of date. We wondered what else might have changed.

Soon another sign revealed further trail rerouting that added even more miles to our hike, increasing the day's distance to 22.6 miles.

"I can't believe we have more than six extra miles to go," he said. "What should we do?"

"Well, Mom is long gone. There's no way to reach her to change our pickup time." I mulled over our few options. Cell phones didn't exist yet.

"Sorry I got us into this pickle," he said.

"That's okay, Dad. We can do it. What do you think? We'll just hike steady and take short breaks." I might not have felt so optimistic about our situation if I wasn't hiking with such a strong, aerobically fit man and seasoned hiker.

"Let's take a break at Kid Gore Shelter up ahead!" he suggested.

Nineteen years earlier, in 1971, Dad had watched the shelter's first few logs carefully positioned in place while traversing this section but had never seen the finished product. He loved visiting Long Trail shelters and appreciated the history of each one, including when it

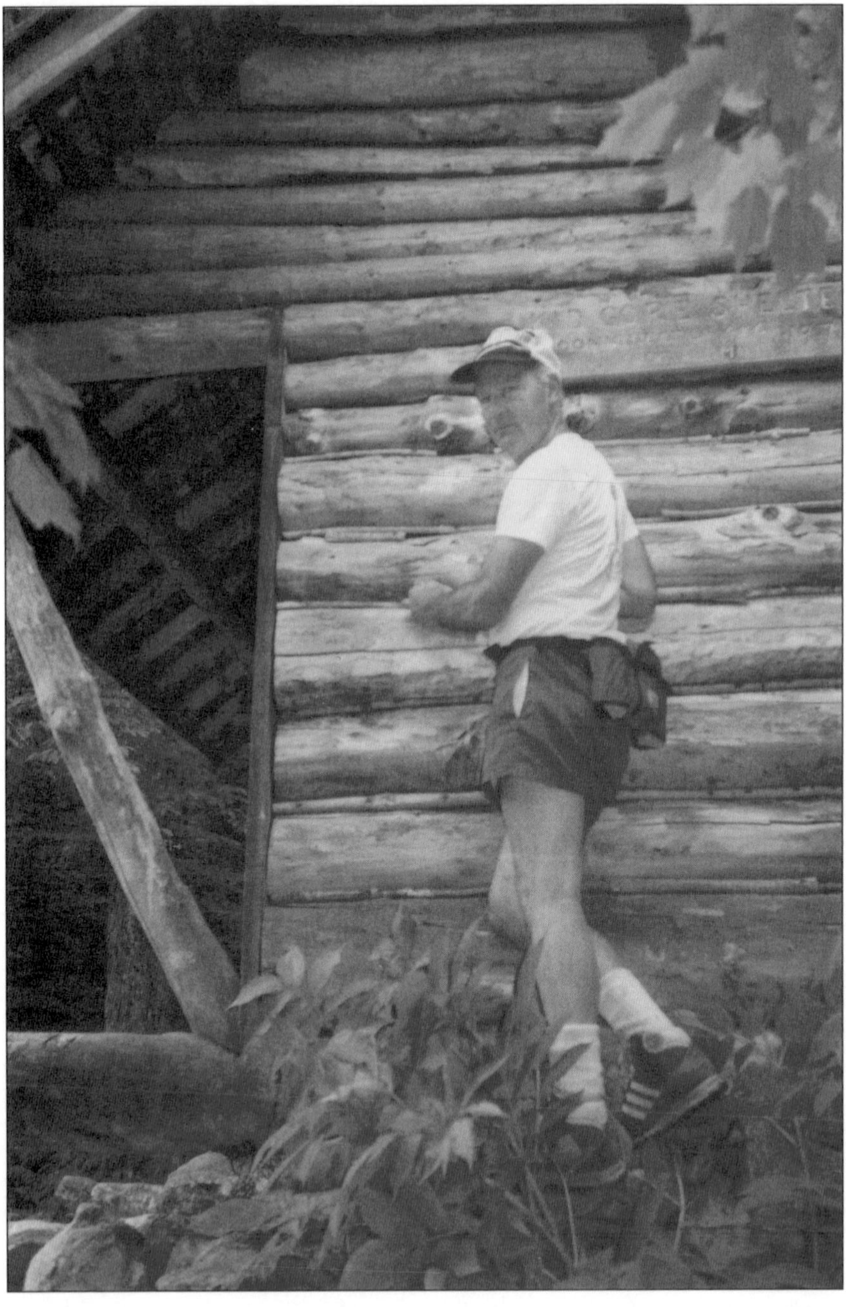

19 years after he witnessed the start of construction, Dad returns to see the completed Long Trail shelter built in memory of his friend, Kid Gore.

was built and whom it was named after. This would be a particularly meaningful stopover, as the log lean-to was named after his friend, Kid Gore, who had been the director of Camp Najerog, a children's summer camp in Wilmington, Vermont.

"What a great tribute to a fine man," he said when we reached the shelter.

After a quick rest, Dad and I climbed steeply to Big Rock, then more moderately to our lunch spot on the densely wooded summit of Glastenbury Mountain.

"There it is," Dad yelled, when he spotted the old fire tower. Making good time due to our persistent pace and disciplined breaks, we were more than half way to our destination with time for me to scamper up the old fire tower to check out the outstanding 360-degree view, and identify Stratton Mountain, Mount Equinox, and the Taconics.

After lunch, feeling renewed, we picked up our speed.

"Let's go," I said. "Only ten more miles. We're doing well."

We quickly descended past the remains of the old fire warden's cabin and then past the relatively new Goddard Shelter that had replaced Glastenbury Shelter where I stayed seventeen years prior.

Taking us completely by surprise, the sky suddenly let loose with sheets of rain which quickly drenched us.

"This is the heaviest rain I've ever hiked in," I cried, feeling the pressure to keep on walking. We had no time to spare.

Raindrops pelted us so hard we couldn't even see, so we gave in and huddled under the thickest spruce cover we could find.

"Just what we need, a gully-washer," Dad exclaimed.

"That really says it, Dad," I agreed.

Soaked to the bone despite rain gear, we happily resumed our quick pace to stay warm. We settled back into a comfortable rhythm over the rolling terrain, still determined to make our goal despite the delay. As we descended Glastenbury's south side along the muddy, soggy path, the sun dried our clothes and raised our spirits.

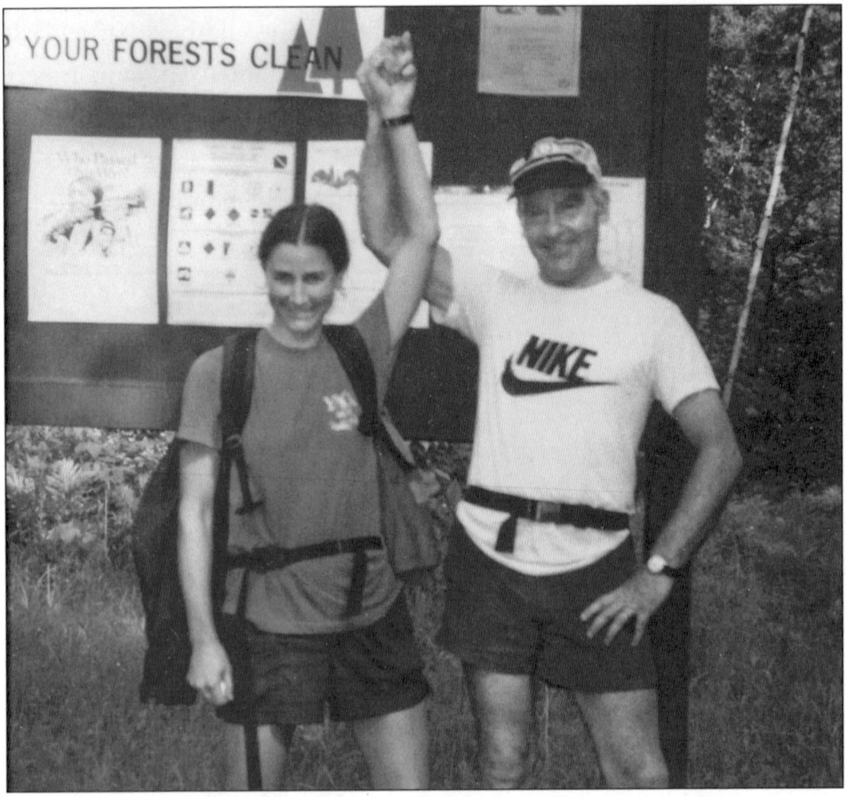

Celebrating our 22.6-mile day on Division 2 of the Long Trail near Route 9 in Bennington.

"I really feel it in my quads," Dad said after a quick thousand foot drop from Maple Hill. Yes, we were ready for our epic day to end.

"Do you hear that?" Dad asked, nodding toward the welcome sound of cars and trucks on Route 9.

We strongly marched the final stretch of trail to the finish line, feeling a mixture of relief and gratefulness, pride and humility—at exactly five o'clock. My mother was there waiting, glad to see us, though obviously unaware of our challenge to make it on time.

"Wow, Dad. We did it!" I said, before a heartfelt celebratory hug.

My usually talkative dad only shook his head and smiled.

EIGHT

A FAMILIAR SMELL GUIDED ME down the long hallway right to Dad where he sat in his wheelchair near the nurse's station.

"Hi, Donna," he said, cheery and animated, with a smooth shave and relaxed smile.

"Hi, Dad!"

As I knelt down to embrace him, the classic scent made me smile.

"Dad, when I was young, I always needed to use the bathroom when you were shaving, of course just when you had your water the perfect temperature..."

He smiled.

I REMEMBERED DAD'S SHAVING RITUAL. He adjusted the cold and hot water knobs, then filled the small, white bathroom sink with hot water. The soft-bristled brush with the Ever-Ready red base sat on the top shelf like a soldier guarding the soap mug and the heavy, stainless steel Gillette safety razor. He turned the razor's metal shaft counterclockwise to open the butterfly gates, and slid a new double-edged blade into it with a metallic *plop*. Then he twisted it clockwise to lock it into place.

Dipping his badger bristle shaving brush into the hot water, then into an Old Spice soap mug, he lathered his face until he had a Santa Claus-like white, foamy beard. He plucked his razor from its high promontory and pulled it through his pronounced black stubble in careful downward strokes.

He puffed out his cheeks like a blowfish for some careful upstrokes. When he came to the difficult area between his nose and upper lip, he contorted his face to pull the skin tight, rinsed his razor, and tapped it gently on the sink's edge.

Afterwards, he tilted his head at various angles, felt with his fingers to make sure he hadn't missed a spot, then applied his distinctive Old Spice aftershave.

NINE

WE SAT NEXT TO a mountain ash tree on the front lawn of the nursing home on a mild, overcast November day. More than half of the saw-toothed ash leaves had fallen, but the bright red berries hung on.

I heard a rumbling.

"Listen, Dad, do you hear that?"

"Yes," he replied with his typical one-word answer.

"Amtrak's a little late today," I said as it came into view.

He watched it intently, no more words. We observed the entire train speed south, Dad absorbed in the moment, captivated by the procession of rail cars.

"I remember when you took Amtrak to Philadelphia to meet me, and then we took the train back to Brattleboro together. We had time to catch up on everything. I'm glad we did that."

Trains had enthralled Dad since he was a young boy growing up at 33 Webster Street in Franklin, New Hampshire, where the lights from the 11:30 P.M. freight train shone through his bedroom window every night. The track was a playground to him and his brother, Bob. They walked the train tracks to go swimming and gestured the universal signal for the engineer to blow the whistle. They saw hobos hitching a ride and fantasized what it would be like to ride the rails someday. Trains were an integral part of their world.

In Brattleboro, Dad timed his walks to intersect with the train passing through the bottom of Main Street. If he was walking and heard the whistle or he sensed "it was time," he'd alter his walking route and just happen to veer in the direction of a passing train.

Throughout his life, whenever Dad had the chance to ride a train—he did. When riding into Crawford Notch over the Frankenstein Trestle he was in awe of the engineering feat involved in building the five hundred foot span that crossed a rugged mountain ravine, especially in the late 1800s. Durango to Silverton, Bellows Falls to Chester, or Morrisville. If there was a train, Dad was on it.

In New Zealand, Dad and I had bounced, swayed, and hung on tight as we viewed breathtaking mountain scenery. We had stood on the edge of the open rail car on the New Zealand Railways train bound for Christchurch from Arthur's Pass—the Tranz-Alpine route. Afternoon sun created magnificent shadows on the velvety, rugged ridges on both sides of the train. Three hilarious Australian guys entertained us for a short time as they searched for the famous Staircase Viaduct. Every time they prepared to take a photo, the train would go through a tunnel and we'd all laugh.

Most people didn't stay long on the viewing platform, so my dad and I had it mostly to ourselves. Not only were we on a train, which we both loved, we felt at one with the train there in the open-air car. We felt the sensation of each bump over imperfect track junctions, the thrill of speeding down long straightaways, and the jolt of braking before numerous tunnels. The cool mountain air inspired us to don one more layer, the stingy warmth of the low setting sun no longer enough. Surrounded by clanging, banging, click, click, click,

Trains—a lifelong passion.

On the train north out of Brattleboro.

we couldn't easily hear spoken words over the noise. We reeled and rocked with contented smiles on our faces and pointed out anything worth sharing.

Further south in New Zealand, the renaissance revival architecture of the grand, ornate Dunedin Rail Station impressed us before we even boarded the train. More than a station, it was a historical masterpiece with copper-domed cupolas set on terracotta shingles, a mosaic tile floor, pink granite supporting pillars, and lofty clock tower looming over the city. We could envision a hundred trains a day passing through in its heyday.

Dad expressed surprise at our small train—only two cars. While he imagined it a lot bigger, he had no trouble immersing himself in this five and a half hour long journey north along the east coast of New Zealand's South Island. Dunedin to Palmerston to Oamaru, the miles clicked by, past sheep, cattle, and deer farms, occasionally through tunnels. Ham salad sandwiches from the café filled our bellies. Enjoying his comfortable seat and smooth ride, Dad chatted with a delightful woman from Christchurch. Staff served traditional afternoon tea just before Timaru—a chocolate chip *bickie* (cookie) with tea and coffee.

"Dad, you told the best train stories—thrilling mysteries with such meticulous details. I remember one story—a load of jewels traveling west by train never made it to Omaha. You wanted us to guess what happened and solve the mystery. We asked you a lot of questions and you gave us clues, as usual. There was no sidetrack this time, but a hidden partition in the roof of the tunnel…

"I don't know how you did it, Dad, how you told us such riveting train stories time and again. We couldn't wait for the next one."

The train never failed to garner Dad's attention, whether we sat inside the nursing home or outdoors. His ears pricked up—Amtrak heading south between one and one-thirty. I could only imagine his thoughts. Perhaps he was transported back in time—to the trestle, tracks, and trains of 33 Webster Street and those carefree days ingrained in his soul. Surely Dad was comforted by counting the cars, hearing the soothing rumble, and listening for the last faint whistle before all was quiet again.

TEN

WALLY, GERDA, and I entered the nursing home and soon found Dad waiting near the nurse's station.

"Your hands are cold," Dad said when I took his hand."

"We just took Gerda for a walk. It's freezing outside!"

We wheeled Dad down the hallway to a quiet room where he sipped his raspberry smoothie through a straw and watched Wally begin to entertain him by impersonating Donald Duck and Porky Pig.

"Wally's crazy," Dad said, as he chuckled at Wally's antics. Dad had enjoyed Wally ever since he met him and once had asked if he had any "Dearborn blood" from a latent gene, because he fit in so well with our family.

"Dad, I don't know how I ever found him," I said, looking in the direction of my silly husband. Wally shrugged his shoulders and picked up the guitar he'd borrowed. Wally was my rock and I welcomed the times he'd drive me to the nursing home and just be with us. He not only livened our moments, he was my pillar to lean on when I wilted in exhaustion after some visits.

"Do you know it's our wedding anniversary, Dad," I said. "Six years ago today."

He nodded.

"Did Wally ask for my hand in marriage?"

"No," Dad said and grinned. "He wanted all of you."

"Remember that day?" I asked.

"It was cold!" Dad said.

"You were going to sing two songs for us but you lost your voice."

I thought about our unique mountain wedding on that brisk February day...

Wally and I had considered snowshoeing up the backside of Okemo Mountain. After all, we wanted a non-traditional wedding—quiet, low key, small—and we had met on Okemo two years prior when we volunteered for a junior high school ski program. We wouldn't let winter stop us from getting married on a mountain.

"Will you marry us on Okemo Mountain?" Wally asked Pastor Rick who seemed bored with traditional weddings.

"Sure, Wally, that sounds great. When are you thinking?" Rick asked.

"February 5th," Wally answered.

"Wow. I was expecting a summer or fall date...but, sure...that sounds like great fun."

Wally and I wrote our vows, met with Pastor Rick, and intentionally kept the plans low key. Dad loved the idea and offered to sing and participate in any way needed. Not surprised by our unusual selection of wedding venue, Mom worried most about being able to stay warm, having become more susceptible to the cold since her heart attack. My brother, David, offered to be the official wedding photographer.

Though no official invitations went out, friends heard about our plans and wanted to participate in our out of the ordinary wedding.

Saturday, February 5th, 2000, nineteen snowshoe-clad adventurers set off into a true winter wonderland up the Healdville Trail. Bright sun reflected off two feet of untracked powder, intricate snowflakes glinting like thousands of diamonds winking and welcoming us all to the wedding processional. Not a cloud in sight, the brilliant blue sky contrasted perfectly with the overwhelming whiteness, fresh snow hiding any imperfections and drifted into whimsical sculptures—nature at its best—on our special day.

White ribbons and bows adorned my Sherpa snowshoes. Daisies and Baby's Breath encircled our heads over my white fleece hat and Wally's cowboy hat. Our packs bulged with extra clothes, hot dogs, marshmallows, Asti Spumante, and fire-starting materials. We all bundled up in wedding attire that was far from traditional—fleece tops and long johns, warm hats and mittens, and insulated boots with gaiters. Our four-year-old yellow Lab Gerda wore a corsage around her neck—our flower girl.

Dad had laryngitis and was under doctor's orders to refrain from talking and unable to sing the wedding songs he'd practiced. He snuck in some short, raspy-voiced conversations with our friends despite his doctor's directives. Corsage pinned to her parka, Mom was in awe, and at the same time voiced she thought it was a little crazy. David generously videotaped the whole event. How did he keep his fingers from freezing in the twenty-degree air?

As I checked on our wedding party members, one by one, I realized the responsibility we'd taken on. Far more than a wedding, we found ourselves in the midst of an adventuresome mission. I assumed my usual role as Outward Bound instructor and safety-minded leader with an all-encompassing big-eye view of our group. "Are you warm enough?" "Slow down, take your time," I suggested to some out-of-breath ones. "Are you having fun?"

While our original goal might have been the top, I realized early on that goal was not practical, considering the varying levels of fitness and experience. As some of our friends labored up a steep section—breathless, sweating, fatiguing—I kept my eyes peeled for the perfect location.

"Here! This is a great spot—it's flat, spacious enough, has a view. What do you think, Wally?" I asked, when I sensed we had ascended high enough for our group and as far as I felt comfortable leading our motley crew into deep snowy woods.

Wally liked it, pointing out a big boulder we could use as an altar. We passed the word, to the delight of many, "This is it!"

"Where's Rick?" Nowhere to be found, our pastor had snowshoed ahead, intent on our original destination. I sent our fittest friend, Larry, up the mountain to retrieve Rick. Meanwhile with our snowshoes, we stomped out a platform and fashioned our niche in this stunning amphitheater framed by shining white birches and tall, stately beeches. Sporting colorful hats and parkas, our group assembled in a horseshoe-shaped array.

"On behalf of Wally and Donna," Rick said, "I welcome you to this place and this moment as Wally and Donna express their love for each other and their desire to live from this day forward as husband and wife…"

Dad and Mom walked me across the snow and we proceeded with our vows.

"Who gives this woman to be married to this man?" Rick asked.

"Her mother and I do," Dad said.

Gerda joined the festivities, proceeding to eat her flowers and declaring an abrupt end to her flower girl role. We all smiled at the impromptu comic relief.

We kept the ceremony purposely brief, needing to move our muscles to warm our extremities in our open-air wedding chapel. Down the mountain we trudged in single file until we reached a lower elevation out of the wind and off the trail to the ideal open spot. Some of us collected firewood, benefitting immediately from the physical exertion. Others bundled up in warmer layers and danced a jig to stay warm. Wally built a fire sufficient to roast hot dogs and keep us warm enough to make a toast with naturally-chilled Martini and Rossi Asti Spumante.

After toasting marshmallows for s'mores, we desperately needed movement and warmth—an indication our celebration was drawing to a close. Down the mountain we flew on snowshoes and quickly warmed. Spirits and energy levels high, everyone declared our snowshoe wedding a success.

When I pass *wedding rock* in my regular hikes up the Healdville Trail in all seasons, I can visualize the colorful snake of family and friends snowshoeing up the trail in deep powder and assembling in a little horseshoe. I think of Dad, our hopeful wedding singer, and Mom, antsy to get moving. I wonder—what other seventy-one-year-old parents could or would do this for their daughter?

DEAR DONNA—

SURE HOPE YOU READ THIS BEFORE LEAVING FOR THE EAST—WILL MAIL IT MONDAY AM—DON'T WANT TO WASTE THE DOLLAR FOR YOUR SOUP OR WHAT-EVER.

IT IS CERTAINLY EXCITING TO REALIZE THAT YOU'LL BE HERE A WEEK FROM TUES OR THERE-ABOUTS—CALL US COLLECT WHEN YOU KNOW THE TIME YOU'LL BE IN SPFLD AND WE'LL SHOVE OFF IN DAVE'S BIG TRUCK TO GET YOU—IF YOU ENCOUNTER A CHANGE OF PLANS GIVE US A CALL ALSO—I DON'T KNOW WHY I NEED TO TELL YOU ANY OF THIS—YOU HAVE TRAVELED—TRAVELED & THEN SOME—SO WE JUST WANT TO INDICATE OUR CONCERN AND SUPPORT FOR YOUR SAFE TRIP HOME.

WE WERE SLIDING ON THE HILL WITH JOSH AT THE FAIRGROUNDS THIS AFTERNOON AND HE REMARKED THAT IT WOULD BE FUN RACING DONNA DOWN THE HILL—THE SNOW WAS LIKE SUGAR—

[illegible] FRIDAY—

SUPPOSED TO HAVE A STORM TUES—HURRAH!! MAYBE WE'LL RUN THAT LIFT YET—VIKING TOURING CENTER IS OPEN—WE'LL GO THERE WHEN YOU ARRIVE.

HAVE A GOOD TRIP HOME—OUR THOUGHTS & WISHES & LOVE ARE WITH YOU. IT WILL BE A JOYOUS RE-UNION & WE LOOK FORWARD TO IT—CAN'T WAIT!!

MUCH LOVE & SUPPORTIVE THOUGHTS

Dad, Mom & all

Sunday letter from Dad on December 15, 1981, to Bozeman, Montana—with a dollar enclosed—as I packed up for my move East with a ride in an 18-wheeler hauling salmon to Pittsburgh.

ELEVEN

"HI, DAD," I said.

"Hi, Donna."

"Let's put on some warm clothes and go outside for a spin. It's cool but sunny and nice. You'll like it."

The brisk air turned Dad's cheeks red and put a smile on his face on a cold February day. Even just going out the door provided a huge lift. We didn't have to go far to let the outdoors work its magic and bless us with its restorative powers.

Renewed and refreshed, back inside we settled in a quiet corner of the Rose Room by the window.

"Dad, I brought some old letters you wrote me... We wrote to each other every Sunday, didn't we?"

"Yes, that's something."

"When I went away to college, you said you'd write to me on Sunday and would I do the same. We started writing to each other every Sunday, week in and week out... and never stopped. You put a dollar in every letter! For a bowl of soup, you said. You didn't have much money when you attended Springfield, and your dad included a dollar in the letters he sent you."

"That's right, soup." He laughed.

"When I graduated from college, we kept writing every Sunday, no matter where I lived."

I thought of my many different homes: North Carolina, Arizona, Montana, Minnesota, Michigan, South Korea. When I traveled I always gave him my itinerary with addresses and dates: Bangkok, Canberra, Bern, Hong Kong, Auckland, Oslo—all over the world. I couldn't wait to reach a post office to check my mail.

"I always felt so loved. Thank you, Dad." I knelt down and gave him a strong hug.

"Here, I'll read a few of them to you..."

Dear Donna,

Sunday evening and my favorite time to think about you and write you a note. It seems good to be able to use the computer that I just got going this morning after talking with you last night. It was so easy. Is it my age or my impatience that gets me to sort of back off and solicit advice and instruction? Good thing you understand me and know that I have my other points that are more commendable, albeit that list is getting shorter each year.

With your busy schedule, I appreciate how thoughtful you are to both of us. Great to have you so close. It's a joy to have you around with so much to talk about and do. How grateful we are that we had three wonderful children as you, Deb, and Dave. Our family is close and we've always been able to communicate and share our love—that's a special thing. You remind me in many ways of myself when I was young—with your determination, resolve, and adventuresome spirit.

Life almost gets more complex as we get older, with the tugs to do so many things that we forget the simple and meaningful things at times. I try to recall often that you should live each day as though it might be your last because time is so precious and it goes so fast. We should try for quality, kindness, and appreciation and not forget the many blessings of God, as often there is no time to pause, for we are striving for the next program or activity and we forget to treasure the moment. We should hopefully not have the maybes *when we leave but take stock time and again as to where we are and avoid that elusive little demon in our lives*—regret. *Whoops!! You'll accuse me of being on a soap box.*

If you are still reading this letter . . . for I have gone on and on, thanks for your patience and love. This is the advantage of the computer for me, to be able to sit down and let my thoughts flow, and thanks to a loving and understanding daughter, know that someone will read them and care. My loving thanks to you now and in the future, Dad.

Dear Donna,

This evening we were walking on our way home from downtown when a huge CN train tooted so I had to backtrack to the station and watch it—91 cars and 6 engines, with special cars that carry automobiles and lots of cars full of lumber, so worthwhile of course.

I look forward to leading a twilight hike on Tuesday evening. I guess I will never get over the desire and fun I have to lead groups and to interact, even in my retirement. It has been a large and rewarding part of my life. Also my work with the Pathways group is fun, working to create something for others that I enjoy myself—a walking path along the Whetstone Brook.

Appreciate your wonderful letters and timely calls . . . adds so much to our lives. Wonder how you are doing. You have undoubtedly been so busy leading your Outward Bound course that you have little time except to deal with your troops—10 boys and girls who are 14 years old. I hope your co-instructor is good—you said he had lots of experience. You may need those mosquito head-nets in the deep Maine wilderness!

Hope this letter meets the deadline for your supply and mail leader to get it to your group at resupply. I bet the youngsters are awaiting letters to let them know there is still a world out there. I recall in my 6-week boot camp many years ago, I couldn't wait to hear from someone and was surprised to realize that life went on as normal. I thought they were trying to kill me, but now I realize it was a toughening up process to prepare us for following orders and overcoming adversity. Amazing what the years can teach you, if you listen and evaluate things so you can improve . . . Your group is getting a taste of that from two excellent leaders and it will put them in good stead for later life, even though now they may just be glad it's over.

On Wed. a Yung-Yung called you from Korea and asked how you were doing. I told her you were in Bethel leading an Outward Bound trip and said you would be in touch with her. That's the only clue, phonetically it sounded like Yung-Yung. I had trouble understanding her, so assure her that your father is almost literate.

I'm sure every once in a while you have a camper who reminds you of Deb. So often I see a young lady who reminds me of Deb's caring and her love for her son.

Hope to see you Monday, though it's a long way to come from Greenville, the end of the world, but we love to see you and will have the fatted calf cooking. Will enjoy hearing about your backpacking and canoe trip.

Always good to talk with you, via print, and share our love and thoughts with an open mind and caring heart. It's a great quality that we can level with each other and exchange thoughts without any judgment problems. It's like unconditional love—it's always there. Kind of rambling but sending love and caring across the miles on a cool, late Sun. night. Just let us know when we can assist in any way. Lots of love and good support, Dad and Mom

"Do you want me to read one of my letters to you? You can read along with me, if you want, Dad."

"Okay."

Dear Dad and Mom,

I'm celebrating my 41st birthday at the Upper Spey Hut on the Dusky Track in Fiordland National Park, in the remote southwest corner of New Zealand's South Island. I read that only those with pioneer spirit in their blood *would venture to the Dusky and that sold me, though Tom was skeptical about my choice. I stashed a special birthday ration of instant cheesecake and canned salmon in the bottom of my pack to last the seven days until March 5th. Today, our 8th day on the Dusky, I made the cheesecake and let it set for two hours. I added the small can of New Zealand red salmon to Hawaiian rice and that was my birthday dinner. Supreme! Four hikers sang Happy Birthday to me and I blew out one big hut candle.*

I took special care to pack particularly good food for this trip, a wide variety of tasty meals and plenty of food (Indonesian-style Satay rice, minted peas, Hokey-Pokey flavor pudding, Thai rice, green beans, Singapore curry noodles, lemon twist tea, chocolate pudding). The psychological lift from good meals is huge.

The two sections above treeline were majestic and we wandered along on tussock and moss and enjoyed views 3000 feet down into Dusky Sound and many fiords. Gale-force winds threatened to blow us over one afternoon—my jacket never buffeted in the wind so much. Some downhills were near vertical steepness and our knees are still recovering.

What a challenging, muddy track it's been, one of the less-traveled and more remote ones in NZ. It's in a rainforest which gets 300 inches of rain a year, with lush vegetation of ferns, mosses, liverworts. With all the wetness, the huts were very welcome sights. The three-wire bridges are really something—two wires for hands and one for feet. Dad, you would NOT like those! Some are long, high, and bouncy, challenging with a full pack.

This track is neither for the meek or the fainthearted, nor for those scared of heights or allergic to mud or rain . . . We were swallowed by mud holes up to our hips and we experienced a rainforest up close and personal, the perfect adventure for my birthday. Tomorrow is our last day on the Dusky Track. I'll talk with you soon! Lots of love, Donna

"Read another one," Dad said.

"Okay, here goes."

Dear Dad and Mom, *June 1, 1994*

What a train journey! I'd read about this renowned trip and looked forward to a relaxed train ride through Malaysia to Bangkok. Dad, I wonder what you would have thought of it.

Maybe because I wanted to break it up and stop in Surat Thani for a couple days, I could only ride second class. How different from first class could it really be, I thought.

Well, it was more like a circus. Upon settling into a thin, torn seat, I found the seat back fell down to a reclining position and wouldn't stay fastened. No chance to change seats as the train was crowded and all seats were reserved. I wedged wads of newspaper so the seat back would stay vertical and that worked temporarily until the newspaper jarred loose. The double seat also swiveled around in a semi-circle and wouldn't stay locked. On top of that, it rocked back and forth from front to back. Many passengers tried to help but nothing worked.

With no air-conditioning in second class, we had to keep the windows wide open for ventilation. That also welcomed in all the dust, dirt, and grime of the surrounding countryside . . . our bodies and clothes turned gray. The noise of this ancient train on rough tracks was deafening with the windows open. This train seemed equivalent to a Korean fourth class train which I called "rattletraps" and avoided whenever possible.

When we reached the tiny border town of Padang Besar, the last town in Malaysia, hordes of Malaysian men and women stormed onto the train carrying large sacks of garlic, biscuits, chips, and other bags. More huge bags came through the windows. I couldn't understand this activity, since all seats were already taken. I crawled over all the sacks to exit and get my passport stamped to depart from Malaysia and then stopped at the train station to buy water, biscuits, and a sandwich.

As I exited the station, I saw our train pulling away. Frantic passengers ran along the tracks to catch it and I was very concerned about being stranded in the middle of nowhere. A Malaysian woman furiously shook her head and hands at me and held up five fingers, signaling for me not to worry, that the train would come back for us in five minutes, I think she tried to communicate. I sat down on the station wall and ate my scrawny sandwich which consisted of two measly pieces of green tomato and a thin slice of processed cheese between two slices of stale white bread, one of which was the heel. When I searched for the train, I found it parked down the track and climbed over all the bags and boxes back to my seat.

I glanced at my passport and noticed only a stamp for departure from Malaysia but no arrival stamp. The one English-speaking woman I knew pointed to the train station—I needed to do both there. The train was leaving momentarily but I had to push and shove and rush to immigration, fill out the forms, get my passport stamped then climb over all the sacks once again to my seat. The train rolled away as soon as I reached my seat . . . whew, that was close.

When we crossed the border into Thailand, all the sacks were passed out the windows to others waiting below. Malaysians leaped from the train and went running back across the border into Malaysia. The border patrol stormed the train and after a lot of loud talking and gesturing, the train pulled out an hour behind schedule. I never heard an explanation, whether it was an everyday occurrence or special to increase the entertainment value of this train ride which was never boring. That's part of the story! It was some train trip. In 14 days I'll be flying from Seoul to New York and can't wait to see you all! Lots of love, Donna

"I hadn't seen you for more than a year, Dad. What a great reunion we had!"

"The best."

GOING AWAY FROM HOME helped me gain an entirely new perspective. I realized that Dad was no ordinary father, rather the exception, and genuinely wanted to stay in touch, continue to show his love and caring, and be there for me. Sunday letters became an integral part of our routines while Dad continued to be an inspiration to me.

Dad relished newsy reports from the jungles of Malaysia, the Great Barrier Reef of Australia, and the hill tribe country of northern Thailand. When four letters from Dad greeted me in Jakarta, I felt hugged in a giant bear hug. Dad personified *faithful.*

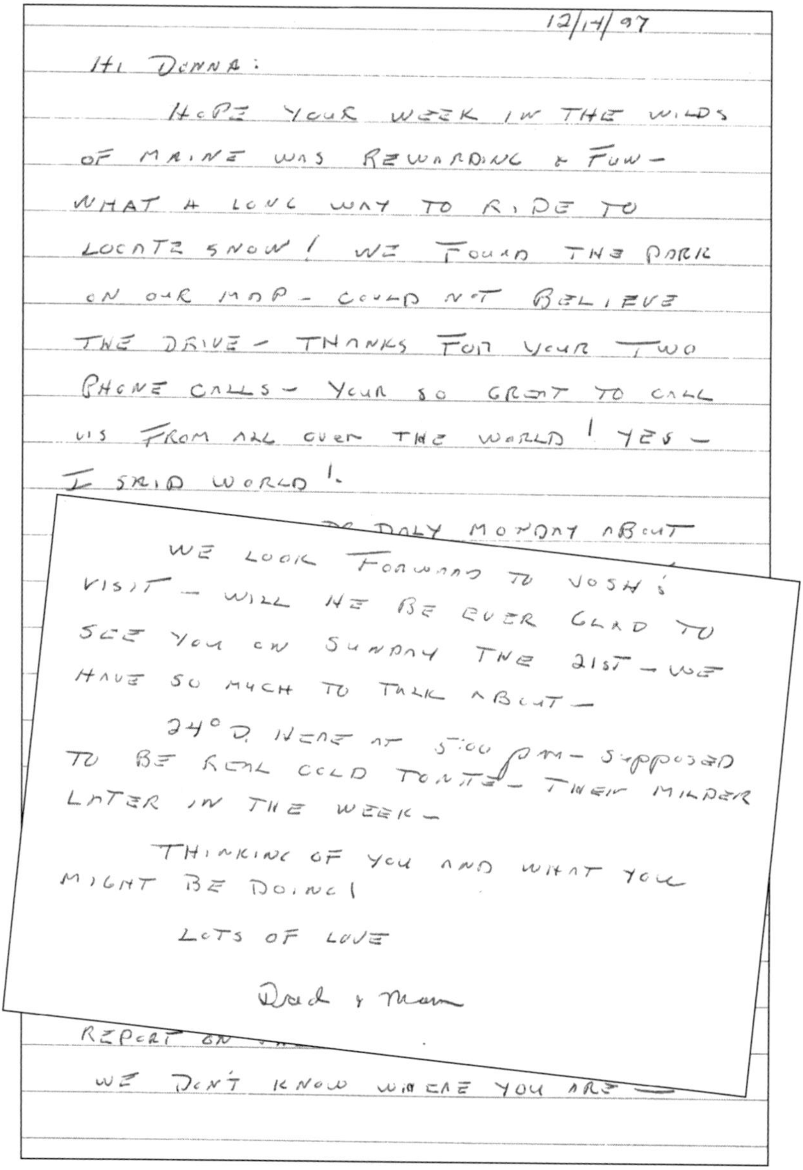

12/14/97

Hi Donna:

Hope your week in the wilds of Maine was rewarding & fun - What a long way to ride to locate snow! We found the park on our map - could not believe the drive - Thanks for your two phone calls - your so great to call us from all over the world! Yes - I said world!.

... Daly Monday about ...

Report on ...

We don't know where you are —

We look forward to Josh's visit - will he be ever glad to see you on Sunday the 21st - we have so much to talk about -

24° F here at 5:00 pm - supposed to be real cold tonite - then milder later in the week -

Thinking of you and what you might be doing!

Lots of love

Dad & Mom

Dad writing to me in Bethel, Maine, while I was on Outward Bound winter staff training.

One week Mom wrote the Sunday letter to me in New Zealand, Dad recuperating from surgery after a burst gall bladder that doctors had misdiagnosed as a pulled muscle in his stomach. I felt so far away and helpless. Reminded of the fragility of life with the sobering news that I almost lost my dad at the age of sixty-six, I treasured his letters even more than ever and saved every one.

No topic was off limits in our weekly epistles which covered the gamut, both humorous and serious—joys and sorrows, triumphs and frustrations, injuries and healings, aspirations and challenges. Above all, there was honesty, caring, respect, and love.

Dad wrote to well over a hundred different addresses while his vagabond daughter wrote only to one: Howard Street. More than thirty years of exchanging letters every Sunday began with our simple "let's stay in touch."

Not many things in life are assured, but Dad's Sunday letter was one of them.

TWELVE

SNOW ACCUMULATED RAPIDLY, making our back roads and the interstate highway slippery, so our trip to the nursing home from our house took us much longer than the usual one hour. It was not a good day to be driving, but we felt the coffee must get through.

"The Coffee Man's here, Frank," Wally announced.

Dad reached for the coffee with French vanilla creamer, took a sip, and gave Wally a thumbs up. Coffee often perked him up, but this day he remained quiet.

"There's already eight inches of fluffy powder this morning—good for skiing," I said. "I think I'll take Gerda out in our woods this afternoon."

"Donna's birthday is coming up in a couple days, Frank," Wally said.

"Dad, remember when you let me skip school on my birthday to go skiing at Mount Snow?"

He nodded.

What a great day it had been...

"WHERE DO YOU WANT to go skiing on your 15th birthday?" Dad asked.

We had skied my favorite ski area, Stratton Mountain, for my 14th birthday.

"How about Mount Snow? I've never been there," I answered, imagining that one of the premier year round resorts in the East would certainly be an adventure.

What could be any better than a midweek birthday ski day with Dad? Off we went to Mount Snow on a sunny, blue-sky Friday in March. Steam rising off the outdoor heated swimming pool immediately set an atmosphere of intrigue, unlike any other ski area I'd been to. Wait a minute! We didn't go to Mount Snow for swimming, lounging, or modeling a new bathing suit.

"Dad, look at that!" I pointed to an impressive mound of snow and ice.

"That's Fountain Mountain," he explained. "It's a water fountain that keeps running all winter and creates a tall glacier. Isn't that something?"

Snow bunnies dominated the bustling lodge scene, women dressed in all the latest fashion, lavish clothing, and accessories. I wondered if they even skied. They looked more like decorations adorning the lodge—every hair perfectly in place, hats not part of their outfits. The glitz and glamour didn't fit our usual style, though "people watching" was good entertainment.

Dad and I caught a chairlift to the top of the Main Mountain where we viewed distant snowy peaks, trees fully laden from the latest storm. Turning, shifting, sliding down the extra-wide trail, we warmed up after the chilly early morning ride to the top. My black metal Hart skis were still shiny, only a couple of months old. Dad skied on his well-used Heads. We loved the near-empty slopes and perfect conditions on this midweek March day.

We skied down the mountain together, but took slightly different lines to grab a pocket of powder—until I caught an edge. A big

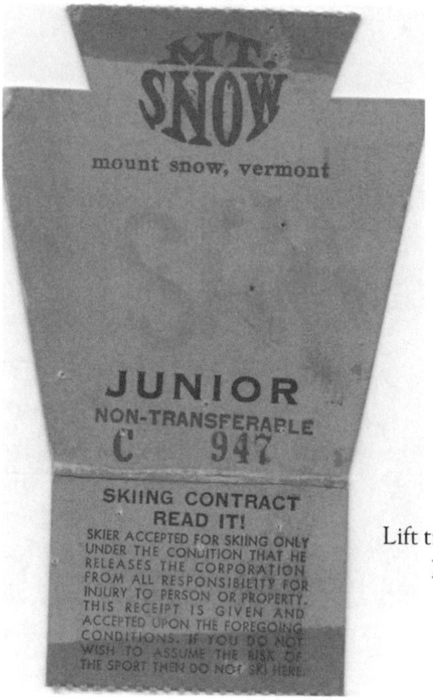

Lift ticket at Mt. Snow—March 5, 1968.

wipe-out. I landed in a snowy heap, one ski off, white from head to toe, and laughing. We explored new trails each run until we found one we liked, then one continuous run all the way to the bottom—to see if we could do it and feel the burn and tingling in our legs. Off to the North Face, our minds cleared—no thoughts of school tests for me or meetings for Dad. We stopped to watch expert skiers fly by and then schussed a steeper run.

At lunchtime inside the bustling Snow Lake Lodge, hot chocolate and our sandwiches from home fueled us for afternoon runs. While our hair appeared matted and tousled, the snow bunnies still had perfect hair, drinks in hand, and pale faces, easily distinguishable from those who had skied hard all morning and had ruddy wind-burned faces.

We hurried back to the slopes to fit in as many runs as we could, challenged to find a little-used slope and a short lift line. We skied until closing, completing a full, invigorating birthday on the slopes. What a joy to downhill ski with Dad.

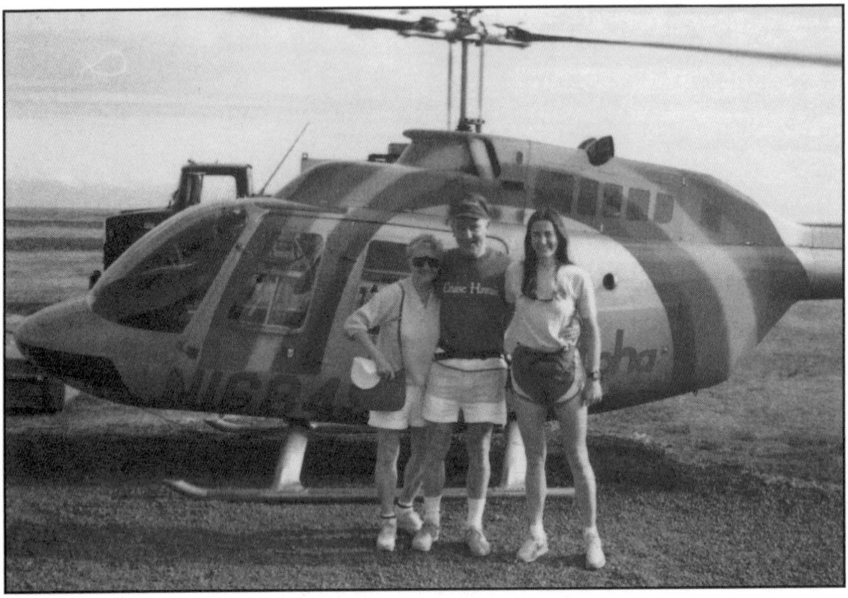

Boarding our helicopter at Port Allen Airport to survey the canyons and waterfalls of Kauai from the air.

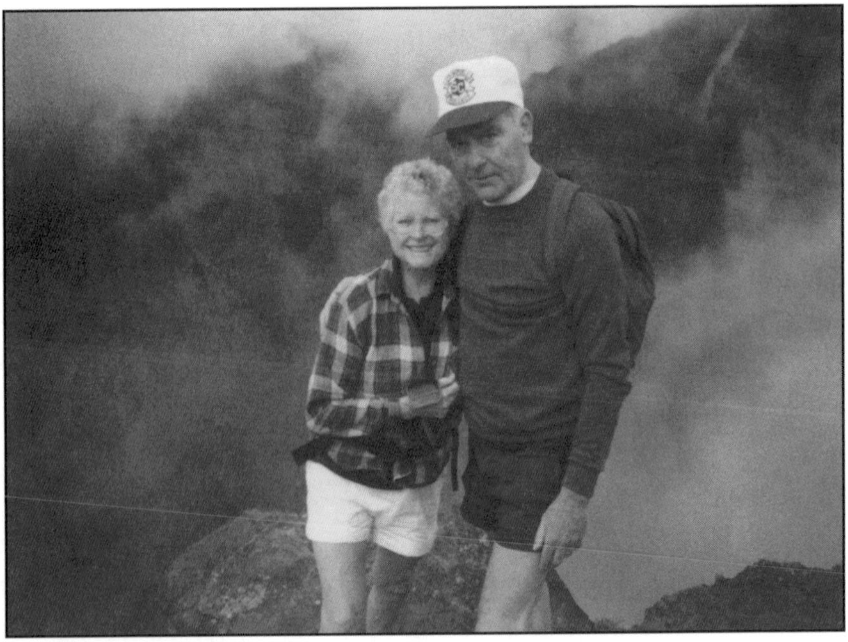

Overlooking Waimea Canyon from the Canyon Trail on Kauai in Hawaii.

THIRTEEN

DAD WAVED TO ME and seemed to recognize me from faraway as I walked down the long hallway.

"Hi, Dad," I waved back.

"Hi, Donna!" He reached out to hug me as I slipped under his good arm.

I wheeled him into the dining room. When lunch arrived, I watched him devour his chicken stir fry, rice, beets, cranberry sauce, and mandarin oranges.

"Dad, it looks like you're eating everything in sight!"

"Yes, everything except the earth itself."

"Reminds me of being at the luau in Hawaii. The food was so good and we kept going back for more. There's some pictures of it in the booklet I made for you—let's find them."

"Good idea."

"Here they are," I said. "We're standing in front of the helicopter that took us for a great ride over Waimea Canyon. That was thrilling."

"I loved that!"

"We had a cloudless day, just like today. Look at the sky." I pointed out the window.

"It's beautiful."

"Look at this one. You wore your new Hawaiian shirt to the luau. I liked the peacocks. Mom loved the mai tais."

He laughed.

After eleven hours in the air to Honolulu, my parents and I boarded a thirty-minute Aloha flight to Lihue on the lush, green island of Kauai. On land at last, I methodically stacked our suitcases, duffels, and packs into a tiny, bright blue, three-cylinder Geo Metro. What possessed me to reserve such a small car for ten days for three adults with considerable luggage? We squished in and headed toward Koloa.

The road turned to dirt, became bumpy and pot-holed before I pulled into the Kahili Mountain Park office at dusk to register.

"I wish I was in a motel," Mom uttered from the back seat, never shy about vocalizing her opinion. She had serious doubts about this rustic location on a secluded hillside behind sugarcane fields. First a miniature car and now dubious accommodations.

My stomach churned as I drove up the hill to the next-to-last cabin. Our Swiss Family Robinson-type cabin felt like heaven-on-earth to me. Not quite utopia to my parents at first glance, soon they praised our homey, spacious, spotless cabin surrounded by lush ferns, noisily-chirping birds, and gurgling stream in the backyard.

The next day we hiked the steep Ridge Trail to a jagged crest with views of wild, green valleys below. We rose from Port Allen Airport by helicopter for a spectacular survey of the island—a full array of waterfalls, canyons, craters, cliffs, and fields. Our pilot hovered close to the canyon walls of Waimea Canyon—"the Grand Canyon of the Pacific." Dad flashed thumbs up, silently but clearly communicating his contentment, in complete awe of waterfalls dropping hundreds of feet below. He loved helicopters and this was one topnotch outing. Our entertaining pilot generously extended the flight to show us intimate views of several more canyons, the Na Pali coast, Hanalei, and Waialeale crater.

On our third day, we wandered the steep dunes of secluded Barking Sands Beach. Golden sand massaged our bare feet while roosters cackled in nearby canyons.

The slow, winding route up narrow Waimea Canyon Drive took us to Kokee State Park where we spread out in "Hala" cabin. Our home for three nights offered us a woodstove, five beds, big kitchen, hot showers, and a barnyard complete with roosters. We played our first round of the card game, Casino, a mere warm-up for the competitive games in the evenings ahead.

Awaawapuhi Trail led us three miles to cliffs overlooking the velvety canyons of the Na Pali coast. For six leisurely hours on an eight-mile "Kokee sampler hike," we forded streams, stood beneath tall waterfalls, and identified and smelled a wonderland of flowers—hydrangea, pink wild begonia, pretty purple glorybush, lantana, impatiens, bird of paradise, awapuhi ginger...and Mom's favorite, the banana passion fruit flower.

The little Geo putted from Waimea to Hanalei where we checked into a clean, airy cottage and I prepared a dinner of baked potatoes with a large salad and plentiful vegetables.

Warning signs at the start of the Kalalau Trail held our attention—"DANGER—CAUTION—hazardous rip currents—streams flood suddenly—PROCEED AT YOUR OWN RISK." Yellow- and black-striped markers showed the safety level in case of a tsunami. Despite the dire warnings we chose to proceed, wearing our sturdy hiking boots to handle the "steep, narrow trail with uneven footing, protruding roots and rocks, mud and slippery surfaces..." that we were advised about on yet another sign. Wow—we'd never seen so many alerts in one place!

We dipped into a valley and forded Hanakapai Stream using the tattered rope strung across it and noticed countless wild cats at the nearby beach. We checked out all the promontories for stunning coastal views and found the perfect lunch spot at which to savor our extravagant crabmeat sandwiches.

"We couldn't have a better day, a more picturesque spot," Dad said, as we sat on the edge of the cliffs enjoying lunch. "Aren't we lucky?"

"Do you think we'll see some whales?" Mom asked.

"Keep a lookout, that would be exciting," I answered.

Dad especially loved the hala trees with their stilt-like roots and pineapple-like fruit. Mom relished each new ocean view and tried to identify every flower. I admired patches of giant sisals.

Later, Mom beat us at Casino back at the inn during a severe lightning storm.

The next day, Fern, the bubbly owner, and her grandson, Tony, welcomed us to the Jade Room at the Paradise Inn B&B in Kapaa—a clean, roomy place with two queen-sized beds, a little kitchen, and unique double-nozzle shower. I cooked dinner of rice, broccoli, and shrimp with salad.

In the morning, Dad shivered and declared it felt like forty degrees! No wonder—cool air flowed right into our Jade Room which was separated from the outside solely by screening… though the thermometer officially registered sixty. We warmed up by hiking through ironwood, swamp mahogany, guava, and eucalyptus groves to the top of nearby Nonou Mountain, the Sleeping Giant.

On our last night, we celebrated my birthday early at a spectacular luau, walking through thriving botanical gardens teeming with peacocks, ducks, chickens, and roosters. The pig, which had been cooking all day in the pit, was unveiled at the Imu Ceremony. Drinks followed under the pavilion with a huge buffet of salads, potatoes, yams, bread, chicken, sweet and sour fish, teriyaki, and the highlight—kalua pig. We returned for more of the tasty meat. Mom reveled in the beautiful evening and especially loved the mai tais. How many times did she go back for a refill? Not that we were counting.

Dramatic drummers, hula dancers, and fire dancers entertained us in the amphitheater, performing all sorts of dances from Japan, China, Philippines, Fiji, New Zealand, and Hawaii.

"This is a perfect, fitting end to our ten days," Dad declared, festive in his new blue Hawaiian shirt. "I've loved every minute of it."

The next day we flew to Honolulu and settled my parents into their B&B in the hills of Manoa, overlooking Honolulu—home for their last four nights, as I prepared to fly on to New Zealand. We walked along Waikiki Beach, then sipped expensive chi-chis on the beachside patio of a mammoth old hotel.

"It's hard to say goodbye," I said at the airport.

"It sure is," Dad said, teary-eyed.

"I wish we were going with you," Mom said, surprising us all.

Her words perfectly reflected the fact that our longest trip to date for our threesome had been extremely successful and could not have been more fun—some of the best times we had ever shared. We had taken the time to truly enjoy each other. No wonder it was so hard to say goodbye.

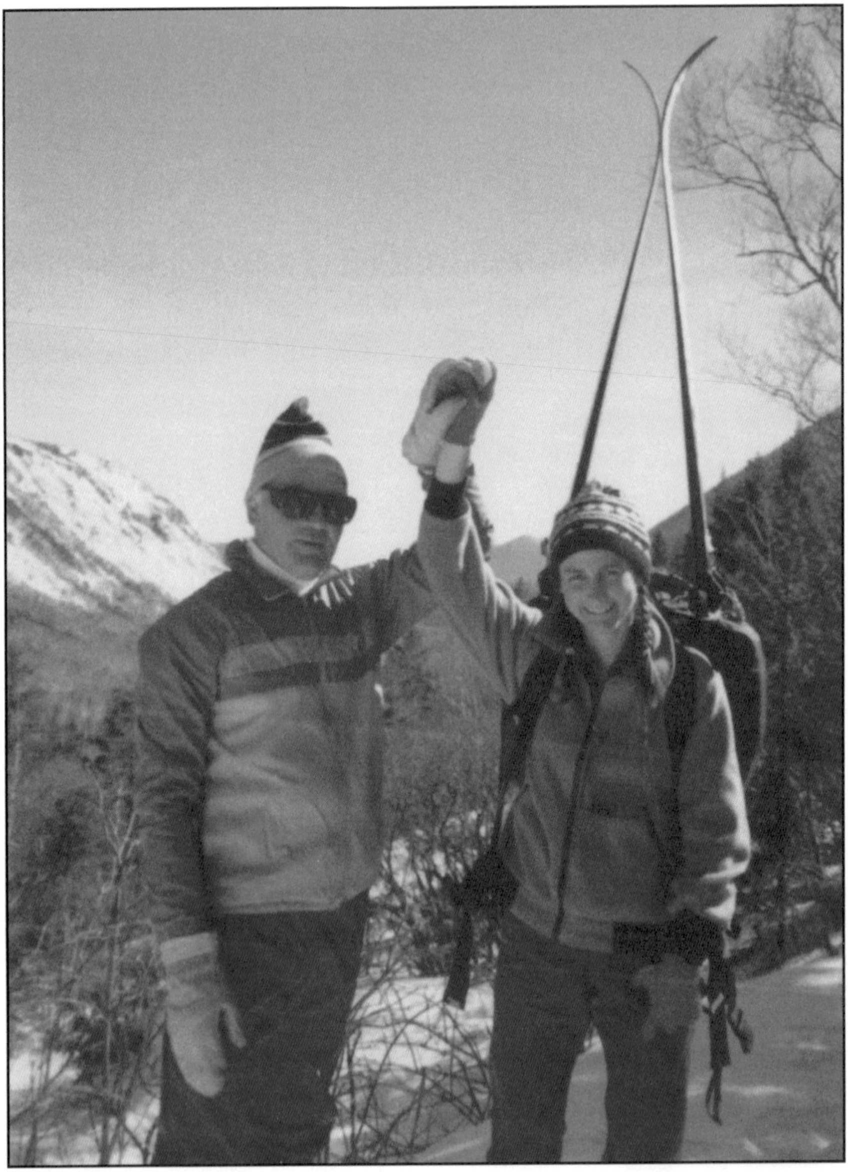

Arriving at Zealand Hut in the White Mountains for Dad's 61st birthday celebration.

FOURTEEN

"WHAT ARE WE GOING to do today?" Dad asked, as soon as Wally and I arrived at the nursing home.

"Well, I think we'll go outside—it feels like spring. We'll celebrate your birthday—Mom sent down some grapenut custard for you. But first, I'll cut your fingernails. They're looking a bit long, like fangs," I said.

Dad's nails were so brittle they flew off and hit Wally in the chest, on his arms, and one to his forehead.

"Frank, those are lethal weapons! I need protection," Wally said, as he raised a writing tablet for a shield. Fingernail cutting had never been so dangerous or so fun.

I gathered Dad's warm clothes from his closet to dress for our outdoor excursion. He stretched out his right arm so I could thread it through the sleeve of his jacket and then hugged me as I pulled him forward in order to tuck it down in back. I zipped up his coat, left arm securely tucked inside, and positioned his navy blue ski hat on his head and a double-thickness mitten on his right hand. After three years of doing this, we had become proficient.

Wally pushed Dad's wheelchair so I could walk alongside with Gerda on a leash.

"You look like Little Red Riding Hood with your hood up today, Dad."

He laughed.

In mid-March snow still lined the roadside though it was melting fast, except for the hard-packed snowmobile trail that crossed near the power line. Even though Dad was quiet I could tell he loved feeling the warm sun on his face and smelling the sweet spring air. Regardless of the season, we heeded the call for fresh air. On this day with the temperature in the forties, we stayed outside for over an hour—far past the stately oaks, the icicled waterfall, and two giant mounds of snow—all the way to the old cemetery. There, sun glinting off frosty spruce trees reminded me of Dad's dramatic birthday celebration at a hut in the White Mountains…

A TIMELY SNOWFALL had covered the hard-packed base and provided ideal conditions for my parents and me to ski six miles to Zealand Falls Hut under a bright-blue sky.

Dad had anticipated this trip to celebrate his 61st birthday for several weeks and he glowed in pure contentment.

We fastened our Rottefella three-pin bindings, hoisted packs, and began the climb up the unplowed Zealand Road, the summer access to the hut. Our packs felt streamlined, even filled with warm layers, sleeping bags, and plenty of food.

We stopped for an orange and snack bars at a Watershed Restoration sign.

"*Gabions*," I read. "Dad, do you know that word?"

"No, I don't," he answered. He loved learning new words and his curiosity was piqued.

The sign informed us that the Zealand River was damaged in a 1959 storm and this spot had become a study area for watershed management. Rock-filled baskets called gabions were installed to reduce scouring and movement of the stream, curb bank erosion, and improve fishing. This type of retaining wall was especially resistant to being washed away by moving water. Gabions—now we knew.

After skiing through a tunnel of spruce and fir to start the Zealand Trail, we tackled the undulating terrain through sunlit birch glades. Mom cruised on her old blue Trak skis while Dad glided efficiently on his red and white Schuppens. Though the temperature was only eighteen degrees, our striding and poling kept us plenty warm. We had the woods all to ourselves, not unusual for a Monday in mid-March.

The trail leveled out across the wetlands on well-built puncheons and over wooden bridges to reach Zealand Pond. Direct rays of the sun warmed us even more—not a cloud in the sky.

"There it is!" I exclaimed, as we viewed the hut for the first time.

"The trail goes straight up!" observed Dad. The hut wasn't far, but sat quite a bit higher than where we stood near the pond.

"We'll take our skis off over there and walk the last part," I said, as I pointed to the last flat spot.

With skis secured to the outside of our packs, we slowly, steadily climbed the steep trail, not bothering to change out of slippery-bottomed ski boots. The climb was worth every hard-earned step. Views of Zealand Notch and Whitewall Mountain opened to the east. Carrigain Notch lay silhouetted to the south between distinctive Mounts Carrigain, Lowell, and Vose Spur.

"WELCOME AND COME IN" the sign read. We obliged. We set down our packs, changed into hiking boots, and savored our sandwiches and cup-of-soup lunch in the comfort of the hut. The kitchen came fully equipped with pots, dishes and utensils, though we supplied our own food.

The bluebird day enticed us back out into the brisk air for an afternoon hike to Zeacliff. I stuffed everything we'd need into my pack so Dad and Mom could climb unencumbered for the more than a thousand-foot elevation gain. Not without some trepidation, Dad and Mom hiked steeply up the Twinway to the much colder, windier Zeacliff. They weren't *winter hikers* but were willing to stretch their horizons with me as their guide and organizer.

We pulled our hoods up and donned our thickest mittens before we broke out of the trees. The scene took their breath away—pure white Mount Washington and the Presidentials in the distance, with Willey, Field, and Tom in the foreground.

I smiled. "That's where I skied through the Pemi last week. I went through the notch at the base of Whitewall to Thoreau Falls and then picked up the Shoal Pond Trail," I said reverently, referring to the vast, roadless Pemigewasset Wilderness, my favorite winter playground.

This was their rare glimpse into that remote, wild winter scene—another world.

As thrilled as they were to stand atop Zeacliff and soak up the expansive views, they were equally glad that the hut awaited us less than a mile and a half away. We descended the steep trail quickly and soon settled in near the little Fisher woodstove in our sweaters and down vests with the kettle on for hot chocolate and tea.

We perused books and logbooks from the shelves before our filling spaghetti dinner with parmesan cheese and fresh broccoli. Brownies with candles honored Dad's upcoming birthday that we celebrated a couple days early.

We were the only guests! We loved our private hut with only the quiet, laid-back caretaker who happily gave us a tour of the recently renovated hut and his brand new, spacious crew quarters.

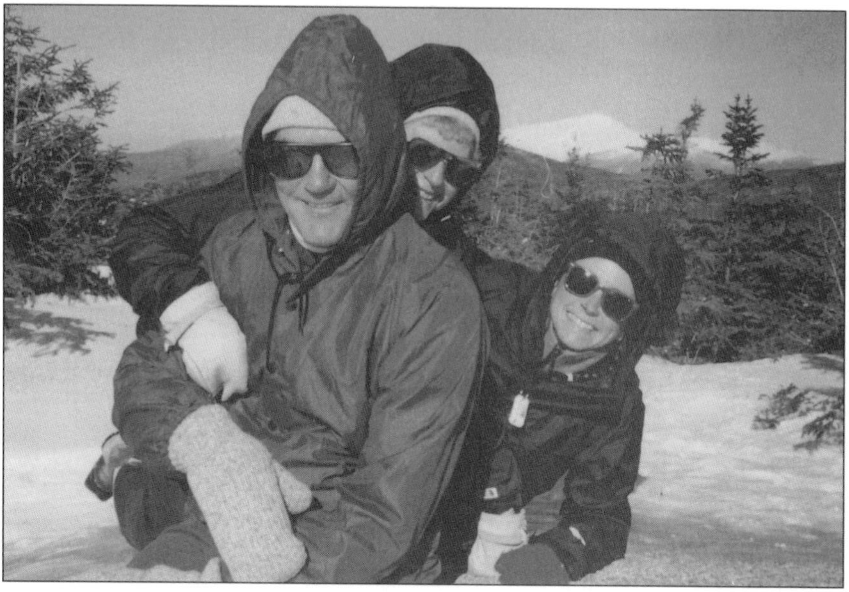

Hoods up and thick mittens on to enjoy views of pure white Mount Washington and the Presidentials from Zeacliff.

With his blessing, we pushed the table and benches aside and lined up our three mattresses on the floor next to the woodstove—a slumber party for Dad and Mom's first overnight visit to this hut. When they visited nearly two years prior on a day hike, they vowed to return. While I doubt they envisioned a winter visit, Dad couldn't have been happier with this destination to celebrate his birthday.

He added his brief entry to the hut's logbook:

> SECOND VISIT TO HUT—HIKE TO ZEACLIFF WAS SPECTACULAR.
> FINE ACCOMODATIONS AND GREAT HOSPITALITY
> THE WARM FIRE SO WELCOME—HOPE TO COME AGAIN
> (BIRTHDAY TRIP FOR DAD)
> FRANK & DORIS DEARBORN
> DONNA DEARBORN

Before lights out, we ventured out onto the porch. The sky was an explosion of color! Sunset was long gone.

"It must be the Northern Lights!" I exclaimed.

We stood in awe, mouths agape at the ever-changing show dominated by pulsating greens and deep, deep reds.

"Over there!" Dad pointed to his left.

"Look!" Mom said, as she gazed to the south.

Red streaks, green ripples, fascinating patterns of colors, unlike anything we'd ever seen. We scanned the sky for a long time, not wanting to miss any part of this brilliant display.

"Happy Birthday, Dad," I said, as I grabbed him firmly around his shoulders, not wanting our mystical evening to end.

MORE THAN TWENTY-TWO YEARS later I learned that the aurora borealis on that night was one of the most striking displays of auroras in recent times. A billion-ton plume of superheated gas erupted from the sun's surface on March 10, 1989. When the gas cloud reached earth a few days later, it set off a geomagnetic superstorm that caused the collapse of Hydro-Quebec's transmission system and knocked out electric power to about six million people. Not only did it produce widespread multi-colored auroras in Europe and as far south as Texas and Cuba, a red glow appeared in the sky over most of the world and some people who had never seen an aurora before worried that nuclear war had broken out.

Standing on the porch of Zealand Hut, we had no idea of the scope of this aurora of historical proportions, only that we felt grateful for the most extraordinary and unexpected birthday surprise in our tiny corner of the White Mountains.

FIFTEEN

I PUSHED DAD'S WHEELCHAIR along the edge of the road. T-shirt weather at last! We drank in sweet, warm air as we strolled past red clover, dandelions, and crown vetch to a precisely laid out vegetable garden at the corner. Thick fingers of water cascaded over the lip of the waterfall where feathery plumes of Ostrich Ferns proliferated and Mourning Doves cooed.

"You look good in your Kansas City Royals baseball cap, Dad! It's your color."

He smiled.

On the way back, Dad waved to a mechanic who waved back. Rich purple lilacs next to one apartment lured us closer and then held us captive in a perfumed trance.

"Breathe in, Dad. It's heavenly." He closed his eyes and breathed deep, as he cradled a flowering cluster.

"I just thought of the time Mom bent over to inspect a lady slipper. It was about this time of year. When she straightened up her pack hit you under the chin."

"I remember."

It happened on the Long Trail…

"Let's do an overnight on the Long Trail," I suggested to my parents as my sophomore year at Springfield College came to a close. While they were veteran day hikers, they hadn't been overnight, and I urged them to join me for a different experience.

"That sounds fun, if you'll organize us and tell us what to bring," Dad said.

"I'll go if you do the cooking, Donna," Mom said.

"It's a deal."

"Where should we go?" Dad asked.

"I'd love to hike from Smuggler's Notch to Jonesville," I said, anxious to traverse that section. "We'll need three days and two nights." I had backpacked south from Jonesville for a week with my sophomore roommate the previous June.

"Sounds good!" Dad said.

We packed our frame packs with three days of food, sleeping bags, and warm clothes. On May 25th, my parents' best hiking partners, Betty and Dick Crosby, drove us and our two-year-old family dog, Angus, to the trailhead on Route 2 in Jonesville where we left our Chevy Impala. They transported us north into Smuggler's Notch where we began our southbound hike.

"I'll see you at the top!" Betty called, as she drove off to the Toll Road with our backpacks.

With only daypacks, Dad, Mom, Dick Crosby, and I hiked up the steep path from Route 108, gaining two thousand feet in less than two miles to Taft Lodge, the largest Long Trail shelter, which sat on a shelf below the Chin of Mount Mansfield. Angus joyfully raced up the trail with us after more than three hours in the car.

At Eagle Pass, we took the short spur path to the Adam's Apple, well worth the detour for the view of nearby Lake of the Clouds, even though clouds obscured the distant views.

"This is the highest point—the Chin," I commented. "Can't get any higher in Vermont."

Jay Peak stood alone to the north.

"Is that Killington?" Dad asked as he pointed south.

"Yes," I said.

We traversed the Lower Lip and Upper Lip and passed the Rock of Terror, a boulder that seems on the brink of plummeting down the mountainside.

As we hiked toward the Mount Mansfield Summit Station we saw Betty up there waving her arms.

"Betty!" Mom called out in delight at our successful rendezvous with Betty and our packs.

Atop Vermont's highest peak, we savored our bologna sandwiches and oranges from home and then hoisted our backpacks which felt noticeably heavier than our day packs. Light rain started as we walked south to The Forehead, the southernmost peak of Mount Mansfield, so we donned our colorful ponchos and said a quick goodbye to the Crosbys.

Betty and Dick returned to their car in the summit parking lot while Dad, Mom, and I descended the very steep, rough path over rocks and ledges. We carefully carried Angus down two ladders where no alternate route existed, even for our clever dog. He stayed calm and didn't mind.

We maneuvered through the two large boulders of the Needles Eye and arrived at our destination. From Butler Lodge we looked down into the Champlain Valley and out to the Adirondacks.

"What a spot! Aren't we lucky?" Dad exclaimed.

"What are those mountains?" Mom asked, as she pointed to the west.

"Those are the Adirondacks," I said. "I love it here. Let's go in and find some bunk space."

We claimed bottom bunks in the impressive, old log cabin, ending our 5.4-mile first day.

I set my Optimus 8R backpacking stove on the rock ledge in front of the lodge to cook dinner for three hungry hikers. Perhaps I was trying too hard to impress my parents, as I spilled the pot of boiling water which was all ready for the noodles. Thankful it was not the cooked dinner that spilled, I started over, supper slightly delayed that night.

The Burbanks, a couple Dad knew from a Vermont Baptist gathering, arrived later. Despite a full cabin, I slept well, unaware of any snoring.

The next morning we slipped on ponchos again as clouds lowered and settled in, contouring across the west slope of Mount Dewey on our way to Nebraska Notch in steady drizzle.

Mom bent over to inspect a pink lady slipper, one of her favorite wildflowers. Her cumbersome frame backpack made it difficult to get a closer view.

"Look how perfect this one is... it almost doesn't seem real," she said.

As she straightened back up, the top of her pack's frame hit Dad sharply under the chin. He reflexively shoved her out of the way, saying "Owww, that hurt."

Mom catapulted into the rain-soaked bushes upside down, unable to get up, with her pack weighing her down and scraggly sumac branches trapping her.

"Oh, my god," Dad said. "I didn't mean to..."

"Mom, Mom, are you okay?" I said, as I rushed to her aid.

I heard indecipherable sputtering.

"Are you okay?" I tried again.

I reached out, gave Mom my hand, and hauled her back onto the trail. All in one fluid motion, she rose to her feet and bolted down the trail away from us, south on the Long Trail. She was fuming, too furious for words.

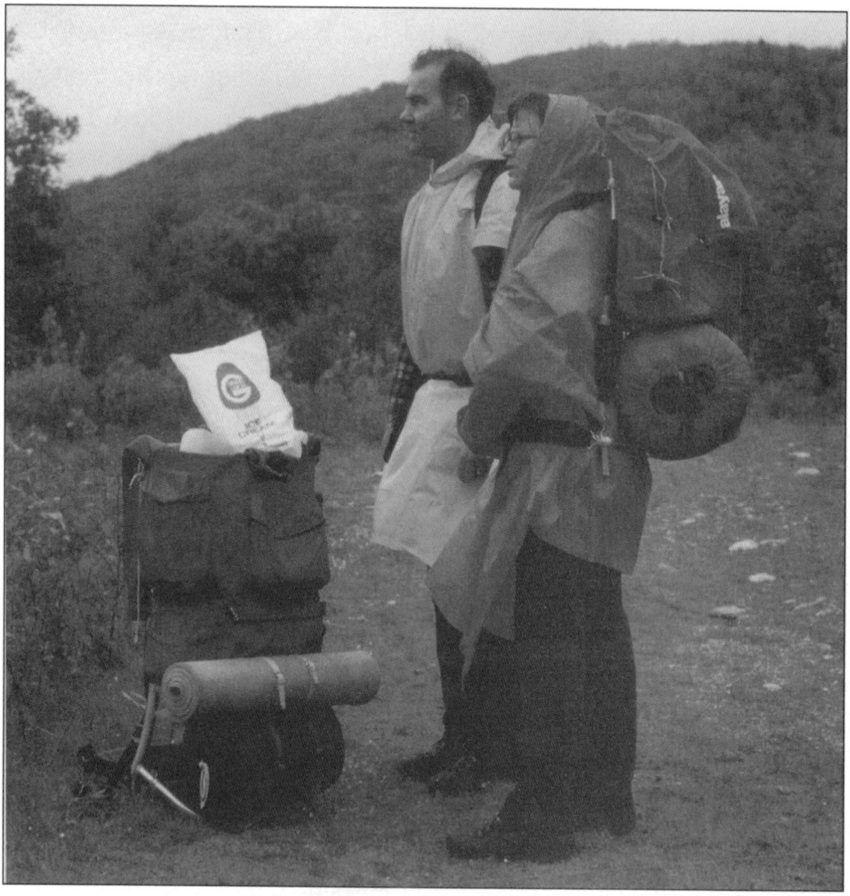

Still raining on day 2, en route to Puffer Lodge.

Dad stood there speechless. "Doris! Doris! Wait!" he called after her.

"I'm sorry! Wait!" he tried again, louder this time.

By then she had sped way out of sight. Dad and I hurried down the trail. At times we glimpsed her red pack ahead, but no matter how hard we tried we could not lessen the gap between us. We didn't catch Mom for over an hour. She still fumed and didn't want to talk. It took considerable explaining and apologizing before Dad was back in her good graces.

In Nebraska Notch we took the Clara Bow Trail as a more interesting and difficult alternate route. We dropped into the boulder-filled notch, barely squeezing our packs under one big rock. When we reached another descending ladder, Angus immediately headed into the thick woods with an alternate plan, hopefully not pursuing a porcupine! After several anxious minutes Angus rejoined us near the base of the ladder, skillfully finding his way to circumnavigate the vertical cliff face.

"Good boy, Angus," I said.

We stopped briefly at Taylor Lodge before climbing steeply to a lookout to view Lake Mansfield below. After two more climbs and dips we ended our 7.9-mile day at Puffer Lodge.

The Burbanks also overnighted at Puffer and generously served us freshly-steamed fiddlehead ferns at the busy camp. With the log cabin full, Angus and I camped in my little orange A-frame tent and kept each other warm on a very cold night.

Our packs felt comfortable and light by the third day as we hiked downhill after the early morning climb to the wooded summit of Bolton Mountain. At Bolton Lodge we viewed Camel's Hump to the north.

The rain stopped as we followed logging roads and crossed several brooks, reaching Duck Brook Shelter and one final viewpoint.

"We're almost there," I said. "Good job, Dad. Good job, Mom."

"It's been fun," Dad said. "Thanks for looking after us. We'll have to do another one."

"It was an experience," Mom said. "I hope the car is still there."

We had dropped a whopping 3400 feet from Bolton Mountain to Jonesville, the lowest elevation of the entire Long Trail—326 feet. Rubbery, tired legs resulted from the unrelenting downhill.

Relieved to see the familiar car at Route 2, we gladly set down our packs. Dad and Mom stood beside the trailhead sign for a final *thumbs up* parting pose, their 24.5-mile maiden backpack journey complete.

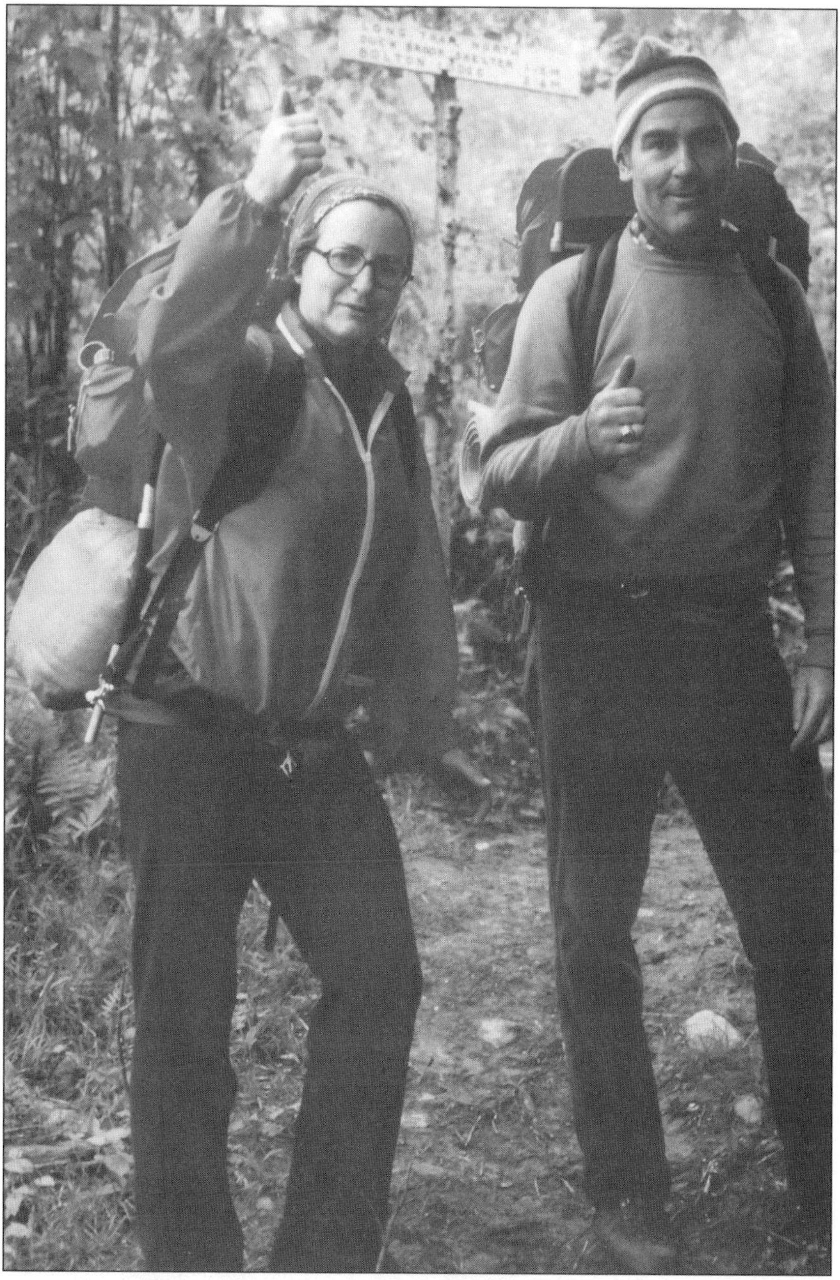

End of our 3-day backpack on the Long Trail's Division 9, near Jonesville.

Dad, with Deb and Josh, hiking the Stratton Pond Trail.

Dad and Mom between the birch trees on Ascutney Mountain in Brownsville, Vermont.

SIXTEEN

"HI, DAD, Happy Father's Day," I said.

"Hi, Donna."

"I made you a new booklet of pictures—*Our Hero: Frank Holt Dearborn. We Love You.* There's one page for each family member. Here's you and David at South Pond." I turned the pages, "Deb and you with Josh in a pack on your back, you and Mom by a beautiful birch tree on Mount Ascutney, you holding me when I was a baby..."

He smiled as he looked at the photographs.

"Mom bought you this pretty striped shirt that will be good for summer."

"Thank you!"

"Here's your card, Dad. I'll read it to you:"

> *Dad- You've been there for me from Day 1. I can never forget that. With your patience you gave me patience. With your strength you gave me strength. You taught me kindness, caring, love, diplomacy, rooting for the underdog. You taught me how to live*

right and live well. You inspired me, encouraged me, supported me. You always had time for me. Not for a day did you ever falter as a father. I thank you for your consistency and your unconditional love. I have known no better person in the world than you, my father, Frank Holt Dearborn.

I love you now and always. Your daughter, Donna

"Dad, here's a story about you that was in the *Brattleboro Reformer* recently. It's called 'Frank Dearborn—a legacy of service and a smile.' Fran Lynggard Hansen wrote it; she was Fran Fairchild. She remembers the Easter egg hunt, especially your kindness to all the kids who didn't find an egg. I'll read some of it to you:"

> Even more important than programs and buildings, Dearborn built relationships with members of the community through the years. This writer remembers Mr. Dearborn and his station wagon appearing every year at the annual Easter egg hunt in the spring. Hundreds of eggs were hidden on the upper field at Memorial Park, along with the grand prize, the golden egg, which held a season's pass to the pool.
>
> Children were lined up on the grass and when he yelled "Go!" ran to pick up the candy eggs and hunt for the coveted golden one. Each year, I was stunned by the numbers of kids and became too overwhelmed to find a single candy egg. The kids moved like a vacuum cleaner over the field and in minutes, the eggs were gone.
>
> Mr. Dearborn would call for the small number of kids who didn't find any eggs, take them over to his station wagon and give each of us a smile, a few pieces of candy and maintained that next year things might be different and encouraged us all to keep trying and to come back next year (*Brattleboro Reformer*, February 19, 2008).

"Do you remember that, Dad? I used to help you hide the eggs."

Dad nodded. He looked at his Father's Day card again and held it tight...

I REMEMBER WALKING down Main Street with my dad who acknowledged everyone with a cheery greeting, a nod and smile, a wave, or sometimes more. Dad looked people straight in the eye.

We had nearly reached our destination of Baker's Bookstore when we noticed a bedraggled man wearing a soiled sweatshirt sitting on a step to our left. Large palms cradled his unshaven face, long unruly hair cascaded over his elbows that rested on greasy, holey jeans.

"Good morning," offered my dad respectfully.

The homeless man's bloodshot eyes raised to meet Dad's, a warm smile creased his face. He nodded.

I might have been afraid and avoided eye contact, but Dad showed me that this disheveled man deserved our acknowledgment and greeting as much as any other person we saw on Main Street that afternoon. Everyone matters; everyone warrants a *hello*, a smile.

I loved walking down Main Street with Dad, who walked tall with confidence and just the right amount of self-assuredness. I walked next to him—a shy, little ten-year-old girl in braids—bursting with pride. I'm with him—he's MY DAD!

We didn't talk about the fleeting encounter with the homeless man, but I never forgot it and saw that it was no isolated incident.

Dad felt particular compassion and empathy for the underdog and the disenfranchised, giving them a voice and showing them respect. He ensured the recreation department offered a summer program for special needs children. Dad gave opportunities to many kids who couldn't get a job because of a learning disability, offering them the chance to help with swimming lessons at the Park or to assist at the Recreation

Center. He gave them responsibility they could handle and in doing so boosted their confidence. One such young gal, Lynne, loved helping with swim lessons and beamed with pride at doing something worthwhile and having a sense of purpose.

Friendly Frank was gregarious and always ready for conversation. Beneath that friendly surface was much, much more—a deep reservoir of love, compassion, and kindness.

Dad looked straight into someone's heart—beyond missing teeth, a limp, strange mannerisms, or odd behavior. He believed in the basic goodness of people and gave everyone a chance.

He hired Herbie, Wes, Peter, and many more who were outcasts, rejects, or people ridiculed for the way they dressed, walked, or talked. They thrived from Dad's kindness and glowed from his attention, comforted they had a friend—one of the few they had, perhaps the only one.

As Herbie the janitor grew older, he moved a lot slower. Cleaning up alone after Saturday night teen dances became overwhelming for Herbie. What did Dad do? He recruited us and we cleaned it together on our way to church on Sundays. We collapsed the heavy, wooden chairs, strung together in groups of three or more, and carted them to the side of the gym. Back and forth across the shiny gym floor I pushed a four-foot-wide swath using the large dust mop. I didn't want to miss an inch of floor, hoping for the prize that would sometimes appear in the dust pile at the end.

We happily helped Dad, with the added incentive of finding treasures beneath the chairs—dimes and quarters, sometimes dollar bills. Now looking back I see the real meaning of Sunday morning floor mopping and one of the many ways Dad reached out quietly, behind the scenes, and without fanfare, pitching in and helping out, as if he didn't already have enough duties.

I learned abundant lessons just by watching Dad. With an open heart, he reached out with smiles, acceptance, and kindness.

SEVENTEEN

DAD SEEMED DOWN as he sipped the strawberry smoothie Mom brought him. He'd hardly touched his lunch of pot roast, squash, and apple sauce.

To cheer him up I pulled out an essay he'd written in 1950 when he was twenty-two years old.

"I'm going to read a little from your philosophical discourse on matrimony that you once sent me in a letter—it's really interesting:"

Marriage is a blending of personalities and it takes a bit of consideration from both partners to make a go of it. One has to sacrifice, to give in, or arguments develop. If you want to go somewhere you have to have acquiescence from your spouse. No going to camps for the summer or engaging in social activities with unabashed fervor. One also has to be thoughtful, doing nice things such as flowers, remembering birthdays . . . Part of a marriage is planning and thinking about the future, about the baby and trips around, socials to attend, different dishes to taste. All the factors are intermeshed into the social phenomenon known as marriage which is stepping into something which is real big . . . it is the turning point of life for a young man.

The hour draws late, the night is dark. The security, peacefulness, and warmth of a well-made white-sheeted bed beckons to the tired, ever-pondering, ever-planning author, so farewell to the keys for another night.

When I finished reading, we had a lot of laughs discussing marriage, Dad's treatise, and the unique woman Dad married—little Doris Brown. Dad said Mom was *overt* in her style of helping him and I was *subtle*—both perceptive and accurate.

"You two have an anniversary coming up soon," I said. "It will be fifty-four years."

"Doris, you're a good wife," Dad said, clear as can be. "Gosh, you look pretty."

"Here are some photos of your 50th anniversary," I said and opened his album. "What a trip the three of us had!"

Oregon had eluded them—the only state they hadn't visited. Exploring their 50th state for their 50th anniversary sounded especially fitting. I planned a trip tailored to their desire to actively explore diverse regions of Oregon and chauffeured them south along the coast and north through the interior for two weeks in May.

"Here you are atop Astoria Column, 164 steps to get to the top," I said, pointing to the first photo. "What a view."

Dad touched all the pictures, one by one, and lingered on some. Snow-capped southern Cascades and sparkling Crater Lake—sea stacks, sturgeons, sage, sand dunes, and sea lions.

"I loved the baby llamas, the lighthouses, and staying at Overleaf Lodge. That was deluxe," Mom said.

"Bridge of the Gods. Dad, I remember you counting the number of cars in the trains that chugged along the Columbia River. You'd give

Young love.

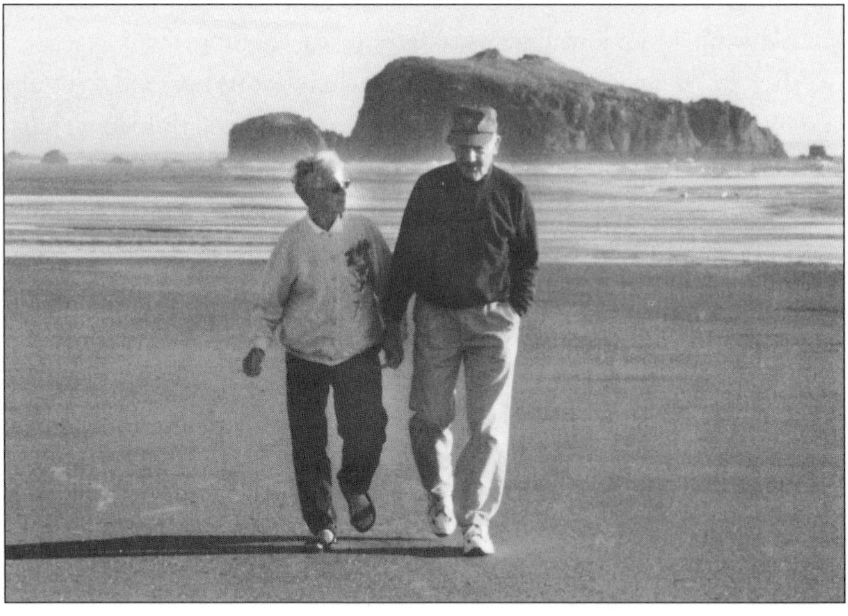

Hand-in-hand on Bandon Beach in Oregon – celebrating 50 years of marriage.

your final tally—'102 cars and eight engines.' We sat on a bench and speculated what they contained and where they were going. There were never-ending trains on both sides of the river, weren't there?"

He smiled.

"Mom and Dad, you look pretty happy in this picture—boarding the train, looking forward to our dinner and murder mystery. That was fun."

Dad shook his head in agreement...

Dad, Mom, and I boarded the Mt. Hood Railroad car at five o'clock—a sellout. Throngs of people waited to board in Hood River, Oregon. The hostess ushered us into our private booth just in time for hors d'oeuvres of smoked salmon and crackers to go with our bottle of wine. Majestic, snow-capped Mt. Hood loomed dreamlike in the distance. With his many questions, Dad immediately gleaned countless tidbits about our waiter Joel's life as a college student. Dad and I savored the exquisite salmon while Mom loved her asparagus spears with angel hair.

After two hours we reached Parkdale where actors boarded the train and immediately mingled with passengers as we started the return journey to Hood River. The murderer roamed amongst us! Who could it be? We embraced our assignment and discussed the plot with the giddy Portland couple across the aisle. One woman halfway down the aisle laughed hysterically and got everyone else laughing too.

Passengers continued to drink and the atmosphere became even more raucous. We had an ideal corner at the quieter end of the train, though when Dad spoke up we became the focus. The inspector raced to our table to subdue Dad and nearly shot him as he pleaded for mercy with his hands raised and a bewildered look on his face. She didn't fire the gun and Dad survived.

At a noisy scuffle toward the other end of the train, some passengers were shot, branded with a "DEAD" tag, and could no longer participate. Our astute friend across the aisle correctly identified the female inspector from England as the cat burglar and murderer. The ideal combination of historic train, captivating entertainment, and fine dining made our five hours pass quickly.

WHILE DAD, MOM, AND I COUNTED our blessings at the time for such a marvelous trip, Dad's stroke a mere one year later had given us a fresh perspective.

This day in the nursing home with Dad, nearly four years after our trip, Mom and I reaffirmed our gratefulness that we had taken the time then and not delayed until another year. We walked and hiked with Dad to his heart's content through abundant state parks, to towering Columbia Gorge waterfalls, past majestic Roosevelt bull elk, and on one special, snow free stretch of the Pacific Crest Trail. We had realized one of Dad's dreams on their 50th anniversary... just in time.

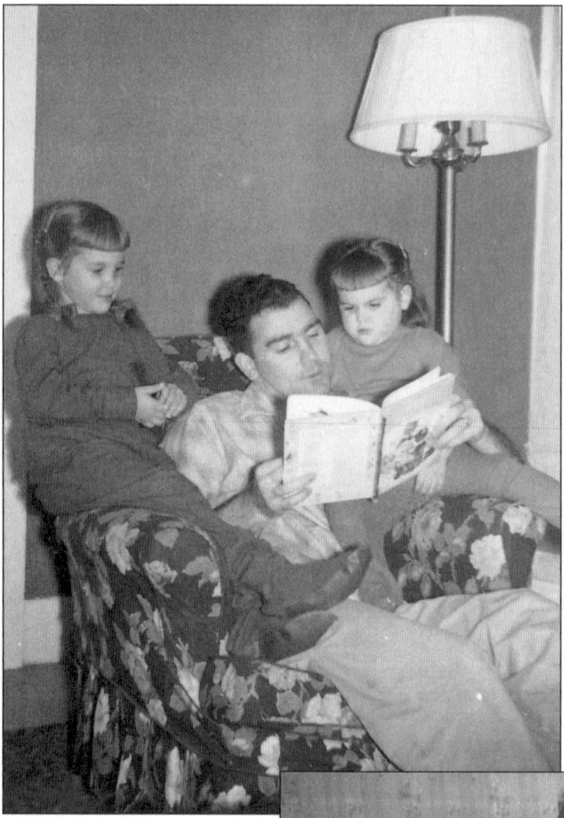

Read us a story, Daddy.

At 198 Western Avenue in 1958.

EIGHTEEN

"DO YOU KNOW the song 'Barney Google,' Frank?" Wally asked as he picked up his guitar. "Sing along. Here goes: *Barney Google with the goo goo googly eyes, Barney Google had a wife three times his size. She sued Barney for divorce. Now he's living with his horse. Barney Google with the goo goo googly eyes...*" I joined in with the words I remembered, singing a song that Dad knew from long ago. He didn't sing but his eyes lit up.

"Dad, remember the time you and Uncle Bob and I were canoeing on the Black River near Franklin. I was in the bow, you were in the stern, and Uncle Bob was sitting in the middle. Suddenly he stood up straight, put his right hand to his brow like this, sort of like a salute, and yelled, 'I see Indian.' Remember what happened?"

Dad smiled at me but didn't answer.

I continued. "The canoe flipped and we all ended up in the cold water. You were too stunned to speak for a minute and Uncle Bob laughed hysterically. We righted the canoe and collected all our floating gear and paddled the rest of the way with no more Indian sightings.

When Mom and Aunt Dot picked us up, they wondered why we all were so wet. The only answer we had was: 'Indians.' Uncle Bob was always up to something, wasn't he?"

Dad laughed and sipped his vanilla smoothie as sun streamed in the windows of the Rose Room on a cold February day, snow still piled up high only four days after the ferocious Valentine's Day Blizzard. It was especially good to see Dad, since the previous Sunday everyone had been sick with the flu and the nursing home was under quarantine.

Gerda moaned in contentment as she curled up tight to Dad's wheelchair and fell fast asleep. I leaned down to pat Gerda's head and could see the patch of smooth skin where no hair grew on Dad's leg. "Debbie, David, and I used to ask you to tell us about that scar, didn't we?"

He nodded.

Back then he told us how he had been hit by a car as he ran across the street without looking, suffered a compound fracture of his tibia, and remained in the hospital for seven weeks with his leg in traction when he was in the third grade.

"Dad, you always had a story for us. I'm going to read you one of mine now:"

STORY TIME

For story time, we piled onto one of our beds in the one large bedroom we three kids shared in our apartment overlooking Western Avenue, across the street from Ziter's Market. Dad had a fascinating story for us just about every night—a mystery, a ghost story, or an adventure story. We requested stories about trains, horses, dogs, tunnels, trucks, bears, and bank robberies. He never let us down.

"One afternoon," he said, "your Uncle Bob and I were confined to our room as punishment for something—I don't remember what. Tired of staying in our room, we made a plan.

First we took the sheets off our bed, tied them together, and attached the whole thing to the bedpost. We opened our window quietly and shimmied down our sheet ladder."

"Who went first?" I wanted to know. I was ten, the oldest, and the best listener.

"Did you make it all the way to the ground?" Deb asked. Chatty, dark-haired Deb with the pixie cut was eight.

"Did you get hurt?" David, the blond-haired, blue-eyed baby, at age five, added.

"I went first, but our timing wasn't very good. We were part-way down when a neighbor saw us and called our mother to ask her if she knew her boys were going out the window."

"What did Nana do?" I asked, thinking of my occasionally stern grandmother.

"She was very mad and scolded us. We had to promise we'd never do that again, and she sent us back to our room."

We learned a lot about Dad's childhood during story time—about the chiggers that kept he and his brother awake all night in their floor-less tent after they had bicycled on their one-speed bikes to York Beach, eating whoopie pies while shooting the .22 rifle in the third ravine at Charlie Slack's place, and driving their Sunday school teacher crazy sending paper air-planes through the window so they soared through the church during the service. And then there were the stories about when Dad fell off the railroad trestle one day and Dr. Beaton put twelve stitches in Dad's chin. That didn't stop him and his brother from walking the trestle. They played hide-and-seek in the beams of the railroad bridge and always waved to the caboose man.

When his father took him and his brother hunting, they never shot a deer, but one of them blew a hole in the fender

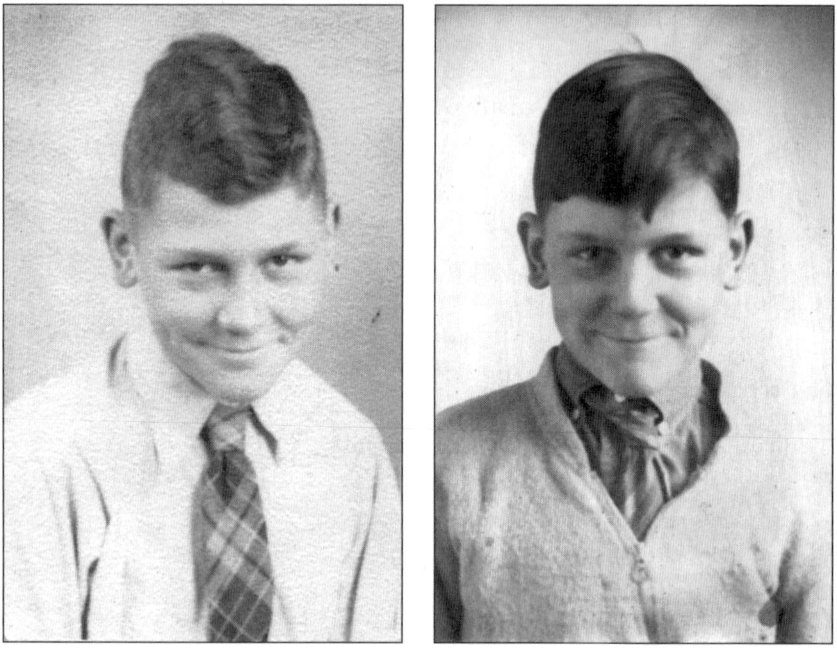

Young Holt.

of the old Hudson car. They told their mother that some darn fool did it and many years later admitted their guilt.

We sat spellbound when Dad recounted one of the scariest times of his youth.

"Bob fell into the river above the Red Dam. He kept going under and coming up and we couldn't reach him. I was so scared. I ran down the path as fast as I could to the nearest neighbor—Gert Nowell—and told her we needed help. She ran to the stream and leapt in, clothes and all, and pulled Bob out—just in time. He was full of water. I can still picture him bent over the cement pillar dazed and scared to death. The ambulance came but he didn't need resuscitation."

"Why didn't he swim to the shore?" I asked. My siblings and I all took swimming lessons at Memorial Park every summer.

"He had never learned to swim—afraid of the water. After that Nana made sure he learned. She scolded him but was so relieved." He smiled at us. "It's good you know how to swim."

Other stories revealed that Dad was just like us. He loved hearing the no-school signal so he could go back to bed or go out to play in the snow. Sometimes he fibbed a little. When he came home from a baseball game at Odell Park with his clothes in tatters, he told his mother he tore them sliding into home plate, but actually he got into a fight. Another afternoon he was afraid to go home with a broken nose because his mother had forbidden him to play ice hockey at Nesmith School.

We especially loved his stories about pranks.

"Bob and I slept in the barn all one summer," he said. "We made it into our clubhouse. We set booby traps on the ground floor to keep our sisters out."

"What kind of booby traps?" David asked, extremely interested.

"At first we had a string attached to the door handle, connected to boards that made a bell ring. Later, we attached a gong to a rope and a trapdoor that opened with debris falling down."

"Did it keep your sisters away?"

"Yes, they screamed and ran back to the house, just what we wanted!"

Back then Dad never ran out of stories and we sat spellbound every night for years. Now the tables were turned—I regaled Dad with stories while he sat captivated by the flood of memories.

On the 33.5-mile-long Milford Track in New Zealand
with MacKinnon Pass in the distance.

Still smiling on day 3 of the Milford Track after 24 hours of rain.

NINETEEN

"HI, DONNA."

"Hi, Dad," I said as I gave him a hug on a drizzly March day.

"It's good to have you here!" he said.

"How was lunch?"

"It was excellent, thank you."

"Mom sent down something special for your birthday—chocolate éclair cake."

"Thank you."

"Ten years ago we celebrated your birthday in New Zealand. What a view above Queenstown from the Skyline Gondola. I'll never forget that buffet—all the choices—lamb, salmon, steak, prawns, mussels, salads, soup, endless side dishes, and the national dessert of New Zealand, pavlova. They brought out a special piece of chocolate cake with strawberries and whipped cream, with candles on it for you. We have a picture of it... here it is."

"That was something," he said.

"Soon after that we started our hike on the most famous walk in the world."

"The Milford Track was beautiful. I loved it."

Hiking the Milford Track was one of the highlights of our three-week trip to New Zealand...

DAD, MOM, AND I BOARDED a tiny boat at Te Anau Downs in New Zealand. Dad raised an eyebrow at me that I knew meant, "We're traveling across an ocean-like lake in this little putter?"

I hadn't realized what a small boat I'd hired, a mere seventeen feet long. Cold water spray from Lake Te Anau instantly splattered us as Vern's boat gathered speed. Dad and Mom cinched their raincoat hoods tight. I helplessly watched the brunt of the spray hitting them—not the picture of happiness I envisioned. What was I thinking?

I had good intentions—to take private transport to the start of the Milford Track at Glade Wharf in order to be there first, not starting the trail with the thirty-eight others who were also hiking the Milford. I wanted my parents to have this magical New Zealand rainforest all to themselves. Now I wondered if we'd even get there. Had I made a big mistake?

Fortunately the ride soon smoothed out, with less spray and fewer bumps. We skimmed over the peaceful waters for the remainder of the forty-five minute trip to the north, a tiny speck on the South Island's largest lake. The rugged Murchison Mountains came into view, then Dore Pass, a vivid reminder why this is my favorite part of New Zealand.

We couldn't wait to start hiking! After taking a family photo at Glade Wharf, we eagerly tramped off into the rainforest. The medieval-looking, moss-draped beech trees garnered our attention along the flat, well-manicured trail. Spleenwort hung from mountain beech. Light-colored totara stood tall and stately, some known to be over a thousand years old.

"Can you believe Maoris hollowed out these trees for canoes?" I said. "Some of them could carry a hundred warriors!"

"Isn't that something," Dad said, shaking his head in awe.

Neatly dressed, he wore a blue plaid shirt layered over a royal blue T-shirt, blue Outward Bound cap on his head. Royal blue shoelaces decked out his blue and brown hiking boots.

He paused and surveyed the long swing bridge across the Clinton River. A few years prior, my adventurous dad had surprisingly developed a fear of heights. What would he think of this bouncy span high above the river? Looking straight ahead, he steadily made his way across.

Sporting a bright red vest and trademark navy pants, Mom bounded across and searched the crystal clear river for more trout; we had already sighted a 2½-foot-long brown trout easing its way along the gravelly bottom of the Clinton.

We all agreed that transporting to the track early had been an excellent idea. Not only was the trail all ours, but we were blessed with the luxury of time so we could poke along and stop often for snacks, photos, and to view distant peaks.

"I've never experienced anything like this," Mom said.

"And to think we almost missed it," Dad said.

I nodded and sighed deeply. We all felt extremely fortunate to be walking the Milford Track. When we had arrived in New Zealand just thirteen days prior, it was fully booked, as it had become customary to reserve a year in advance! Besides becoming a worldwide favorite, the Milford is like a pilgrimage to many Kiwis.

Our names went on the waiting list in case of a cancellation. While crushed, we switched our focus to the Routeburn Track, a less famous trail with an equally stunning landscape.

Luckily, five days later, we learned that three slots had opened and I quickly altered our schedule.

Now, after three hours of leisurely walking 5.2 miles from Glade Wharf, we arrived at Clinton Forks Hut.

"Are we the only ones here?" Dad asked me.

"Yes, it's all ours, for now. Claim your bunks! You get first pick."

Like kids, we investigated every inch of the hut, then plopped our packs in the most remote corner where we secured three bunks. Three communal bunk rooms contained forty bunks with mattresses. A drying room adjoined the dining room where there was a coal stove for heating.

"I'll make some soup," I volunteered. Vegetable soup tasted delicious as a mid-afternoon snack and held us until dinnertime.

I chopped vegetables for dinner and claimed a fire ring, one of eight built-in cooking burners in the hut's kitchen. To cajun rice and beans, I added dried mixed vegetables, then steamed cauliflower, onion, zucchini, and carrots. It tasted great all mixed together, and we still had room for dessert—creamy butterscotch pudding plus Cadbury chocolate squares.

Soon, the full hut bustled with trampers from all over the world. Dad happily chatted with Aussies, Kiwis, Germans, and an American couple with their two-year-old daughter carried in a backpack.

The different English accents confounded and amused Dad. With questioning glances, he looked to me for a translation. Strange accents coupled with unique Kiwi vocabulary words gave Dad a conversational challenge unlike any he had ever had. One by one he learned the American equivalent of many words: *knackered* (tired), *torch* (flashlight), *ta* (thanks), *jumper* (sweater), *dunny* (toilet), and *billy* (cooking pot). We laughed over some phrases, such as *rattle your dags*, which means "hurry up"—from the sound that sheep make when running, caused by dried feces striking together. This was my third time in New Zealand, so I understood their accent and expressions. It was a foreign language to Dad—a true education.

Hut warden Colin recited the standard regulations of the hut. We were relieved we were not in the most precariously-perched building which had one edge already seriously undercut. The previous rainy night, Colin had been awake until 1 A.M. monitoring the dangerously-high river. Dad, Mom, and I went outside.

"Look, there's Orion upside down," I pointed out. Standing out amidst the multitude of stars on this clear night, it was exactly opposite from *The Hunter* in the northern hemisphere.

Sandflies nibbled at our ankles and cut short our star-gazing. The renowned black flies are plentiful along the Milford Track, loving the damp conditions in Fiordland's rainforest which receives over three hundred inches of rain per year.

Bedtime at nine o'clock came with a heightened sense of adventure, knowing an evacuation call could come at any time during the night if the river rose higher than the one meter mark!

In the six o'clock darkness, I put the water on to boil for tea and hot chocolate. No one else yet up, we tiptoed around and packed up in the dining room.

Thanks to Mom we had a banana to share for breakfast. I never took them backpacking, finding them fragile with a heavy leftover peel. I couldn't turn Mom down when she volunteered to be guardian of the bananas to ensure that we'd have one perfect banana to share three ways each morning. Successfully sequestering three bananas in her pack's top pocket, Mom presented one firm, undamaged banana to complement our first breakfast of oatmeal and raisins.

A glorious morning greeted us, clear and cool at 7 A.M. First out of the hut, we relished having the trail to ourselves at least for a while.

"Those are tomtits," I identified the cute, little black birds with a yellow breast that darted back and forth across the trail. Mom loved watching them.

Wood pigeons, the largest birds with iridescent green heads and prominent white breasts, whirred and flew away upon our approach.

We recognized bellbirds by their beautiful bell-like song and green and black markings. Fearless dark gray robins with creamy white breasts walked down the trail just ahead of us. The tiniest bird of all, the greenish-yellow rifleman, entertained us all along the way. Acrobatic fantails opened and closed their tails at lightning speed and snapped up insects in midair. One perched right on my walking stick. Bird paradise!

"There's the eight-mile mark," proclaimed Mom. We made it a fun game to search for all thirty-three wooden peg markers.

"There it is!" I pointed. "That's where we're going tomorrow, the highest point of the Milford—Mackinnon Pass."

The pass looked clear and distinct, and I tried to overlook the gathering, descending clouds. Were they predecessors of the rain in the grim forecast? I didn't like what I saw.

As we gained elevation up the Clinton River valley, waterfalls leapt down sheer walls, one after another. We shivered from the cold spray when we walked close to one thunderous falls and stood in awe at the wispy, dainty threads of others in the distance that dropped more than a thousand feet from glaciers and lakes above.

Glaciers scoured out classic U-shaped valleys throughout Fiordland National Park, one of the largest national parks in the world. Clinton valley appeared all the more imposing because of the narrowness of the valley and closeness of the steep granite walls.

Six robust rainbow trout slithered along in the aquamarine waters of the Clinton River.

"It's so clear, so pretty," Mom said. "Those trout are over two feet long! Can you believe we can see all the way to the bottom?"

Rain gradually intensified to a steady drizzle, forcing us to don rain gear. Our beautiful royal blue sky turned dull gray.

With a mile to go, we shared our favorite Crunchie Bar, a distinctly New Zealand honeycomb-type candy bar covered in chocolate.

"Dad, Mom, how about if I quickly hike the rest of the way to Mintaro Hut alone so I can claim two bottom bunks for you. I'll get a choice bunkroom for the three of us."

"Sounds good, we'll just poke along," Dad agreed.

I saw Mackinnon Pass become enshrouded in clouds—no longer clear and inviting. I hoped the skies would clear by morning. The trek over the pass the following day was the one day on the Milford Track we wanted good weather!

Just before noon I arrived at quiet Mintaro Hut and claimed two lower bunks for my parents. I dashed back down the trail in the steady rain and when I met Dad and Mom we moved swiftly toward the protection of the hut. I quickly boiled water for instant pumpkin soup and tea to go with crackers and cheese, Maureen's scroggin', and Digestive Biscuits for a filling lunch, then boiled more pots of water for seconds on hot drinks and to fill our water bottles.

The rain forced everyone inside so all mattresses were quickly reserved. Dad and Mom loved our private, little nook—prime property in one corner of the bunkroom.

Dad loved the camaraderie of the hut—talking, kidding, sharing stories, and making more friends—truly in his element! He developed a special rapport with Michael, a policeman from Australia, sharing hours of good conversation. Dad still couldn't believe he was in New Zealand! And I felt so lucky that they wanted me to guide them around my favorite place on earth.

The next day I anxiously ran outside to view the morning sky. Still pouring rain! Nineteen hours and still no sign of dissipating.

On another track, we would have waited out the storm, but in this strictly-regulated hut system, we needed to continue to the next hut. With no other option, we bundled up in our rain parkas and stepped out into the pouring rain, first ones out of the hut just before seven.

Despite the dismal forecast, I maintained hope and believed the weather would improve. How could it get worse? After skirting Lake

Mintaro, we crossed the Clinton River once again on a swing bridge. The two-mile climb commenced, up the first of nine long switchbacks.

I led, followed by Dad, then Mom, who preferred taking up the rear. Dad copied my Kiwi-style outfit, shorts over long johns. Not impressed with that look, Mom stuck with her navy blue long pants. Rain jacket hoods temporarily sealed out the cold rain.

Taking small steps, we inched by fallen trees covered with moss and lichen. We nodded our heads in silent acknowledgment of the fifteen-mile marker on the fourth switchback.

As the trail curved in a tight hairpin turn, I glanced over my shoulder. Thick clouds swirled around two blue forms with heads down to escape the full force of the rain. Their shoulders hunched as a protective mechanism, almost like a turtle trying to withdraw into its shell.

This sight haunted me. What am I doing? I thought. What daughter would expose her parents to such dismal conditions? These are my parents!!

The voice of reason and calm countered—Donna, such is the nature of a backpacking trip. You accept the weather you're given. You have no choice.

I remembered this section from five years prior when I hiked it in ideal weather and had thought how perfect it would be for my parents. It couldn't have been more different.

I could stand the silence no longer. I stopped and turned around.

"Mom, I have a quote for you. I think you'll like it."

"Mmmm," she grunted.

"It's by Mark Twain—'I'm glad I did it, partly because it was well worth it, but mostly because I will never ever have to do it again.'"

"You're right, I will never ever have to do this again," she agreed and couldn't help but laugh.

Starting up the sixth switchback, we confronted the full force of wind and rain above tree line. Looking forward to the shelter in the pass, we slowly, steadily trudged up the last few switchbacks. How could it possibly rain the entire eight miles?

We reached the 3520-foot-high pass marked by a giant cairn that honors the discovery of the pass by Quentin Mackinnon and Ernest Mitchell in 1888. Conditions at the exposed, windswept site made a break completely unappealing, clouds obscuring Mount Hart and Mount Balloon on either side of the pass. Our cameras remained undercover and we could only imagine the view.

The guidebook notes: "If the weather is fair, the pass is a place trampers like to spend extra time; otherwise, they can't get off it fast enough." We raced to the protection of the lunch hut.

We burst through the door of Pass Hut which was tied down with cables to weather the harsh elements, two hours after we left Mintaro Hut.

"We're the first ones here! How about some hot chocolate?" I asked.

"Sounds wonderful," said Dad, his spirits boosted at the mere mention of a hot drink.

"That's a great idea," added Mom.

What a relief to be out of the rain, to temporarily shed our sopped jackets and slip into dry fleece jackets. In the unheated hut, warm hats remained on our heads.

We devoured cookies and chocolates, and heavenly hot chocolate to fuel us for the four-mile descent into the Arthur Valley. I wrapped my hands around my parents' cold hands, first my mom's and then my dad's. I enveloped their hands as the guide preventing hypothermia as well as the daughter infusing them with warmth and love. We joked about being in near-survival mode at the one spot we wanted clear conditions.

A guide in the next room prepared hot drinks, snacks, and a heated room for the pampered hikers who had yet to arrive, a reminder why their hike cost a thousand dollars and ours cost less than a hundred. *Guided Walkers* stay in comfortable lodges equipped with hot showers, drying rooms, and bedding and are served three farm-style meals each day. We were *Freedom Walkers* or *smellies*, since we tramped without the luxury of showers in our huts.

Before leaving the pass we all visited New Zealand's most scenic outhouse, a stone structure perched high on the edge of a precipice. On a clear day one can sit in the outhouse with the door open and gaze out upon expansive views back down the Clinton Valley. I envisioned the Clinton River flowing through the grand U-shaped valley, surrounded by towering granite cliffs.

A *kea*, a high mountain parrot, flew in to visit us at the outhouse. Keas constantly scavenge for food and are pesky thieves, but this one seemed to respect that we already had enough adversity, as it simply called its raucous *keeea* call and flew off.

"Ready?" Mom asked, knowing we had six more miles to hike.

"Let's do it," Dad said.

"You know the good part about the rain?" I said. "Twice as many waterfalls, twice as big."

We cinched our hoods over warm hats and stepped back out into the rain. The first few minutes we battled against the wind as we descended past tarns, anxious to reach tree line. Plants such as the cushion plant and vegetable sheep hugged the ground and caressed rocks, their protective mechanism to survive. In twenty minutes we reached greater shelter of the bush, surrounded by mountain cabbage trees with sword-shaped leaves. The rocky track forced us to concentrate on each step. Waterfalls tumbled in torrents from thousands of feet above.

Before we knew it we had descended three thousand feet to the valley floor. Large keas perched on the roof line and greeted us at Quintin Hut, the third overnight hut for the guided walkers. We snacked at the day-use shelter for independent trampers, before descending Gentle Annie Hill and hiking through thick forest to Dumpling Hut.

"There's the hut!" proclaimed Dad, with obvious excitement as we reached our home for the night. Dad maintained his cheery attitude despite hiking in the rain for nearly eight hours.

A building never looked so beautiful!

"Let's go to the upper hut," I whispered when I noticed the lower hut bustling, already one big drying room—everything wet. No one knew about the upper hut. We had first pick in the empty upper hut and settled into yet another private corner.

We could finally get out of our wet gear! What a relief to be under cover and take respite from the rain which had poured for over twenty-seven hours straight by that point. We had navigated the 8.7 rugged, wet miles up and over Mackinnon Pass.

At three o'clock we wrapped our hands around mugs of hot soup and cups of tea. Hungry again by five, we gathered round the huge dinner table to share stories one more time in our third hut—our last night on the Milford Track. Dad was still talking when Mom and I went to bed at nine.

"Do you think we can make it to the end in time tomorrow?" Mom asked, after she was snuggly tucked into her sleeping bag. Concerned not only about the distance we needed to hike the next day—11.5 miles—she worried about the deadline. The Milford Track ends abruptly in remote rainforest of a westerly arm of Milford Sound and the only way to return to civilization is by boat. We had booked a boat leaving Sandfly Point at two o'clock sharp.

"We'll be fine, Mom. We'll get a good early start."

My alarm beeped at 5:45 A.M. to signal the start of our last day on the Milford. Others were also up early on this last morning, all trying to make it to Sandfly Point on time.

We shared our last banana with breakfast before we set off from Dumpling Hut just before seven.

"Good job with those bananas, Mom," I complimented her for keeping the three bananas from becoming squashed.

"Thanks for letting me bring them."

Mom was on a mission—to reach the end—and on this day we counted down each mile marker. We didn't miss a single one, starting with number twenty-two not far from the hut.

No rain for the first two and a half hours! We appreciated the reprieve, short as it was, until we donned rain jackets once again for the rest of the day. Lush vegetation throughout the Arthur Valley, tree ferns and silver beech trees lined the track, as on our first day.

Stoat traps caught our attention and we used them as another navigational aid to gauge our progress. Years ago New Zealanders introduced *stoats*, a small, weasel-like animal, to help quell the rabbit population explosion. Their plan backfired when the stoat population soared and they became a threat to native birds such as the tomtit and rifleman by raiding their nests and eating the eggs. An intensive trapping program commenced using traps baited with eggs. In this section of the Milford we judged our headway according to which stoat trap we walked past, as 120 traps were placed all along the trail, numbered and marked with bright orange triangles, trap number 120 not far from the end.

"There's stoat trap number seventy-five," Mom announced. She loved spotting them.

"Only forty-five more to go," Dad calculated. He enjoyed doing the math.

"The egg's gone!" I reported. I liked looking inside.

We peered into some traps to see if a stoat had been captured. We never saw one. Most traps still had the egg, but some had no egg and still no stoat.

We plugged along all day with only brief stops. Mile twenty-eight. More than a hundred years prior, prison gangs had blasted the track out of the perpendicular rock wall. Paradise and grey ducks swam by.

We stopped at Giant's Gate Falls near the thirty-mile peg—only three miles to go. Giant's Gate looked appealing as a lunch spot in

Reaching Sandfly Point—end of the Milford Track—on time.

sunny weather, but we purposely kept our cracker and cheese break short, since we easily became chilled.

"Where's the thirty-two-mile marker?" Mom asked. "Did we miss it?"

"I thought we would've covered a mile by now," Dad said.

"There it is! That was one long mile," Dad added.

We soon passed Doughboy, the shed next to Lake Ada, and took one last look up the long, narrow lake. Only a mile to go and it was a little past one o'clock. We'd make it.

"Stoat trap number 120!" Mom triumphantly announced.

A few minutes later we arrived at Sandfly Point. Heartfelt, soggy hugs communicated a mixture of relief, joy, and gratitude. It was 1:30 and we had plenty of time.

The rain didn't stop us from posing at the unique finish sign adorned with old shoes, sneakers, sandals, and hiking boots. We had completed our pilgrimage tramping the most famous walk in the world, 33.5 miles on the Milford Track from Lake Te Anau to Sandfly Point, quite an achievement for Mom and Dad, the oldest hikers in our group of forty-one, though at sixty-eight and sixty-nine, much fitter and better prepared than most of the young college students.

At two o'clock we boarded the small, packed boat for the twenty-minute ride to Milford Sound. Luckily we had a roof over our heads, as the rain poured harder than ever.

"Nice beard, Dad," I kidded, referring to the gray stubble and extremely rare four-day beard on my usually clean-shaven dad.

We're going on a cruise in Milford Sound at three o'clock? Maybe we'd rethink that.

As bad as the weather looked, we really did want to go on the cruise, for this is the outstanding landscape that Rudyard Kipling described as the eighth wonder of the world. We couldn't miss that. It is also one of the wettest places in New Zealand and the guidebook says, "You can pretty much expect to see Milford Sound in rain or drizzle."

We quickly sped into the large twenty-stall bathrooms to change out of all our wet clothing and into proper *cruise attire*, which to us meant something dry.

As we walked the plank onto our boat, sun broke through the clouds. We stayed on the deck and soaked it up for two hours as we cruised the dramatic ten-mile-long fiord dominated by majestic Mitre Peak which rises over five thousand feet right out of the sound. Tremendous waterfalls—Bridal Veil, Stirling, Fairy, Bowen—thundered down the sheer walls. Milford Sound at its best. Fur seals basked in the sun on Seal Point and we basked in sheer appreciation of being there.

TWENTY

LOOKING SHARP in his royal blue Denali baseball cap, Dad reached out to pet the newest member of our family on his lap—little eight-week-old yellow Lab Ella with the coffee-colored ears, pink pads, and brownish tip on her tail. He stroked her soft, silky coat until she fell asleep, shaded by the mountain ash tree on this unusually warm April day. Gerda rolled on her back in the cool grass before nuzzling in close to Dad for attention which he readily provided, unconditional love flowing in both directions.

"Gerda, you're a good dog," Dad said.

Later, even though Dad was fairly quiet, he ate all his fish with tartar sauce, mashed potatoes, brussel sprouts, and coffee ice cream with a hearty appetite.

"Let's read this poem in your booklet you always loved—'Success' by Bessie A. Stanley:"

He has achieved success who has lived well, laughed often, and
loved much,

Who has gained the respect of intelligent men and the love of little children
Who has filled his niche and accomplished his task
Who has left the world better than he found it, whether by an improved poppy, a perfect poem, or a rescued soul
Who has never lacked appreciation of earth's beauty or failed to express it
Who has looked for the best in others and given the best he had
Whose life was an inspiration, whose memory is a benediction.

"It's a great one, isn't it?" I said. "She won a contest with it in 1905."

He nodded his approval.

"I brought this plaque of yours with me today."

Dad ran his fingers over the raised ornamental border of the ornate plaque as I read the inscription and the newspaper story:

1966
CITIZEN OF THE YEAR
FRANK H. DEARBORN
A TESTIMONIAL OF SINCERE APPRECIATION
IN HONOR AND WITH DEEP APPRECIATION OF THE DISTINGUISHED
AND UNSELFISH SERVICE GIVEN TO THE COMMUNITY WHILE SERVING
WITH OUTSTANDING LEADERSHIP, VISION AND ABILITY

PRESENTED JANUARY 23, 1967
BRATTLEBORO AREA CHAMBER OF COMMERCE

Frank H. Dearborn, for nearly 10 years superintendent of recreation at Brattleboro, last night was named Man of the

> Year by the Brattleboro Area Chamber of Commerce at its 60th annual meeting attended by about 300 persons.
>
> Last year's winner of the Man of the Year award, Henry Z. Persons, presented the 1966 award to "a dedicated worker who knows no hours—beloved by children, youths, adults and Golden Agers."
>
> Dearborn "works well with problem youths," a citation said, "equally well with town teenagers who respect his leadership and understanding."
>
> Dearborn, a graduate of Springfield (Mass.) College, accepted the award—a large plaque—and referred to a new Recreation Department activity here: the Senior Center for older citizens' recreation. Dearborn, 38, said that in the older people he had "never seen such appreciation or delight." He added that now someone is "paying some attention" to them (*Brattleboro Reformer*, January 24, 1967).

"Dad, I remember going to Golden Age Club meetings with you at the Grange Hall on Canal Street. At Christmas we sang 'Rudolph the Red-Nosed Reindeer' for them. You played the ukulele, I played the piano, and Deb sang with us. That was fun. They loved having us come!"

"They did," he said and smiled…

Dad had a special rapport with senior citizens. With endless patience he listened, counseled, and helped work out rifts between seniors and sort out petty arguments. They wrote him letters of apology and thanks. Dad visited with seniors often and led sing-a-longs. They adored him.

A picture appeared in a December 1964 *Reformer* with the caption "Dearborn, beloved by 'his girls,' was honored at a surprise party

Dedicating the swimming pool at Living Memorial Park in Brattleboro.

Croquet with Francis Morse, Mildred Space, and the seniors in Dummerston (1960).

Opening of the Senior Center at Sam's in 1965.

and presented a money tree for his new home before more than 50 Golden Age Club members and guests." One of the *girls* gave a testimony: "You have always been so generous with your time and advice for eight years... with gratitude and affection—the whole group of us."

Dad also loved working with kids. As a father-figure to teens frequenting the recreation center, he went into their world to shoot hoops and play ping-pong. He took them under his wing, listened sympathetically, and offered them common sense answers.

He was a smiling presence at the top of the stairs at teen dances and a cheering voice while directing Winter Carnival ski races. Kids gravitated to Dad as their role model, maturing and gaining confidence under his supervision.

Dad trusted them. Certainly he had disappointments, when kids smashed lights at the pool or spray-painted the walls. Someone stole all the money from the ski-skate exchange one night. Still, he didn't stop trusting or lose faith in people. Dad had patience with poor decisions and gave second chances after *talking it through* in a calm, supportive manner.

Dad gave young people a chance, for many their first job. Sandy started working for him when she was thirteen, returned every summer to work for him all through college, and became a highly esteemed recreation therapist for seniors. She said he taught her so much about living life and how to provide recreation for all ages, especially our elders, and remains an inspiration to her and so many others.

Dad had a special touch with people, an openhearted style that fostered cooperation and communication. His kind, gentle manner served him well in interactions with parents, softball and basketball league players, board members, and townspeople.

He was always willing to contribute, to give his time and expertise—at PTA meetings, on a high school panel discussing problems taking place in teenage homes, at dinners, in college classes, at student clubs, on numerous boards. "Thank you for giving so generously of your time. We know you are a busy man!" He was.

Passionate about working with people, he chose the perfect profession and influenced so many—from youngsters to senior citizens.

"Congratulations, Frank," wrote one longtime employee. "The people who have worked for you and with you have always thought of you as the 'Man of the Year.' It is good to know that others recognize this."

TWENTY-ONE

I ARRIVED AT THE NURSING HOME in time to see Dad punch the beach ball with vigor at exercise class. I loved watching him execute an athletic overhead motion with his strong right arm and laugh when he connected for a powerful hit. Despite being confined to a wheelchair, with so much taken away, he was making the best of what he did have—true to his lifelong philosophy. I marveled at the sight.

"Dad, Kristin should get combat pay the way you're all whacking that ball at her!" He laughed. "Makes me think of the time you visited my tennis and racquetball classes I was teaching at the University of Minnesota."

"That was a good visit. I remember the bridge that ended," he said.

"Yes, that was a little nerve-wracking."

Our three days together had given us many stories…

"WELCOME, DAD," announced one of the huge signs that adorned my small room in the big white house I shared with two other graduate students at 829 Marshall Street in Minneapolis where I was pursuing my PhD in Exercise Physiology. Dad arrived on my doorstep at just the right time. How I struggled—overwhelmed with teaching and studies, stressed with not enough money, and depressed due to a recurring knee injury that kept me from being able to run. What a gift—a visit from Dad.

With all my classes at the University of Minnesota in session, he knew this was no vacation. Always embracing new experiences with passion and exuberance, he wholeheartedly immersed himself in my world, excited to observe me teaching tennis and racquetball and to sit beside me in both huge lecture halls and intimate seminar classes.

Despite my room's sparse furnishings of hand-me-down drapes, a bed covered with my old patchwork quilt, and a small table for a desk, my easy-to-please dad was content. We'd make the most of our three days before he had to catch his flight to Oklahoma City to attend a national recreation board of trustees meeting.

"Here's your bicycle, Dad," I said, as I handed over the three-speed Schwinn I had borrowed for him while he was in town, since my 1962 Volkswagen Bug wouldn't start reliably. No hardship for my dad, he relished the thought of bicycling everywhere. We pedaled to the university during morning rush hour on the first day, stopping at a big intersection where all cars had stopped. I cautiously led the way across the intersection, Dad following closely behind.

When we reached the middle of the crossing, I heard the blare of a police loudspeaker, "You two went through a red light. You need to obey the traffic signals even if you're on bicycles."

All eyes focused on us. I dreaded the moment the cop caught up with us to ticket us, and breathed a sigh of relief when he didn't follow up on his warning.

"Sorry, Dad. That's an embarrassing way to start our day!"

Dad seemed completely unfazed.

We managed to make it without further incident to the university tennis courts, scene of my first class to teach. At age fifty-three, Dad still played well.

"Let's warm up, Dad, before my class arrives."

How great to stand on the tennis court once again with my original mentor and practice partner. The slow warm-up didn't last long, for soon we were smashing crosscourt forehands back and forth with such pace that any bystander would think we were trying to annihilate one another. When I finally missed one into the net we laughed.

"Wow, that's just like old times, Dad."

"That was really something," he said with a big smile.

"Okay," I barked at the arriving students. "Everyone warm up—some ground strokes, some volleys."

When everyone had arrived, I announced, "We have a guest appearance from an accomplished tennis player from Vermont, my dad—Frank Dearborn."

"He came all the way from Vermont for our class?" one student kidded, impressed he joined us.

Late in the school term I was teaching doubles strategy and positioning to primarily freshmen and sophomores. I positioned my dad as my partner at the net for the first demonstration, as I taught how a doubles team moves to adjust to each hit of the ball. He deftly moved to cover the alley and expertly shifted to the other side when we pantomimed a lob going over his head, taking his role seriously and following all my instructions. True to form, he couldn't keep a straight face for long. Sometimes just a facial expression or a shrug of his shoulders got the class howling. Fully present, as in all his activities, he easily fit in with college students more than thirty years younger who were sad to say goodbye to our celebrity guest.

For my next class, we bicycled to the racquetball courts.

"This will be fun, Dad. You'll pick it up fast."

"I'm ready to learn and I'm lucky I have a great teacher."

Before the students arrived I taught Dad the basics. Athletic and coordinated, he should catch on fast, I thought. I hit the blue, bouncy racquetball towards him.

"It's just like flubber in the movie. How do you control the darn thing?" he said.

It really wasn't fair, instantly going from a tennis racket in his hand to the shorter-handled racquetball racket. Not surprisingly, he swung and missed the first few times. I tried to keep a straight face, but couldn't help bursting with laughter.

"Watch the ball, all the way into the racquet," I suggested, trying to help him succeed.

He finally connected, only to watch the ball bounce high off the walls at unpredictable angles. Each miss made him more determined to master this new sport, yet the harder he tried, the funnier it was. Relieved that no one else was watching, we could only laugh until tears rolled down our cheeks. Though baffled that he didn't catch on immediately, he kept trying.

"I think I'll just observe this class," Dad finally said.

His brief racquetball career started and ended on the same day, a humbling experience for my active dad.

We headed toward my next class.

"Here it is, Dad," I pointed to the door to my most difficult class, organic chemistry. "This professor seems intent on failing everyone in the class."

We entered from the top of the large stadium-like classroom and walked steeply down to the middle of the room ringed by blackboards. Well over a hundred students settled into their seats by the time our stone-faced professor appeared.

Wearing a short-sleeved white shirt and black pants, the pale, pencil-thin man started right in lecturing about organic compounds and filling blackboard after blackboard with his scrawl of boring words and molecules. He proceeded quickly through a lot of material while everyone furiously tried to take notes. Finally, he filled the last blackboard all the way to the bottom, which signaled the end of class. Notebooks closed and students climbed the stairs to freedom and release from organic compound overload.

I sat in my seat for a few extra moments and took two deep breaths. Dad leaned over and whispered, "I'm really impressed. I guess the students understood everything?"

"No, they probably understood very little or maybe none of it."

"Then why didn't anyone stop him and ask a question?"

"Because they don't even know enough to be able to formulate a question."

That pointed out how detached and aloof our professor was and how we struggled in survival mode, trying to grasp even the most basic points. Our professor had literally left us in the dust from the first day. My dad couldn't imagine a model of teaching and learning so different from his own. A group worker and team player, Dad advocated talking things out. If you didn't understand, you asked; give and take existed in his world. Interactions and class participation, learning and humor abounded in the classes he occasionally taught at Greenfield Community College, the University of Massachusetts, and Springfield College.

After dinner that evening, Dad suggested we take a short walk.

"Let's go investigate that construction site we passed earlier today, Dad." I'd noticed him looking at it before.

"Let's go." He was already halfway out the door.

With the workday over, we weren't surprised to find the site deserted. A large gate left open enticed us to explore further, though we did question the easy access onto the bridge still under construction. We walked until the bridge ended abruptly in the middle of the Mississippi River and noticed the long drop to the water without any barriers or railings. Definitely not a safe place to be! This area would not be open to the general public, someone out for an evening stroll.

It was fascinating to observe this work in progress, even more so once we realized it was off limits. Had someone forgotten to close the gate? The sun set, increasing the chill of the evening air and reminding us that we'd better start home.

Upon retracing our steps back to the gate, we found it tightly shut and secured with a stout padlock.

"What do we do now?" Dad asked.

Jokingly I said, "I can see the headlines now—'University of Minnesota grad student and her father arrested for trespassing.'"

A few minutes later it wasn't so funny. We had carefully searched the entire chain link fence for any holes or openings. Anything! A small space existed between the gate and the start of the fence, though much too small to squeeze through. The barbed wire on the top of the high fence ruled out scaling the fence. Maybe we could yell to someone. Could we get their attention so they could help us? There was no one around, this project isolated and far from any residential area. No phones. We were on our own to figure out a solution.

"There's gotta be a way out!" exclaimed Dad, starting to shiver.

"I agree, Dad. We're not going to be trapped in here all night! We'll find a way out."

But I didn't feel as confident as I sounded. Questions raced through my mind. How will we get out? Did someone purposely lock us in, to penalize us for trespassing? Was someone waiting nearby to see what we would do? Would we really be arrested? Was there some way out besides the locked gate? Would we have to spend the night?

We searched every inch of the fence line again, more slowly and thoroughly this time. Nothing. We shouted for help, but no one came to our rescue. By this time darkness had fallen and we didn't have a flashlight. After all, we went out for a short after-dinner evening stroll and planned to be home well before dark.

In desperation we reconsidered the small space between the gate and the start of the fence.

"Dad, I'm going to try to squeeze through here, even though it doesn't look big enough. I don't know what else to do."

By sucking in a huge breath I managed to make myself skinny enough to push through the tiny space.

"Dad, you can do it," I encouraged. Dad took a mighty breath in and barely maneuvered himself through the opening and heaved a major sigh of relief. We walked back to my room feeling relieved not to be trapped in the construction zone for the night.

The next day Professor Anderson welcomed my dad as a visitor to our graduate course, "Computer Application to Statistical Analysis." Only a handful of graduate students circled a small table for this more intimate seminar, a sharp contrast to the impersonal organic chemistry lecture the previous day.

"I'm not sure I know anything about this subject," Dad commented on the intimidating course title.

Realizing our topics were far afield from my dad's expertise, my professor veered off the usual subject matter to involve Dad in a lively discussion to begin the class. It was Dad's kind of class, with dialogue and interaction. Professor Anderson was an excellent teacher and communicator, a man very much like my dad. Dad fit right in.

Dad and I packed a lot into our three days—bicycling my favorite loop around Lake Harriet and Lake Calhoun, climbing to the top of the University of Minnesota football stadium in between classes, eating mud pie at my favorite restaurant, and just plain talking.

All too soon, the time came to take him to the airport to catch his flight to Oklahoma City where he would meet up with many recreation colleagues scattered across the country. Dad knew that once I turned on my old Volkswagen Bug engine I couldn't turn it off, as it needed a cooling off period of about two hours before it would start again. Accordingly, we hugged and reluctantly said our goodbyes before loading everything into my red beater. At the airport Dad quickly unloaded his luggage while I kept my finicky bug idling. I quickly hugged him goodbye again.

I felt blessed, not only to have Frank Holt Dearborn as my dad but to have him with me for three days at this unsettled time in my life. Dad reinfused my world with sunshine and love. What perfect timing to have a visit from the one person who had always encouraged me, praised me, and believed in me. His sphere of positive energy was contagious, overflowing to give me hope, trust, and a renewed positive outlook.

TWENTY-TWO

DAD LOOKED HANDSOME with a smooth shave and wearing his new bull moose T-shirt and khaki pants. He cradled a little white poodle that seemed content in his arms while three other dogs raced around the nursing home dining room between the wheelchairs on *Oodles of Poodles* Day.

"Let's go outside for a stroll—it's nice out," I said, when the poodles had gone home. Dad waved to the maintenance man mowing the expansive front lawn who seemed to spare a nearby patch of white clover. A Ruby-throated Hummingbird paused at a feeder oscillating in the breeze.

As we made our way along the driveway, new light-green growth at the tips of spruce branches caught our attention. "Feel it, Dad, it's so soft and silky," I said, as I lowered the fresh sprig to his fingers.

We settled underneath the sprawling beech tree which provided us ample shade on this warm June day.

"Happy Father's Day, Dad! Here's your card I made—I'll read it to you:"

Dad—Father's Day is a chance to recall many of the reasons I have always thought I was the luckiest one—to have you as my father. I often tell stories about what my father taught me *and* what my father did with us growing up . . . *and* how my father influenced me. *Your influence goes on and on, Dad.*

I realize more and more as I grow older that I had no ordinary childhood. We were lucky to have parents who were fully involved and always there, who cared about all the things we were doing and actively participated in all aspects. Other people are amazed when I tell them my childhood experiences and about all the things we did together.

So I cherish the memories of Stratton Mt. skiing, football and running races in Mr. Clark's field, Yankee Stadium, the flat tire on the way to Fenway Park, foul-shooting contests, playing catch, Maidstone camping, cross-country family trips, skijoring and hot-dog roasting, tomato soup and grilled cheese sandwiches, Ho Chi Mǐnh Trail . . .

Every day of my life I've had the comfort and good fortune to feel the love of my faithful Dad. What a great gift to a daughter.

To my Champion Dad. I Love You - Donna

"Let's play catch, Dad. You're *Buttonhook*, Wally's *Butternut*, and I'm *Buttercup*."

"Ready, *Buttonhook*," *Butternut* said. Dad looked up and caught the tennis ball. We tossed the ball around randomly in a game that resembled hot potato. I received a pass from *Buttonhook* and moved my left arm in a big arc away from my body as I threw to *Butternut*.

"That reminds me of your left-handed hook shot, Dad, I mean *Buttonhook*. You knew how to do it!" I said.

Now and then one of our shots broke a window on the garage door. Our basketball court in the driveway was pretty narrow because of the retaining wall, but we made do.

The fun we had on the basketball court…

"How about some one-on-one, Dad?" I said one afternoon after junior high school got out. Ever ready for an athletic challenge, Dad rarely turned me down.

"I'm ready," he replied. "Let me just change my clothes."

A firm believer in wearing the proper clothes for each occasion, Dad was known to change clothes five or more times a day when he switched activities. Despite our ribbing, he held fast to his principles and continued to employ a specialized wardrobe, even for mowing the lawn.

A few minutes later, Dad dashed through the door with light blue T-shirt, navy shorts, white socks, and white sneakers, his basketball outfit for the day.

I had first possession and drove hard for the basket. Dad blocked, grabbed the rebound, and took the ball out. He dribbled deftly across the court to his left, arced his left arm out and up, and released a picturesque left-handed hook shot from his fingertips that swished through the net. At thirteen I wasn't tall enough to block it.

"HOW do you MAKE that shot?" I asked, impressed once again.

He just smiled. Lean and lightning quick, he continued to employ a dazzling hook shot from each side and an enviable one-handed jump shot. During his junior year of high school, Dad was a playmaking guard on the Franklin High School Class B state champion basketball team. Underdog Franklin defeated St. John's of Concord 48-23 at the University of New Hampshire's large arena. The first time any of them had played in anything other than a small gym, little Franklin High claimed the upset victory—New Hampshire State Champions!

Dribbling to the retaining wall, I turned, leaped, and sunk a one-handed jump shot.

"Good shot," Dad said and smiled. He loved watching his kids succeed.

Plenty of hollering emanated from the narrow driveway when our neighbor, Peter, and my sister, Deb, joined us. Sometimes the deciding shot was a long heave from the sloped, grassy strip above the retaining wall.

When I played on my high school varsity basketball team as a sophomore, Dad faithfully practiced with me at the recreation center's regulation court—an old wooden floor with a perfect, glossy finish. This massive, impressive arena was surrounded by a rickety, old balcony that creaked eerily when wind blew through the tall, ancient windows.

Witnessing the enthusiasm and intensity that Dad put into our one-on-one games in the rec center gym, no one would have guessed he was forty. My slightly-built dad streaked across the court with the competitive spirit of a kid.

When we'd had enough one-on-one, we practiced foul shots. The playing field was equalized—it didn't matter who was taller or stronger or quicker.

"Best of ten," he'd say while passing me the basketball. "Take your time. Don't rush."

Dad shagged while I shot my ten, then I'd do the same for him. I perfected my foul shot under his watchful eye.

My left toe up to the foul line, I'd bounce the ball twice, spread my fingers, focus my eyes on the rim. I'd take a relaxed breath and loft the ball just barely past the front rim, the same ritual each time. Dad emphasized the importance of foul shots and we practiced hundreds.

"That's the only way you'll get better," he coached. "One foul shot could mean the difference in a game."

Sometimes I made ten out of ten, but usually eight or nine, as he challenged me to a foul-shooting contest to test me under pressure.

Despite all the skills Dad taught me on the basketball court, in retrospect what I treasure most about our basketball practice is the gift of his complete attention and his time.

TWENTY-THREE

I WAVED TO DAD in the nursing home dining room.

"It's good to see you," Dad said in a quiet voice, as he gave me a strong hug.

Despite his sleepiness, he ate every morsel of his beef burgundy, mashed potatoes, and carrots. When we wandered outdoors, a wall of hot, humid air greeted us so we paused under the large canopy of a maple tree near the well-kept lawns and apartments of the Birches, Gerda at our side.

Lumber sat neatly-stacked to our right, while on the opposite side of the road corn grew tall and sturdy in precisely-spaced rows. "We used to play hide-and-seek in the cornfield near the ski jump, didn't we? If we had knobby off-road tires on this wheelchair we might be able to go that way."

We stuck with our usual route. On the way back, Gerda leaped into the holding pond next to the waterfall for a swim, paddled effortlessly to the middle and back, then sounded her impassioned bark for a stick to be thrown. Despite being cooled somewhat from the spray when Gerda shook, we sought shelter from the sun's baking rays under the mountain ash tree that had grown substantially larger and provided us even more shade in this fourth summer we sat beneath it. Special to us, this tree was one of our indicators marking each new month as we had followed the rhythm of life in nature and experienced every season four times since Dad moved to Vernon Green Nursing Home. The sun had risen and set well over a thousand times, as birds flew south, snow fell, flowers bloomed, and corn grew tall in a seemingly timeless, regenerative natural cycle.

"I brought you these fresh blueberries from the Miller's Farm Stand—they were just picked."

He sampled one and reached for more.

"These are really good, Dad, aren't they?"

He nodded and continued to eat them until they were all gone.

I handed Dad a photograph. "I brought you this enlargement of one of my favorite photos of you, Mom, and me. We're standing on top of Galehead Mountain when we celebrated your 35th anniversary—twenty years ago."

Dad took the laminated photo and studied the three strong pairs of tanned legs, our upraised arms, and contented smiles…

Dad sat proud as a king at the head of a long wooden table inside Galehead Hut deep in the White Mountains of New Hampshire. As raindrops drummed on the roof, other hut visitors coveted the special anniversary dinner I made for my parents—fresh broccoli with noodles and salmon. Everyone carried their own supplies into this self-service hut and most meals were Spartan. Not ours! I willingly carried the extra weight and took the time to prepare something unique, fresh, and slightly more complex than the average backpacking meal.

On September 8th, we were a few days late celebrating their August 30th anniversary with a traditional hike. That morning the thick canopy had shielded us from slight drizzle as we started our hike from

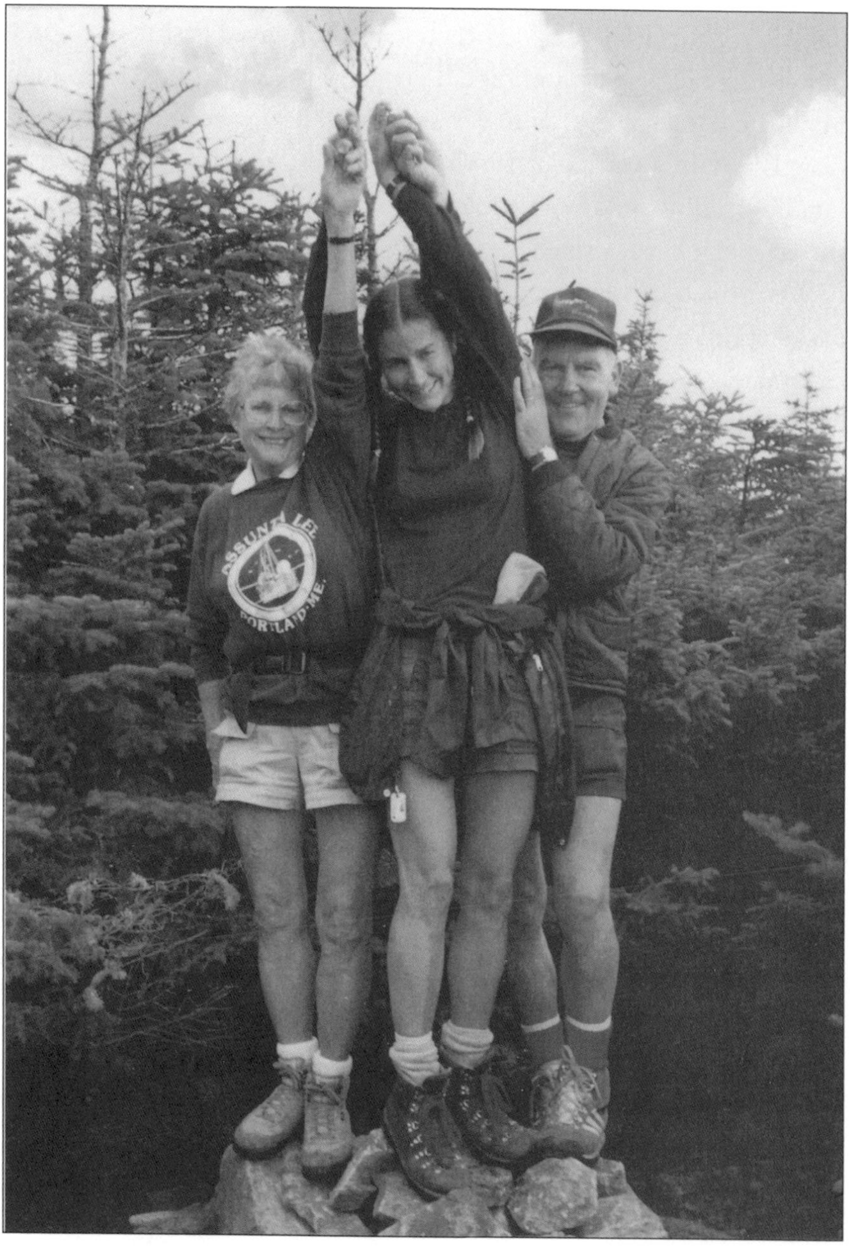

A favorite photo—atop Galehead Mountain in the White Mountains of New Hampshire.

Gale River Road. Maple and beech leaves displayed flashes of color, a tantalizing preview of coming fall attractions. While water rose high in all the brooks, stepping stones still showed so we could safely cross Gale River. In a particularly lush, green forest we bent to touch saturated, soft moss and observed fat water droplets balance tenuously on the edge of a large, striped maple leaf—in no rush.

We arrived at Galehead Hut after nearly three hours of hefting packs uphill over slippery roots and rocks. Dad happily set down his red frame pack, anxious to change out of his damp, white turtleneck into warm, dry layers and relax in the hut.

True to form, my mother was antsy for more activity—*relax* not in her vocabulary.

"The sign over there says 'South Twin Mt. 1 mile.' What do you think? It's early," said Mom.

My practical father remarked that it was raining and foggy and we wouldn't see a thing from the summit. Dad was accurate, yet my sense of adventure and curiosity prevailed as I sided with my mother.

Against the better judgment of my dad, the three of us climbed steeply over rocks into a thicker fog. Were we crazy? The simple one mile on the Twinway was anything but easy, rising over a thousand rocky feet to the top of 4902-foot-high South Twin Mountain.

A sharp wind chilled us instantly when we peeked out from the last scrawny trees. Bent over to keep our center of gravity low, we reached the cairn and sign on the windblown summit, an obvious landmark even in the thick fog.

"Well, we did it," Mom said quietly. Her curls glistened with moisture from the fog. Everything was damp.

"It's an experience," Dad said, in typical understatement.

We had merely a few feet visibility, though now and then we could make out a nearby ridge for a couple seconds as clouds swirled and raced by.

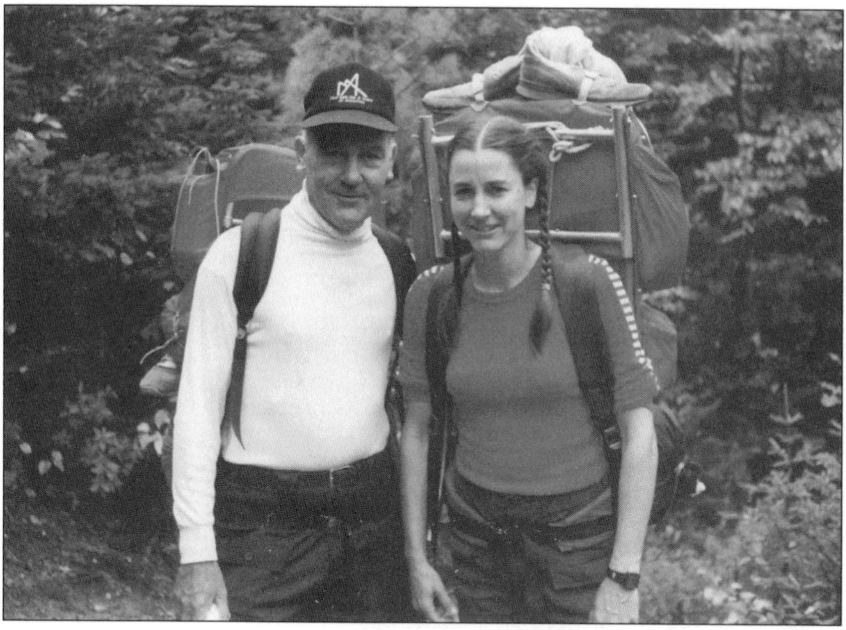

Backpacking up the Gale River Trail.

Dad appreciating their 35th wedding anniversary trip to Galehead Hut.

"This is wild. How about one picture, Dad? I'll set up my camera," I said.

Despite damp, uncoordinated fingers, I set up my camera for a ten-second delayed exposure of three of us huddled under my dad's poncho on the summit. Fog disrupted the camera's auto focus, so the photo is blurry which accurately tells the story of what it was like that nasty, gray, wet September afternoon on the summit of South Twin.

"Let's head down and get dry," I suggested. It was no place to linger. "We'll have to return someday."

We descended the steep path twice as fast as we climbed, highly motivated to reach the protection of the hut. Soon we were toasty and dry, our wet gear hanging everywhere.

Dad still had plenty of time to relax and converse with the few hikers who had ventured out on this rainy Tuesday. He certainly deserved to relax and savor his anniversary meal.

The next morning we embarked on a day trip that excited Dad. The sun poked out briefly as we hiked to Thirteen Falls via the Twin Brook Trail. We lingered in a sun-dappled birch glade for lunch and then climbed up the Franconia Brook Trail back to the ridge near Garfield Campsite. Halfway there, rain started to fall again.

"Do you want to climb to the top of Garfield?" I asked. It's about a mile farther, all uphill."

Dad and Mom conferred briefly.

"No, we'll pass on that today," Dad said.

They had had enough of rainy, windblown White Mountain summits. Instead, we hiked the half-mile spur trail to the shielded top of Galehead Mountain where at the time there was a limited view. We balanced atop the summit cairn in a perfect pose—arms raised, hands clasped, smiles all around. Three pairs of strong, sleek legs cushioned by sturdy hiking boots, clad in short cargo hiking shorts, the style of the day. It remains one of my all-time favorite photos.

TWENTY-FOUR

I GAVE DAD HUGS from all of us when I greeted him in the front entryway of the nursing home, a spacious, uplifting area with a lofty ceiling.

"Hugs are good," he said. I beamed upon hearing his voice.

A short while later, he seemed to delight in holding Gerda's leash as we made our way down Stebbins Road.

"My sled dog," he said and laughed, as Gerda pulled him for short spurts. What fun.

"'Vehicles Turning,'" Dad said, reading the sign. He seemed interested in everything around us and I never knew what would attract his attention.

Canada geese honked overhead and a little chickadee chirped a clear *phoebe* call. Acorns fell from tall oaks and bounced off the pavement all around us. Sumac blazed red and distinctive three-leaflet clusters of poison ivy proliferated along the roadside.

"We'd better steer clear of those leaves, Dad! You've had some pretty bad allergic reactions in the past," I said as I gave the patch a wide berth.

"You're right."

We took a break near a bench in front of a sugar maple tree aglow with golden yellow and burnt orange leaves. Because of Dad's strong connection with the natural environment, these peaceful times outside meant even more—vital parts of our visits that fostered relaxation and closeness.

"I found this poem named 'Youth' by Samuel Ullman on your desk, Dad, so I put it in your latest booklet. It was a favorite of General Douglas MacArthur."

> *Nobody grows old merely by living a number of years. People grow old only by deserting their ideas. Years may wrinkle the skin but to give up interest wrinkles the soul.*
>
> *Worry, doubt, self-distrust, fear and despair . . . these are the long years that bow the head and turn the growing spirit back to dust.*
>
> *Whatever your years, there is in every being's heart the love of wonder, the undaunted challenge of events, the unfailing childlike appetite for* what next? *and the joy of the game of life.*
>
> *You are as young as your faith, as old as your doubt; as young as your self-confidence, as old as your fear; as young as your hopes, as old as your despair.*
>
> *In the central place of your heart, there is a recording chamber; as long as it receives messages of beauty, hope, cheer, and courage, you are young. When the wires are all down, and your heart is covered with the snow of pessimism and the ice of cynicism, then and only then—are you grown old.*

"That's well said, isn't it? You've always been young at heart, Dad."

He nodded.

Even with few words spoken that day, I knew he appreciated Gerda's and my presence. I tried to stay attuned to Dad—to listen, observe, and ascertain what I could do for him. If he couldn't tell me what he wanted or needed, I attempted to sense and understand subtle cues, to be there for him, to *hear* him. That's the least I could do—Dad was always the best listener…

I've never forgotten the time Dad took time out of his busy schedule to drive an hour to pick me up at my college dormitory, take me out to lunch at Friendly's, and listen to my woes…Nothing could have been better than a father-daughter heart-to-heart talk.

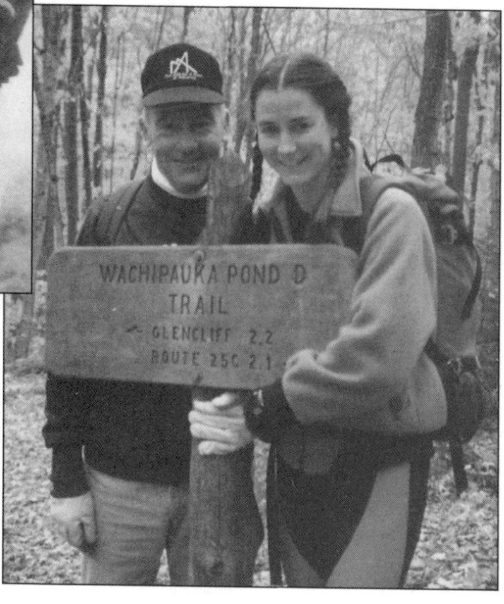

"It's only when you grow up and step back from him…it's only then that you can measure his greatness and fully appreciate it."
Margaret Truman.

He listened and nodded. Instantly I felt better, enveloped in love. “Hmmm,” was all he said for the first few minutes, listening intently to each word, in his typical calm, deliberate way. With puffed-out cheeks, he ruminated, like a cow chewing its cud. He took his time, pondered, and asked questions. That was his way, never telling us what to do, rather guiding us through the process of arriving at the solution ourselves. Often a simple question from him solved our dilemma.

Dad was a master at empowering us—respectful of our choices and supportive of our decisions even though they might have been harebrained or different from his. Could he remember he was once an imperfect kid or an adolescent who made questionable choices? He seemed to take all our questions seriously—no dilemma too foolish or silly.

No matter how busy he was, Dad always made time to listen. Embraced by his gentleness and kindness, cradled in a sphere of love and acceptance, no wonder we felt like the most important person in the world in his presence.

As usual, Dad didn’t say what I should do about my troublesome boyfriend. Together we concluded that my boyfriend was immature, even though he was ten years older than me. Always a diplomat, Dad gave people the benefit of the doubt, even this difficult boyfriend.

Taking time out of his demanding schedule to be there—to listen—Dad came through again, just when I needed him.

TWENTY-FIVE

MY PUP, ELLA, and I hiked up the overgrown pathway to Root Beer Ridge on a sunny, clear September day. I'd been there many times, usually on skis, so I knew there wouldn't be a root beer stand waiting for us there. I always wondered how it got its name and one day I finally found out. While charting the original route on a warm summer day, Stanton Allaben commented that he could go for a nice, cold root beer float. It's true—that's how the trail became the Root Beer Ridge Trail.

It's very wild countryside, the perfect place to go on a day when we didn't want to see another soul.

Ella stopped abruptly as we reached a wood plank bridge over a small stream with slow-moving, shallow waters. The hair stood up on her back and formed a ridge. She isn't a Rhodesian Ridgeback, one of those pretty copper-colored dogs. No, Ella was pure six-month-old Labrador, seen in her voracious appetite, active nose, and boundless energy.

Beavers had dammed up this stream by hauling branches, mud, and debris to create a huge berm. I acknowledged the presence of beavers

Hiking the Root Beer Ridge Trail.

to Little El, even though we didn't see one. We quietly moved through this area on alert in case there were beavers working, but only saw skinned branches and teeth-marks in trees only partially felled.

The day felt perfect—with no deadlines, appointments, or agenda. A perfect day for a fall ponder. Deep piles of maple, oak, and beech leaves crunched underfoot.

We had a clear view from the top, down into wild Mount Tabor basin with nothing man-made in sight—a comforting scene. We followed the ridge to the north for some time. Fortunately I wore long pants to protect against the abrasive hobblebush branches that sprawled into the trail.

We hadn't taken a break for over an hour so I sat down on a log. As I sat there, breathed, and let myself be there deeply in that moment, an unexpected upwelling of joy took me by surprise. Molecules of joy surged into my cells, displacing molecules of sadness. I felt it happening within my cells. With a graduate degree in biochemistry I understand a little bit about cellular reactions, yet this phenomenon stretched beyond my wildest biochemical dreams. I loved the sensation of joy, so strong and uplifting. Even more so, I loved feeling the sadness pushed out.

"All is well with the world," Dad loved to say. I felt my dad rejoice at the sadness being exiled. He wouldn't want us heavily burdened with sorrow.

Dad had tread on this very path a number of times—he would have hiked there if he could. I couldn't help think of him, someone who truly epitomized joy.

I readily relinquished the heavy load of sadness from my cells.

My feet hardly touching down, I bounced lightly down the remainder of the rustic path—the lightness and airiness of joy a delight, little Ella by my side.

On the way to the nursing home the next day to see Dad, I wondered if the joy-filled cells would hold. This was a major test, going where sadness usually peaked.

Even after three and a half years and over three hundred visits, the knot grew larger in my stomach the closer I got.

I said hello to everyone as I walked the long corridor to find my dad at the end. I knew most of the residents, cleaning crew, maintenance men, kitchen staff, nurses, and aides, and they all knew me.

I reached my dad and gave him a cheerful smile and hello, followed by a giant bear hug. He was glad to see me, as always. I held his hand as I read to him, told him stories, and asked him if he needed or wanted anything. As on most days, Dad spoke few words.

The time came to say goodbye.

"I'm going back home to Chester now. I'll see you soon, Dad," I said.

He nodded.

"I love you. You're the best, Dad. The best."

In the moment of leaving, sadness crept back into my joy-filled cells as much as I willed it not to. Saying goodbye to my dad in the nursing home was sad—it's just the way it was.

Together with Aunt Ella on our 1966 family vacation to Kansas.

TWENTY-SIX

I GREETED DAD with a big bear hug and he said how about another one. I obliged. After all, you can never have too many hugs.

Dad sipped his Dunkin Donuts coffee I brought and began to eat his shrimp wiggle, one of his favorites.

I glanced over at Dad's dessert. "That rainbow sherbet appears to be melting fast," I said.

"I know. If I had wanted soup I would have ordered soup," Dad said, in quick reply. We laughed. Dad's sense of humor was still intact, despite strokes, seizures, and more setbacks.

We noticed the sky had suddenly turned black as hefty gusts whipped debris against the windows of the Rose Room and generated an eerie humming sound.

"We're not going outside today," I stated the obvious. "I'm glad we don't live in Kansas. What's that remind you of, Dad?"

"Tornado," he said without hesitation.

"Remember that night?"

"Yes."

In the middle of a stormy August night at my aunt and uncle's home in Kickapoo, Kansas, I awoke when I heard loud talking and laughing and raced to the living room. Our family of five, with our cherished Aunt Ella, traveled from Vermont to Kansas about every other year—essential that Mom spend time with her two sisters and we three kids reconnect with our cousins on Mom's side of the family.

Storm warnings had dominated the television news just before we all went to bed. A tornado sounded thrilling and intriguing—completely foreign to us Vermonters.

The whole family had gathered in the living room, apparently woken by all the commotion.

"What's going on?" we all asked in unison.

Dad explained that when a full bladder had roused him from a deep sleep, he heeded the call and proceeded groggily to the bathroom. Without turning on any lights, he had groped his way back through the living room and seen lightning illuminate the entire sky when he glanced out the large picture window. "I saw a twister! Just like in the news—the classic black funnel approaching!" Dad said.

Uncle Bob, a prison guard at Leavenworth Federal Penitentiary, took over the story. "I heard, 'Tornado! Tornado!' I thought I was dreaming. But then I heard it again. 'Tornado! Bob, quick! A tornado's approaching!' I raced into the living room to see it for myself and I prepared to lead everyone to the basement. I said, 'Where, Holt?'" Our relatives always called Dad by his middle name, *Holt*.

"Holt pointed out the picture window," Uncle Bob continued. "I looked for the approaching tornado…" He slapped his knee and started laughing.

Dad blushed.

"What?" I said. "What did you see?"

"Just this tree," he said.

We all looked out the picture window. Indeed, their rather scrawny pin oak tree looked very much like a funnel. Lightning had dramatically silhouetted the oak tree and to Dad it certainly appeared to be a tornado. We didn't have to rush to the basement after all.

"It's a false alarm. Holt sounded the tornado alert," Uncle Bob said to all the sleepy cousins assembled in the living room.

Even though Dad felt sheepish from awakening everyone in the house in Kansas with his tornado warning, he laughed the hardest—always a good sport and able to take the ribbing that continued for years.

DAD NEVER SOUNDED another tornado warning and Uncle Bob never let him forget the tornado in disguise.

"Uncle Bob said the poor pin oak tree died shortly after from embarrassment."

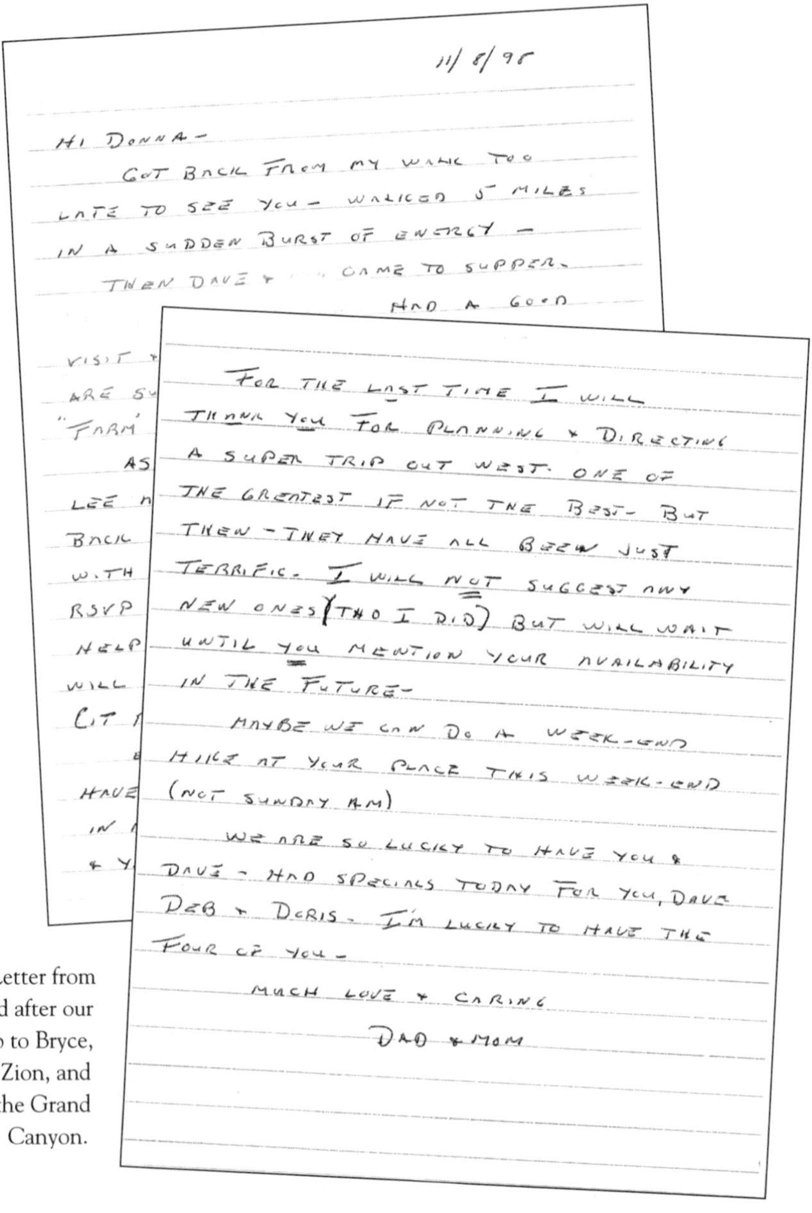

11/8/98

HI DONNA—

GOT BACK FROM MY WALK TOO LATE TO SEE YOU— WALKED 5 MILES IN A SUDDEN BURST OF ENERGY—

THEN DAVE & ... CAME TO SUPPER.

HAD A GOOD

VISIT ...

ARE S...

"FARM' ...

AS...

LEE ...

BACK ...

WITH ...

RSVP ...

HELP ...

WILL ...

CIT ...

HAVE ...

IN ...

& Y...

FOR THE LAST TIME I WILL THANK YOU FOR PLANNING & DIRECTING A SUPER TRIP OUT WEST. ONE OF THE GREATEST IF NOT THE BEST— BUT THEN—THEY HAVE ALL BEEN JUST TERRIFIC. I WILL NOT SUGGEST ANY NEW ONES (THO I DID) BUT WILL WAIT UNTIL YOU MENTION YOUR AVAILABILITY IN THE FUTURE—

MAYBE WE CAN DO A WEEK-END HIKE AT YOUR PLACE THIS WEEK-END (NOT SUNDAY AM)

WE ARE SO LUCKY TO HAVE YOU & DAVE— HAD SPECIALS TODAY FOR YOU, DAVE DEB & DORIS. I'M LUCKY TO HAVE THE FOUR OF YOU—

MUCH LOVE & CARING

DAD & MOM

Letter from Dad after our trip to Bryce, Zion, and the Grand Canyon.

TWENTY-SEVEN

I BOUNCED IN to the nursing home with a smile that belied the sadness that I felt. After Dad's lasagna lunch, we settled in the Rose Room and listened to some hymns on my CD. The Latin hymn, "Dona Nobis Pacem," sounded so beautiful in its simplicity, just three words repeated over and over—translated into English, "give us peace." When "How Great Thou Art" started, I sang along and Dad listened intently:

O Lord my God, When I in awesome wonder,
Consider all the worlds Thy Hands have made;
I see the stars, I hear the rolling thunder,
Thy power throughout the universe displayed.

Then sings my soul, My Saviour God, to Thee,
How great Thou art, How great Thou art.
Then sings my soul, My Saviour God, to Thee,
How great Thou art, How great Thou art!

Dad had been extremely quiet for days; no wonder Mom looked haggard and seemed depressed. She had been visiting Dad regularly in the nursing home for nearly four years. I worried about her as we fast approached the tenth anniversary of her heart attack that had come with no warning when she was sixty-eight.

Dad's latest photo booklet I had made lay open on his tray to the page of Grand Canyon pictures. He ran his fingers over the same photo my eyes were drawn to—Mom and Dad waving and smiling as I took their picture walking along the North Kaibab Trail.

BUNDLED IN FLEECE JACKETS, our troop of seven descended steeply down the South Kaibab Trail into the Grand Canyon on November 1st—still dark at 7 A.M.

What a miracle! Eleven months prior, on December 1st, reservations opened for all of November the following year. Since we knew that all beds at Phantom Ranch for the entire month usually sold out within one and a half hours, I called promptly at 7 A.M. Success! I reserved seven bunks for two nights for our crew.

Plans took a back seat, our excitement short-lived, when Mom suffered a heart attack two weeks later. Grateful she survived, we had no illusion she would be able to hike from the rim to the river and back again less than a year later.

As unlikely as it had seemed at Christmas time, here we were—all of us! Mom's cardiologist gave his full blessing. She had returned to her regular hiking regimen with no shortness of breath, seemingly no side effects, and feeling better than ever.

Beyond experiencing the jaw-dropping canyon views from the rim, we wanted to journey to the heart of the Grand Canyon and intimately feel its pulse.

Dad hurried down the dirt pathway, knowing we had bunks awaiting us at the intriguing oasis of Phantom Ranch and could settle in for two nights. He smiled as he carefully skirted piles of mule droppings.

Mom gladly hiked on foot instead of riding four feet higher on the back of a mule, especially since mules like to walk on the outside of the trail, closer to the sheer precipice. Protective of Mom, I kept a close eye on her, cognizant of the fact that we were going farther away from medical help.

Appreciative of the clear, crisp morning, all seven of us bounded down the trail to stay warm. For this family reunion of sorts, cousin Linda, her husband, Leonard, and their daughter, Lynnette, journeyed from Kansas, while my good friend, Baerbel, joined us from Michigan. We stopped to strip down as the sun rose and warmed the early morning air. Around each bend pink and orange canyon rocks and intricate spires came into view.

Impressive, sure-footed mules passed us on their way to the rim. Views in every direction continued to astound us—plateaus, mesas, deep purple cliffs—the scale so vast and incomprehensible. The Colorado River appeared as a faraway thin, brown thread when we first saw it, somewhat intimidating to realize how much more elevation we had yet to descend.

With pride and renewed appreciation, I watched Mom stride confidently along. Completely self-motivated, she gave encouragement and praise to her niece, Linda, a less-experienced hiker than she was. I checked out Dad who was in his element, simply in awe and grateful for the opportunity to be there. I reflected on this western canyon trip with my parents in its sixth day and already outstanding even before we arrived at the grandest of all canyons. We had hiked the red clay walkways down into the expansive amphitheater of Bryce Canyon National Park, past pinnacles and hoodoos, giant columns and spires, and witnessed the sun's first subtle rays from Sunrise Point portray the canyon in warm morning light—a glowing burnt orange. We had stayed in the heart of Zion National Park at the historic lodge and felt a part of it all, dwarfed beneath massive monoliths.

Halfway down into the Grand Canyon, we started to meet hikers ascending to the rim and stopped to chat with some of the more talkative ones anxious to share their tales. Shortly after passing the Tonto Trail, we saw our route across the mighty Colorado—the Kaibab Suspension Bridge. Switchback after switchback snaked over the landscape and led to the bridge.

After crossing the suspension bridge, we passed pueblo ruins of Anasazi Indians who had lived in the Grand Canyon for hundreds of years nearly a thousand years ago.

Phantom Ranch! The original four stone cabins and lodge built in 1922 stood beneath cottonwood trees which lined Bright Angel Creek. We reached our oasis in the desert after seven hours on the trail, thrilled to reach the canyon bottom and find our bunkhouses. Four dormitories each contained ten bunk beds, bedding and towels included. We five women hikers claimed our spots in a simple, clean dorm with bathroom and shower. Dad and Leonard bunked in a nearby men's dorm. The North Kaibab Trail toward the North Rim beckoned some of us for a relaxing, flat saunter up Bright Angel Creek amidst towering canyon walls, flat ground welcome after our steep, unrelenting seven-mile descent from the South Rim.

Ravenous and first in line at 6:30 P.M., we relished the all-you-can-eat family-style spread of veggie-beef stew, corn bread, salad, cake, coffee, and tea. Dad savored the evening, conversing with travelers from all over our country and around the world. Later, Ranger Seth entertained us with a fascinating canyon geology presentation. Thrilled to be at Phantom Ranch and realize our longtime dream, we wanted to experience everything in this unusual setting.

Monday morning dawned—a beautiful, clear day to all do as we pleased—no agenda. No one in our group took a rest day. Some of us hiked two miles north on the North Kaibab Trail into a narrowing

Exploring the North Kaibab Trail near the bottom of the Grand Canyon.

canyon, walls becoming higher and steeper, before opening up again. Scenery changed around each bend of the inner gorge. The immensity overwhelmed us. Four of us opted for the vegetarian dinner served at 5 P.M. while three ate stew at the 6:30 seating, connecting with new friends from Germany and St. Louis.

Flashlights and headlamps illuminated our way the next morning as we set off in the dark at 6 A.M. to cross the Colorado on the Bright Angel Suspension Bridge, commencing our 9.8-mile journey to the rim. Fleece jackets, gloves, and hats kept us toasty in the frigid inner canyon.

After an hour we turned off headlamps and watched sun filter through the canyon, though we remained in the shadows for some time. Cliffs blazed in new shades of orange, red, and yellow. Mom marveled at the progression of the sunlight, anxious for it to reach us while Dad pointed out features he didn't want us to miss—the Devil's Corkscrew and precariously-perched columns.

We followed Garden Creek to a distinctive plateau and on to Indian Garden Campground. The sun had not yet reached us, helping explain why the temperature still did not register higher than thirty degrees. Colder than we envisioned, we needed our warm layers even as we climbed.

We'd hiked five miles, yet still had three thousand feet to climb, more than two-thirds of our elevation to go. Luckily, our breakfast of scrambled eggs, bacon, pancakes, fruit, coffee, and tea fueled us properly for the long climb—no one needed snacks. Dad scanned ahead to find moving specks in the distance—descending hikers—to show us where the trail meandered across many switchbacks, weaving us in and out of several different canyons.

A welcome landmark, Three-Mile Resthouse brought us a mere three miles from the rim. Mom loved spotting some of the buildings of Grand Canyon Village, a sign the finish line was in sight. *Essence of mule* seemed to be more pervasive in this area. Still in the shade, continuous changes in light and color mesmerized us as the grade increased—the steepest yet as we hiked the final 1.5 miles. After a seven-hour climb, we set foot on the rim with energy to spare, grateful for perfect weather and thrilled to complete our loop which wasn't as strenuous as we'd imagined. We declared it the perfect time of year to be hiking the Grand Canyon.

As we headed home, we reflected on our journey to the Southwest, filled to the brim with stories and memories, scenes and conversations. Mom thrived, this accomplishment a testament to her full recovery. Dad glowed with thankfulness. We treasured our moments, reminded once again not to take anything for granted.

TWENTY-EIGHT

A BLACK FLY dive-bombed into Dad's mashed potatoes. We looked at each other and laughed. I extricated the tiny pest and Dad finished his lunch with no more airborne invasions.

Just as we opened Dad's latest Father's Day booklet, one of Dad's old recreation colleagues from northern Vermont walked in.

"Hi, Frank," said George Plumb.

"Hi, George."

"It's great to see you again, Frank. It's been too long. We had a lot of good times together at conferences, meetings, and visits."

"We were just looking at this article, when Dad received the Professional Award for Meritorious Service in New Orleans," I said.

"That was well-deserved," George said.

> "Dearborn has richly earned the complete respect, admiration, and love of his entire community, young and old alike. He is a constant inspiration to his fellow professionals everywhere.

> Frank Dearborn truly personifies the best of America and the best of the recreation and parks profession," the citation said.
>
> The award is significant since it goes to an individual from a small town whose accomplishments are less well known or publicized. The commitment and contributions of these individuals may involve a far great effort and personal sacrifice than those from larger or more affluent communities or organizations since they have fewer resources upon which they can draw (*Brattleboro Reformer*, November 1, 1979).

"I've always admired you, Frank. You practiced what you preached and participated in a wide variety of recreational activities—biking, tennis, hiking, skiing... You were never too busy to help a young professional entering the field and were always quick to give credit to others. You were a mentor to me."

"Keep up your good spirits," George said, when it was time to go.

After George left, I flipped to the end of Dad's booklet. "Dad, I'm going to read a little from your retirement article that was in the *Reformer*. It's a good one: 'He's had an unending passion for recreation.' I remember the Board of Selectman proclaimed your last day of work as *Frank H. Dearborn Day*. That's quite an honor."

> When Frank Dearborn walks out of the Gibson-Aiken Center for the final time this afternoon, he won't be leaving with regrets. What he will be leaving is the legacy of a man who devoted the last 33 years of his life to developing recreational pursuits for the townspeople of Brattleboro and beyond. Dearborn will retire as director of Recreation and Parks today, looking nearly as fit as he did more than three decades ago when he came to Brattleboro to develop Living Memorial Park into the quintessential recreational facility it has become.

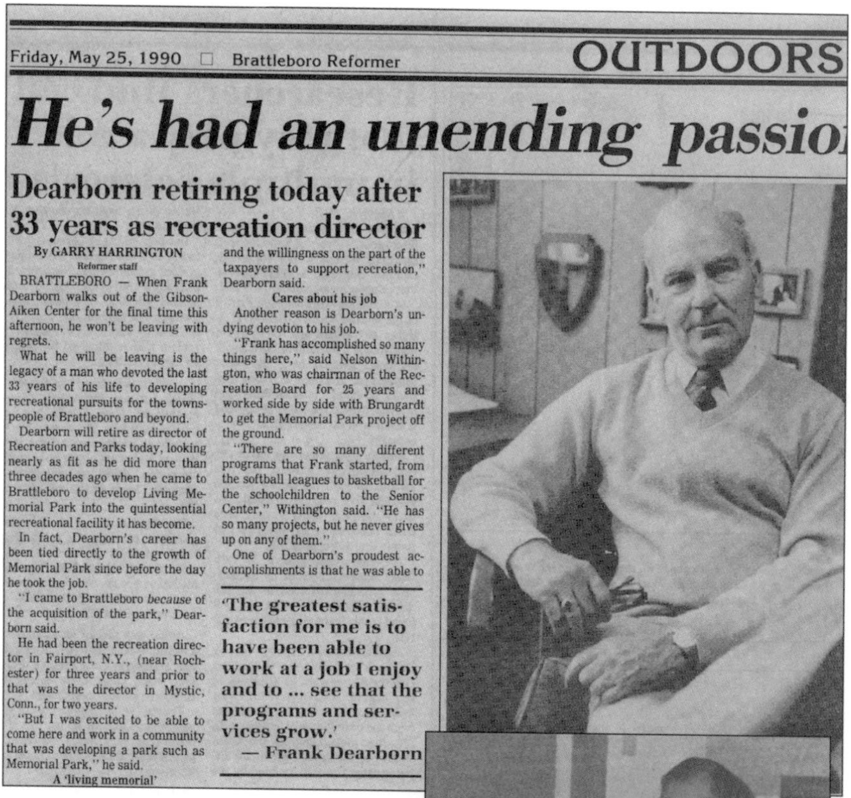

Friday, May 25, 1990 □ Brattleboro Reformer **OUTDOORS**

He's had an unending passio

Dearborn retiring today after 33 years as recreation director

By GARRY HARRINGTON
Reformer staff

BRATTLEBORO — When Frank Dearborn walks out of the Gibson-Aiken Center for the final time this afternoon, he won't be leaving with regrets.

What he will be leaving is the legacy of a man who devoted the last 33 years of his life to developing recreational pursuits for the townspeople of Brattleboro and beyond.

Dearborn will retire as director of Recreation and Parks today, looking nearly as fit as he did more than three decades ago when he came to Brattleboro to develop Living Memorial Park into the quintessential recreational facility it has become.

In fact, Dearborn's career has been tied directly to the growth of Memorial Park since before the day he took the job.

"I came to Brattleboro *because* of the acquisition of the park," Dearborn said.

He had been the recreation director in Fairport, N.Y., (near Rochester) for three years and prior to that was the director in Mystic, Conn., for two years.

"But I was excited to be able to come here and work in a community that was developing a park such as Memorial Park," he said.

A 'living memorial'

and the willingness on the part of the taxpayers to support recreation," Dearborn said.

Cares about his job

Another reason is Dearborn's undying devotion to his job.

"Frank has accomplished so many things here," said Nelson Withington, who was chairman of the Recreation Board for 25 years and worked side by side with Brungardt to get the Memorial Park project off the ground.

"There are so many different programs that Frank started, from the softball leagues to basketball for the schoolchildren to the Senior Center," Withington said. "He has so many projects, but he never gives up on any of them."

One of Dearborn's proudest accomplishments is that he was able to

'The greatest satisfaction for me is to have been able to work at a job I enjoy and to ... see that the programs and services grow.'
— Frank Dearborn

In his Brattleboro Recreation Department office.

Presenting former Senator George Aiken with a fly-fishing rod at a dinner in his honor in Putney.

"I never expected to stay this long," Dearborn admitted. "My plan was to stay for a reasonable length of time, but I was so into the development of the park that the best bet was for me to stay. We got entrenched in the community in every respect—good schools and recreation and we finally stopped considering moving anywhere else. Brattleboro is a pretty good place."

It certainly is a better place thanks to Dearborn.

"Frank has accomplished so many things here," said Nelson Withington who was chairman of the Recreation Board for 25 years. "There are so many programs that Frank started, from the softball leagues to basketball for the schoolchildren... He has so many projects, but he never gives up on any of them."

"Frank took the master plan for the park and carried it out almost to the letter," said Corky Elwell, Brattleboro town manager for 29 years. "Frank is a very creative guy, but with a lot of practical sense. More than anything else he had a touch with people. Even though some may have been adversaries, he endeared himself to them and has been able to make great progress."

"The greatest satisfaction for me is to have been able to work at a job I enjoy and to be motivated enough to see that the programs and services grow," Dearborn said. "That couldn't have happened without great community support."

George Plumb of the Vermont Recreation and Parks Association said that thanks to Dearborn, "Brattleboro is viewed as a model community of what a great recreation program should be. He's one of the outstanding people in our field."

Dearborn said he'd like to be remembered simply. "I just want to be remembered as the guy who came and stayed," he said, "and as one who for 33 years contributed to the growth and stature of the recreational facilities" (*Reformer*, May 25, 1990).

Dad smiled at me. "Thanks for reading that to me."

"I remember what you said on the day you retired: 'My life is recreation. I do it, I live it, I love it, and I'll continue to do it.' I love that, Dad!"

Receiving the Brungardt Award in 1977 from Mrs. "B," Theresa Brungardt, a pioneer in the recreation field and one of Dad's significant mentors.

Dad presenting George Plumb with the Brungardt Award.

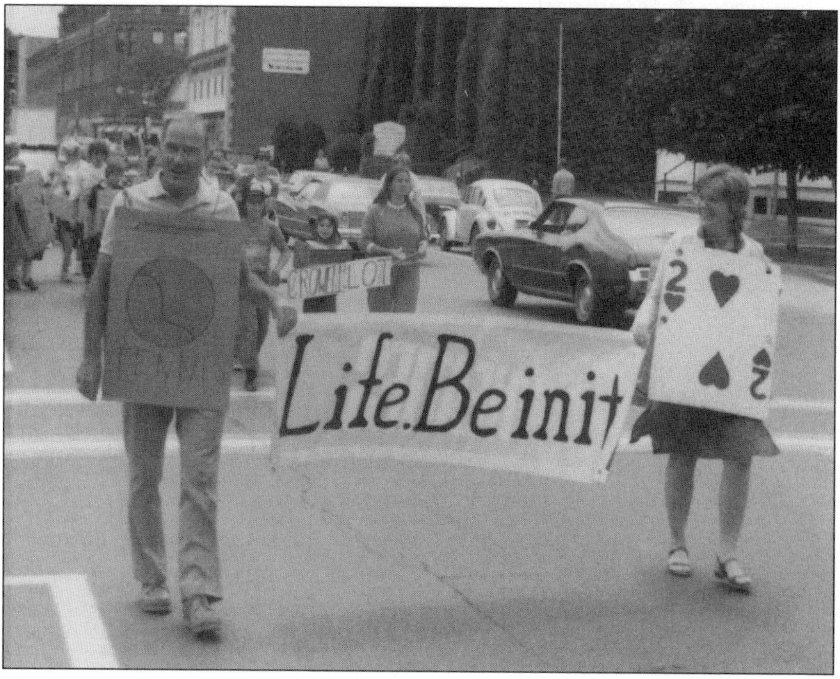

Leading the Recreation Department contingent down Main Street in the Alumni Parade.

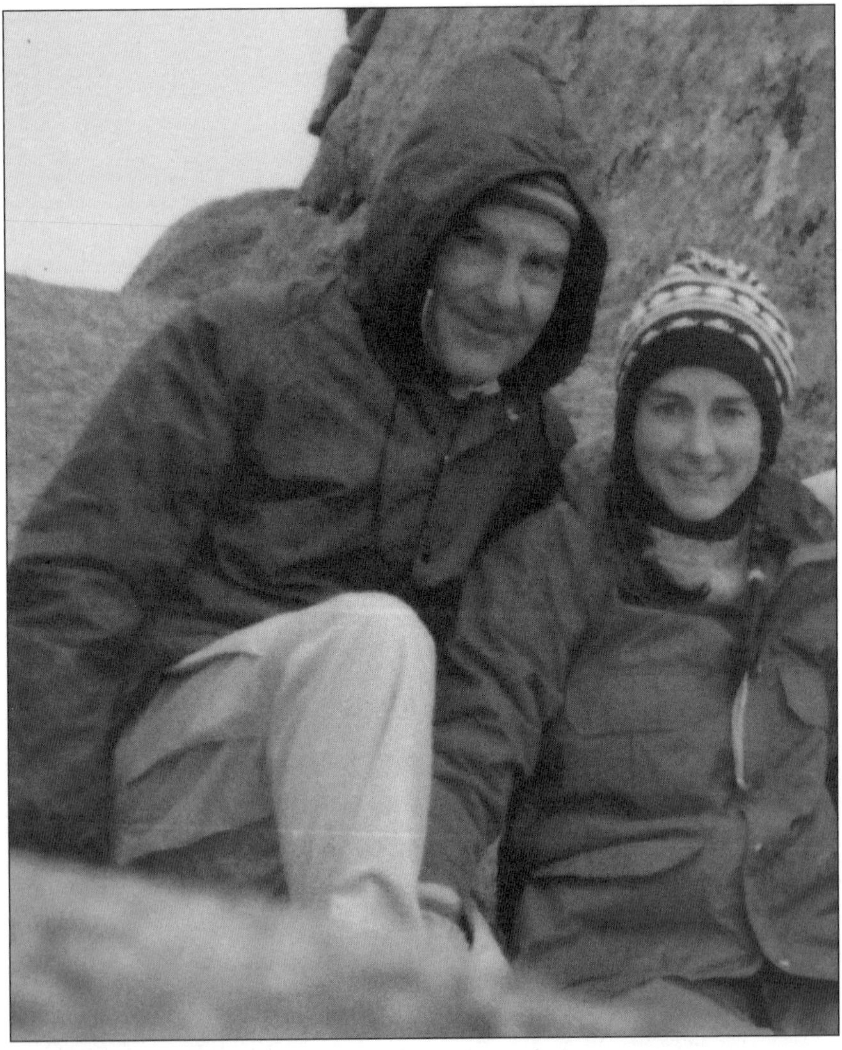

Bundled up at the top of Mount Garfield in the heart of the White Mountains.

TWENTY-NINE

TOWERING, BILLOWY white clouds rolled up and over Franconia Ridge, dramatically flowing toward Ella and me on the rocky barren summit of Mount Garfield. In an instant, my view into the vast Pemigewasset Wilderness was blocked by a sea of puffy clouds that settled into the great horseshoe formed by narrow Franconia Ridge, the broader Guyot-Bond ridge, and the Garfield ridge we stood on. It was picturesque, but allowed me only a fleeting glimpse of the stunning peak foliage from one of my favorite White Mountain vantage points.

Winds intensified as little Ella sat and posed for a photo at the top of this 4500-foot-high peak. Just as I pressed the shutter on my pocket-sized Canon camera, a big gust lifted Ella's floppy ears into a horizontal configuration, and she looked more like an airplane ready for takeoff than a yellow Labrador.

Seeing Ella sitting there, windblown and shaking, I vividly pictured my dad starting to shiver on that very rock outcrop, exactly twenty years prior.

On that cool September day in 1987, my good friend JB, Dad, and I hiked steadily up the Garfield Trail for three hours to view peak foliage from the magnificent Garfield summit. The weather being mild at the trailhead, Dad had dressed in his stone-colored zip-off nylon pants and royal blue T-shirt. Mom was visiting two of her sisters in Kansas, so Dad hadn't hesitated when we asked him to join us for a daytrip on a trail he'd never hiked. Initially the grade is moderate, as the trail follows an old road used for access to the former fire tower, crosses two brooks, and passes through a birch forest.

Dad moved up the trail deliberately, not wanting to miss a single detail. His wide open brown eyes soaked up all the sights near and far—the maroon-tinged hobblebush at our feet as well as colorful views in valleys to the north. He delighted in kicking through deep piles of earthy-smelling fallen leaves. Dad's smile broadened when I pulled out the GORP.

The temperature dropped significantly as we ascended the final quarter-mile rocky section to the exposed peak, so we ducked behind the cement foundation, the only remains of the fire tower that once rose from Garfield's summit. The welcome walls protected us from the wind and enabled us to quickly slip into our jackets. Wool hats replaced baseball caps.

Looking down into the wild Pemi, bright patches of red, orange, and yellow stood out on the lower slopes beneath the dark green of the spruce and firs at higher elevations. Familiar mountains loomed nearby, particularly grandiose Mount Lafayette which dominates five-mile-long, serrated Franconia Ridge that ends in the sharp point of Mount Flume. We identified less prominent, tree-covered Galehead, Guyot standing alone, and then the impressive cliffs of the Bonds. Dozens of peaks awaited identification if we'd had the time and could keep from becoming chilled.

Clouds rolled in and snow flurries swirled about. Dad felt cold, even with warm hat, gloves, and my giant green parka on and was ready to descend. We all agreed that he would start hiking down slowly, then JB and I would leave the summit a few minutes later and catch up with him. Dad anxiously headed below tree line and out of the wind to the warmer, lower slopes. I savored what remained of the views, lingering on the wild summit in awe and contentment, one of the best views in the White Mountains.

About fifteen minutes had elapsed since my dad had left the summit before we bounded down the tricky, rocky section to catch up with him. We'd reach him in no time, I thought. JB flew down the mountain barely touching the ground, agile and quick, as if he had shock absorbers in his legs. I descended quickly, a little more conservatively than gazelle-like JB. We hurried in order to get warmer, even more important, to catch my dad. Where was he? We assumed he must have been motoring faster than normal in order to stay warm and increased our speed.

Eventually we met some hikers ascending the mountain. Surely they would have passed him. "Have you seen a friendly, fit, gray-haired man about five feet eleven, wearing a long green jacket and a navy blue hat? He would have said hello to you."

I expected them to say "yes, he's just down the trail."

"No, we haven't seen anyone heading down the mountain," they replied. For the first time I felt uneasy that Dad might not be ahead of us on the trail.

Two other hikers appeared, also heading up the mountain. They had not seen the gray-haired, gregarious guy in the green jacket either.

I was on full alert instantly. Shivers tingled up and down my spine. My stomach tensed in a knot. Why wasn't Dad ahead of us on the trail? What had happened? Where was my dear dad?

"JB, I'm running back up. I'm taking my pack in case I need something in it," I said without delay.

"I'll head slowly up the mountain. We'll find him," answered JB.

In peak fitness at age thirty-four, I sprinted up the steep trail. Adrenaline surged and boosted my pace to top speed, equivalent to my fastest kick at the end of a five kilometer road race. When the conditions became even colder and windier, with considerably less visibility, I intensified my search. I had to find my dad.

Various scenarios coursed through my brain. Did he take the wrong trail off the ridge? Did he somehow get off the trail? Is he injured? Did he fall? Is he cold? I knew he had to be worried, wondering why we hadn't joined him on the way down. What would I tell my mother?

It was also September 26th, my sister Deb's birthday. She had been gone four years, yet it still felt raw, unbelievable that she was no longer with us. It would have been her 32nd birthday.

I nearly reached the top of the mountain and had not found my dad. What did he have with him? I had the only map and compass as leader of our group. At least he had water and some snacks, but he didn't have much else in his small pack—he was wearing it all. I had brought extra warm layers for anyone who needed them, but that did little to help him—he was alone! I thought I would have found him by then. The pointy summit cone of Garfield loomed ominously nearby, no longer a friendly, inviting mountaintop.

Thick, rain-laden clouds rolled in to make the conditions far more eerie and frightening. I became increasingly worried, surrounded by the dangerous combination of conditions that can lead to the sudden onset of hypothermia: wet, cold, and windy. I was well aware of the insidious nature of hypothermia, having seen fingers rendered useless from an abrupt loss of dexterity. I had seen deadly wind whip away precious body heat to cause stumbling, shivering, and mental confusion, further signs of a decreased core body temperature.

I fought to stay positive, as Dad modeled so well. I rejected the images that haunted and bombarded me, pictures of him lying injured somewhere, cold and unable to walk. As long as he generated heat by moving, he'd stay warm. I held on to that image.

Just as I reached the junction of the summit spur trail and the Garfield Ridge Trail, I saw a speck in the distance coming toward me. Could it be my dad? I couldn't tell at first, as a bundle of clouds immediately obliterated the speck and then quickly passed through. I hiked toward it.

"DAD!" I shouted as loud as I could, hoping it was him.

It was. I ran to smother him in a giant bear hug. His arms encircled me, complete relief and joy radiating through them. Words were not immediately forthcoming.

Dad's words were choked as he told me his story. Not easily ruffled, my fifty-nine-year-old dad was visibly shaken this time. Near tears, he recounted the details, how he had hiked for a long time at a moderate pace and wondered why we hadn't caught up with him, unaware that he'd taken the wrong trail.

Eventually he met a couple on the trail, but not until he had descended a considerable distance. They helped him realize that he was going the wrong way. He told me how foolish he felt. He was scared and more worried by the minute as he backtracked toward the Garfield summit and saw the ridge become totally socked in, questioning if he could find the correct trail he'd missed. Feeling helpless and completely alone, he wondered where we were and worried that we'd drive away without him. Of course, that was totally out of the question. I would have gone for help and searched all night, whatever it took to find my dad.

The mystery was solved—he had taken the wrong trail off the summit, a completely different trail than the one by which we ascended the mountain. He hadn't considered that there was any other way down off the mountain; he took the only trail he saw and hiked quickly to get warm. He was hiking toward Mount Lafayette, an even higher and more exposed peak. If he hadn't bumped into the couple, that's where he was headed, a chilling realization. If I had thought there would be any confusion following our trail back down the mountain, I would never have let him leave before us.

After our emotional reunion we took the correct trail off the summit. I didn't let my dad out of my sight for the rest of the way down the mountain.

"Okay," I said, releasing Ella from her windswept summit pose. "Let's go."

We started our descent, twenty years after my dad thought he'd be spending a cold, lonely, miserable night lost on the flank of Mount Garfield. I paused just beneath the rocky summit cone at the trail junction and understood how Dad could have veered slightly left on the well-beaten Garfield Ridge Trail and missed our trail. It's a confusing, tricky spot just at treeline, and not well-marked. Distinct, powerful memories swirled in my mind as the high winds pushed us around. I saw my ruddy-complexioned dad standing there in his navy blue hat with light blue stripes knit by my mother, green parka hood pulled snugly over it. I missed my best hiking partner.

Ella frolicked and sniffed, drawing me back to the present as she does so well. She gave me a look that reminded me we still had five miles to go to the trailhead and we'd better get moving. She had climbed her first big mountain and performed impressively for only seven months old. We had stayed overnight at the Garfield Ridge Campsite to spread the mileage over two days as the conservative option for my young companion.

Breathing in the sweet aroma of a balsam fir, I joined Ella in appreciation of our stellar, late September day, as my dad would do, as my dad would want us to do. I didn't let Ella out of my sight either.

Four days later when Ella and I visited Dad in the nursing home, I brought him a photo from our latest adventure on Garfield.

"Ella climbed her first four thousand footer, Dad."

"That's good."

"I thought of you!"

THIRTY

PURE POSITIVE ENERGY. Labrador Gerda and I were not only bringing it to the nursing home, we embodied it. Like a powerful magnet, everyone gravitated toward us, as we slowly walked the long, familiar corridor. Hands reached out to pet Gerda's soft-as-duck-down fur. I smiled. They smiled back. I waved. They waved back. Hi, Ray. Hi, Vivian. Hi, Milly. Hi, Randy. Hi, Ken.

We entered the Rose Room at the end of the long hallway in anticipation of seeing Dad.

There he is—he's sleeping. Our globe of positive energy moved into his space.

"Hi, Dad," I whispered.

His eyes focused directly on mine.

"Good to see you, Dad," I said slowly and clearly as I looked into his eyes.

"Good to see you, too," came the emotion-laden reply.

That was a very big sentence for my dad. I no longer expected words or answers to my questions. I didn't expect anything.

I wheeled him over to our quiet, private corner. Gerda sat in perfect posture with adoring eyes on her grandfather, their twelve-year bond still very much intact despite the drastic upheaval in our worlds.

"Should we give her a biscuit, Dad?"

"Yes."

Gerda stretched out beneath his chair, positioning her head perfectly to catch the sun's warming rays as we gazed out the large picture window to an exquisite winter scene that could not have been more perfect.

Large, wispy snowflakes filled the air, slowly and softly landing on the birdfeeder and the bench just outside the window. For a while we just watched this *movie*, perfect for my nature-loving, outdoorsy dad.

"How would you describe this, Dad?" I said. "Can you think of words to describe these snowflakes?"

I offered some words—slowly, softly, and reverently—so not to break the spell.

"Wispy. Delicate. Feathery. Magical…soft, light, complex, fluffy, tranquil…"

Dad nodded his head "yes" for some.

He said "yes," it seemed, for ones that struck him as the right words, ones that he would have voiced.

We savored the peacefulness, deeply immersed, observing hundreds of fragile, fleeting snowflakes.

"It's good to be with you, Dad," I said, breaking the silence.

He stared out at the snow without answering.

"We're doing the best we can, aren't we? You taught me that. You always did that so well. Think positive and do the best you can every day, every moment." I hesitated. "Do you still think like that, Dad?"

"Yes, I do," he replied.

THIRTY-ONE

DAD SMILED and reached out to accept the coffee Wally brought.

"It's about twelve degrees out there . . . and windy," I said, as I held Dad's hand. I wheeled him to a quiet corner where he needed no help eating all his roast pork, cous cous, carrots, and vanilla pudding.

"Wally, Gerda, Ella, and I just got home from the Grant. Remember Merrill Brook Cabin? You and Mom, Wally and I stayed there for my 50th birthday five years ago. This year there was so much snow we thought we were staying in a cave."

"Ella was really nervous going across the suspension bridge, Frank," Wally said. "It was her first time. We had to coax her across."

"We almost didn't go because of Wally's melanoma surgery, but he felt up to it at the last minute. Show Dad your scar," I said.

Wally lifted up his shirt. "They took a big chunk out of my back—twenty-four stitches—and they said they got it all."

"We thought of you and Mom a lot while we were at the cabin."

"Remember the pee bottle I made you, Frank?"

Dad laughed.

"While we were at the cabin, I wrote this story about our trip five years ago. Do you want to hear it?"

"Yes."

TWENTY-TWO BELOW

The hefty padlock secured the rugged, steel gate behind Dad, Mom, Wally, Gerda, and me. Cell phones ceased to work. Deep, fluffy powder surrounded us and high snow banks towered over us as we drove slowly along the Dead Diamond River. Seven miles of slippery logging roads lay between us and our parking area near Monahan's Bathtub. With enormous respect for this harsh environment, we stowed chains, shovels, and a tow chain on top of our gear in the back of the truck. No other cars, no other people, just moose and rabbit tracks. Eerily beautiful, yet also intimidating.

Mom sat silently on the car seat beside me. At the gate I had switched places with my dad, transferring to the driver's seat of their Honda Accord since I knew these narrow, slick roads and had a higher comfort level than Dad. He gladly handed over his keys and hopped up into the Chevy truck beside Wally.

Loggers barreled down these roads and had the right-of-way, roads plowed solely for logging. On full alert to every sound, I kept a watchful eye out for the giant rigs that took up the entire roadway, knowing we'd be forced to yield and pull over or perhaps be forced to back up a long way if there were no turnouts nearby.

When I had initially revealed my 50th birthday wish, complete with the invitation for my parents to accompany us, Dad embraced the idea of joining us in the Dartmouth College Grant.

"Sign me up!" Dad said immediately, keen to venture into unknown territory with fresh scenery. He had complete faith in me and never turned down an adventure that I planned and guided, knowing I'd organize it just right for him and Mom.

A week later, Mom agreed to go. Justifiably reluctant due to increased cold sensitivity from her heart attack, she felt less comfortable being in remote areas far from medical help. No wonder she might be having doubts or second thoughts now. I didn't dare ask.

Wally drove our truck in the lead, while Dad hung on tight. I may not have sufficiently warned Mom of the perils of these logging roads and noticed she practically held her breath until we made it to our parking spot. We crept up one long incline and rolled down the other side, hoping not to meet a full load of logs. Around one more bend—we had made it without meeting one of the beasts.

My thoughts segued from treacherous logging roads to trail and cabin unknowns. Would the trail be packed? How long would it take to get there? How would we cross the bridge with the sled? What not to forget to pack on the sled at the last minute.

We hopped out into incredibly cold air, glad to stretch our legs after the four-hour drive from home. Our nostrils twitched, exposed body parts cried out for cover, and cold quickly seeped into our bones. Unaware that the temperature had drastically plummeted, we found ourselves smack in the middle of a deep freeze and a quick check of the thermometer revealed minus twenty-two degrees!

Back home Mom had said she would go as long as the temperature wasn't below twenty degrees. Fair enough. Plus twenty degrees! We weren't only a couple of degrees off, we were forty-two degrees lower than her comfort level.

"Sorry, Mom, I had no idea it was going to be this cold," I said.

"Okay, let's go," Mom said, in her typical resolute fashion. She wasn't about to stand around and talk about it. We had driven 180 miles and over four hours from home. Who wanted to turn around now?

"Here are your snowshoes and poles," I said. "It'll take me a few minutes to load the sled. There's the trail." I pointed the way to the Dead Diamond River.

Cold quickly chilled our extremities, making it difficult, almost painful, to secure snowshoe buckles and straps. We needed to move and engage our muscles in vigorous movement to produce heat—immediately. I made sure Mom's snowshoes were securely fastened, crucial to send her on her way pronto. Dad gladly stood there and let me tighten his buckles, not wanting to part with his fluffy navy blue fleece mittens which were too bulky to maneuver the hard plastic buckles on his Tubbs.

"All set, Dad," I gave him the go-ahead.

"Thank you!"

If I invited my parents to join us in this harsh, remote environment, I needed to take good care of them. Dad was two weeks from his seventy-fifth birthday; Mom had just turned seventy-four.

"We'll catch up with you in a few minutes," I directed, keeping a watchful eye on everyone. Mom was already on her way.

"I know! I don't worry about you catching me," Mom said, always happy to start with a lead and let us catch up.

Gerda started to lift one paw and then another, as she did in only the coldest of temperatures. After I gave her a warming caress on each paw, she wisely trotted after Dad who hurried to catch up with Mom.

I loaded the sled in record speed, not taking time to load it perfectly, since it was more important to get moving, and I could return later to the truck for the rest of the supplies. Wally locked the truck and we sped off to catch Mom and Dad. We soon saw them approaching the bridge.

Blood coursed through our vast arterial networks, eventually reaching the capillary beds of fingertips and toes. It might have been minus twenty-two degrees, but we felt warm.

"How are you doing?" I called ahead to my parents. "Are you warm enough, Mom?"

"Yes, but I have to keep moving," she replied without interrupting her smooth, steady rhythm.

"How are you doing, Dad?" I asked.

"Great! It's beautiful. Look at the blue ice floes and some tracks over there crossing the river."

"A pair of coyotes," Wally informed us.

With our team approach, we lifted, pushed, and pulled the sled up the gangway and across the jouncy suspension bridge. I stopped to take in the scene upriver toward the wilder Hellgate region, at least ten river miles distant. This was one of my favorite havens, the ideal place to celebrate my 50th birthday. No big parties for me—just give me my snow-draped Grant. I felt the chill of even colder air settled into this isolated river valley and moved on.

After trudging up the long hill, we hit the junction of the snowed-in Dead Diamond Road. With all the layers I wore, I felt completely warm—on the verge of sweating, fingers and toes finally pliable and fully operable. We turned right along our spruce- and fir-lined path.

"There it is!" I rejoiced when we arrived at Merrill Brook Cabin, a cute and inviting lone log cabin built in 1961 by Dartmouth students. Looks are deceiving! From the outside it certainly didn't have the appearance of a stone-cold building that wasn't much warmer inside than out. With no one having used it for several weeks, how could it have been otherwise? Cold had settled deep into the giant logs that formed the framework of this forty-two-year-old cabin.

As soon as I unlocked the door, Gerda burst through as the advance sniffing party, disappointed to find no one home, then curious to determine who had been there and what they had left behind. We didn't have to read the inside thermometer to realize that we would shed no layers immediately. Instead, we added another warm layer, even as we bustled about the cabin getting organized. With Wally's one hundred percent attention focused on heating up our frigid dwelling, he expertly started a fire in the old woodstove.

Dad said he had never experienced such cold inside a building. A wry smile creased his face. He embraced the challenge and adventure of it, completely trusting that we would eventually be able to strip down and lounge in comfort next to the woodstove.

Mom stayed fully bundled, not quite as trusting as Dad that we would soon have a warm cabin, and busied herself unpacking, then laying out their sleeping bags on bottom bunks.

"Good job, Wally," Dad said, as the mercury rose ever so slowly. Every degree was a victory.

By dinnertime our cabin was ninety degrees warmer than when we had arrived four hours earlier, a comfortable sixty-eight degrees. Pasta and homemade tomato sauce with venison hamburger topped with parmesan cheese filled our bellies.

50th birthday celebration complete, packed and ready to leave Merrill Brook Cabin in the Dartmouth Grant in northern New Hampshire.

Luscious, fudgy brownies made by Mom was the perfect packable birthday cake.

With the temperature outside still well below zero, Dad questioned how he could possibly go outside to pee in the middle of the night. Wally went to work immediately to fashion a custom pee bottle out of a plastic jug.

"That's perfect. Thank you. You saved my life!" Dad joked.

By candlelight, the domino game "Chicken Foot" kept us well-entertained until late. I didn't win one game—no respect for the birthday girl! Dad won most of the games, my games-master mother a close second. Though it had been a very heavy game to haul in on the sled, it was worth every ounce for the hours of fun it provided.

The next day we cross-country skied north along the frozen Dead Diamond River and stayed pleasantly warm as long as we kept moving. Hot soup hit the spot. More explorations, card games, a tasty chicken and rice dinner, brownies, and continued Chicken Foot competition filled our dynamic day.

Exhausted from laughing, exercise, and fresh air, we retired to our individual bunkrooms. I tucked my parents into their sleeping bags, pulling their zippers the last few inches to make sure they were snug and toasty on their two bottom bunks, just as they had tucked me in for so many years.

I FELT GRATEFUL AND HONORED that my seventy-four-year-old parents joined us at this rustic spot for my 50th birthday. I appreciated that they were fit and strong enough to do it, still young-at-heart and spirited. With the ensuing events of 2003—Dad's stroke a mere six months later—this trip and these memories became immeasurably dear. We had no idea this would be my dad's last big adventure with us.

THIRTY-TWO

DAD'S KEY LIME CHEESECAKE looked delicious! He must have agreed, as his corn beef and cabbage, and then the cheesecake, quickly disappeared off his plate.

He looked out the window and seemed to be enthused about going outdoors, so I procured extra afghans and layered them on to ensure Dad would be toasty. With a thick navy blue mitten on his right hand, Dad waved to a smiling woman in a long wool coat and then the worker driving the food cart. Warmth from the sun balanced out the cold air—our spirits lifted once again. Only when ominous black clouds built up did we reluctantly move back inside, but by then it was nearly time for the Sunday afternoon church service.

We had time to catch up on Dad's page-a-day Bible verses calendar. One caught Dad's attention and he held the page to study it as I read: "'I lift up my eyes to the hills. From whence does my help come? My help comes from the Lord, who made heaven and earth'" (Psalm 121:1).

At the two o'clock service Anna opened with a prayer. Anna and her husband, Larry, volunteered once a month to offer the church service at the nursing home. Nine residents sat silently in a semi-circle and perked up when Larry's booming voice echoed through the Rose Room. Only two joined in singing "Onward Christian Soldiers," one of Dad's and my favorites. I hoped my singing would inspire Dad to sing a few bars, but he sat there quietly, seeming to appreciate the hymn. Larry's enthusiastic rendition struck a chord, his strong voice reminiscent of Dad's hearty tenor sound.

Other regulars presented the church service on alternate Sundays. Rick brought his guitar, handed out song books in large print for anyone to sing along, and walked around the room serenading each resident with his guitar accompaniment and radiant smile. Charlie and Norma faithfully walked up from The Birches once a month to offer prayers, verses, and music.

"Dad, let's read one prayer I found on your desk."

"Okay."

"'Lord, may I seek You earnestly and patiently in the faith that—as in times past—You will make Your presence felt and bring me peace. Help me to fight a good fight, surmounting my limitations with a zest becoming one of Your followers. Amen.'"

DAD HAD LIVED HIS LIFE in congruence with the Bible since he was young and church fellowship meant a lot to him. Extremely active and involved in the First Baptist Church, Dad assumed many roles within the church (moderator, deacon, trustee), sang in the choir, and occasionally gave the sermon. All through college he taught Sunday school and led the youth group at Hope Church in Springfield, MA.

Spirituality and his religious beliefs played a vital role in his life—inspiring him, guiding him, and comforting him. He studied the Bible regularly and thoroughly in order to better adhere to its tenets.

Dad believed situations which were not to his liking or beyond his control were this way for a reason and used his religious conviction to guide him through tough times. "Trust in the Lord with all your heart, and do not rely on your own insight. In all your ways acknowledge him, and he will make straight your paths" (Proverbs 3:5–6).

Dad's beliefs empowered him to be eternally optimistic and deeply fulfilled. "So faith, hope, love abide, these three; but the greatest of these is love" (1 Corinthians 13:13).

He had often written to me about his spirituality and beliefs…

Dear Donna:

Had a lovely Palm Sunday service today—good music, sermon, and also attendance. I love to sing in the choir and see lots of people join in the church program. I love the message of Easter, that we will live again and be united with our loved ones in Heaven. Never fail to think of Deb and how great that will be. I always say the 23rd Psalm with Deb in mind when I jog. Many times in the evening just before I go to sleep I recite to myself that favorite Psalm—The Lord is my shepherd…. She's always in my thoughts and my faith gives me the strength to deal with it.

I appreciate your willingness to talk about your life as you see it at this time. We have always been able to talk about issues in depth which is a rare thing that few people can do. It's got a lot to do with background, education, and how you are brought up in your family. I never had the background in my family but through college, church, and my work I have learned to discuss and talk things through—sort of group work style.

We all have to know that there is a purpose or goal to life. I find my purpose through the church or belief in God (spiritual) and I have many favorite scriptures, passages… I have studied and discussed my beliefs ever since Springfield College . . . been involved in church, Sunday school, and church work since 1948. Life doesn't make sense without a God. The sense of purpose, love, peace, of sharing with a faith is so much a part that I can't imagine how life would be without it.

We are humans subject to all the problems of the world but God gives us strength to deal with these terrible things. We are better people with love and faith, when we face life's adversities with God as our companion and support.

Whenever things get tough or I get frustrated, I can share my stress or frustration with God and know that it will be alright. I feel I have everything now—I don't need to strive or demand or seek. All I need to do is do God's will—the life of Jesus shows and tells how—love my neighbors—love my God with all my heart—2 greatest commandments.

We all have our highs and lows. If we can put it all in perspective—I think that after all these years I have done that—but my faith has done it, nothing else.

I recall visiting with your Gramp a couple of years ago sitting on a bank beside a stream. I told him that if I were to die tomorrow, I would have no regrets, for I was at peace with the world. I always enjoyed my work, family, and church. There really isn't anything else. This idea of accumulating, striving, desiring, and regretting is bad—bad. The quality of your life—personal and spiritual fulfillment are really by parts.

You have our unconditional love and support. I will always be there—we just don't want to interfere. Hope you can read this letter, for I think faster than I write—better too, I hope. Will be most interested in your thoughts, study, and insights. Much love as always, Dad

THIRTY-THREE

DAD WELCOMED WALLY, Gerda, and me in the front entry way of the nursing home, looking sharp with a good shave and striking red plaid shirt.

"Happy Birthday, Dad! You look good. Are you going to talk with me?"

"Certainly."

I loved his reply.

Coffee perked him up, plus a small bag of Cheetos that Wally brought.

"I made you a new photo booklet for your birthday—*Happy 80th Birthday*. Here you are all tucked in for the night at Carter Notch Hut, in your sleeping bag with a turtleneck, ski hat, and gloves on. Was it that cold?" I asked.

"Yes, it was!"

"I remember you turned the wrong way coming back from the outhouse that night. Mom and I were sound asleep and we didn't know you were lost."

He laughed.

I pointed to another photo of Dad, Mom, and I. "We're standing on top of Mount Hight."

"Look at the view," Dad said.

"Do you remember the party for your 70th birthday and how we tricked you?"

He nodded and smiled.

"It was the day before your birthday. Wally, Gerda, and I were at your house for a visit. I suggested we take Gerda for a walk downtown and you liked that idea. We strolled along Wantastiquet Drive, to Tyler Street, and Walnut Street. As we neared Main Street, Wally had an urgent request—he needed a bathroom. You suggested the Senior Center. When we got there you walked through the door to show Wally the way. Remember what happened?"

"Surprise!" Dad said, now teary-eyed.

A large contingent of family and friends had shouted "Happy Birthday" and "Surprise," as Dad entered the room. He'd been completely speechless, further proof that it came as a complete surprise. No one had ever seen Dad so stunned. When someone presented him with the microphone, he had no words for several minutes, in awe and humbled by the large group assembled to honor his 70th birthday.

"You were astounded, weren't you? I brought the video from that day. Do you want to watch it?"

"Sure."

Right away Dad named a lot of the people he recognized at his party—"Lois, Frank Hickin, Bob Dearborn, Donna, Doris, David. And that's me, Bill Appel, Wally…" He gave us a running commentary as he seemed to relive those moments.

At the party, Dad had eventually overcome the shock and given a lengthy speech filled with gratitude. Everyone had enjoyed a bountiful lunch buffet with sandwiches and salads, cake, coffee, and punch. Dad had relished sitting and talking with all the guests, including his three sisters and brother.

"Dad, there's Bill entertaining everyone, telling the story of how you two got lost in Dummerston on one of your Thursday hikes. What a great friend he was."

"The best."

Dad had led an impromptu sing-a-long of familiar songs—"You'll Never Know," "Anchors Away," "You Are My Sunshine"—and had crooned many old favorites with Luella playing the piano.

I became choked up watching Dad sing on the video. He hadn't sung for nearly four years and it had been one of his favorite things to do. I missed that!

The video completely captured Dad's attention for over an hour.

"This is the book of memories I gave you that day. When I sent out invitations, I urged everyone to share a remembrance or anecdote about you, and the contributions came streaming in—from Kansas, Florida, North Carolina, and all over—heartfelt stories, recollections, and tributes. Let's read one letter. I like the one David wrote…"

A little note to my dad on his 70th birthday . . . I remember you having a lot of time for us. We had so much fun camping and traveling . . . I don't remember you ever getting too mad either. But I do remember when Deb and I threw water over the shower stall and tape recorded it—you got a little mad. Another time when Deb and I were supposed to be going to bed; you and Mom were downstairs watching TV. We were making noise upstairs and you told us to keep quiet. What was happening—Deb kept walking in front of my bedroom door like an old lady and I would break out laughing. I told you why I was laughing. After a while, she did it again and you came running upstairs to catch her and she jumped in bed. I yelled for you not to spank her because we were having so much fun and I don't think you did too much. We used to test you sometimes.

When I was younger I had heroes like Wilt Chamberlin, but as I got older I started seeing that my one true hero was my own

Dad and David hiking up the Falling Waters Trail in Franconia Notch.

dad who was always there and someone to look up to, someone I wanted to be like more than anyone in the world. If people are born again, I would like to have you for a dad again. Dad, I love you through thick and thin and I always want you to know that.
Love, David

"David—he's a good son," Dad said.

"That's a good letter. What a day, Dad. Quite a gathering of good friends and family."

"It was fun."

THIRTY-FOUR

DAD AND I cross-country skied together each year to celebrate our two March birthdays—mine on the 5th, Dad's on the 16th. We were open to others joining us, but it always ended up the two of us, plus Labrador Gerda. One day during the second week of March, two Pisces set off for a birthday ski in the wilds of Weston, Chester, or Londonderry.

One March, there'd been almost too much snow. We could have opted for the ease of a groomed area, but we yearned for the rustic and peaceful experience of skiing in deep woods and, most important, to be able to bring Gerda along.

"I love this picture of you, Dad," I said, as I pointed to Dad skiing over a bridge near Moses Pond in Weston with his skis level with the top of the hand railing in four feet of snow.

"Gerda," he said, tapping on the next photo.

"Yes, Gerda had to be third in line. I can't believe how deep it was! Catamount Trail markers were at about ankle height," I said.

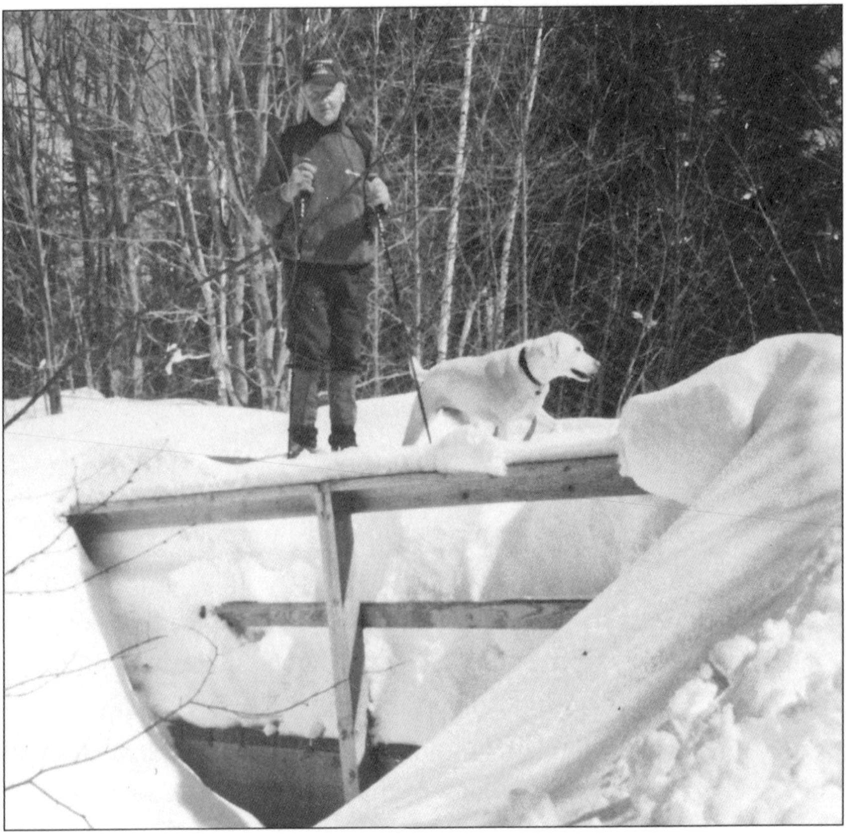

Plentiful snow for our birthday ski near Moses Pond in Weston, Vermont.

Under a brilliant blue sky, we had the trail to ourselves on this midweek day. Gerda would burrow her nose in the deep powder alongside the trail and then promptly rejoin our packed route. When we ventured onto the unpacked backcountry trails, we wallowed in a seemingly bottomless white world, yet skied deeper into the alluring woodland. Spruce and fir boughs laid low with snow surrounded and sheltered us in a secluded cathedral at our lunch spot.

"Here you are sitting on my ensolite pad at lunch, so beautiful. We never saw a soul that day, did we?"

He nodded.

"Dad, Ella and I skied there yesterday on the perfect birthday ski day. We thought of you a lot!"

Ella and I reached the parking lot in Weston to find one car with skis still atop the roof. When I surveyed the trail and found it a bit icy, thawed and refrozen into ridges, I understood why others had gone for a walk instead of a ski.

Not to be deterred, I clipped into my bindings and off we went down the trail. The black leash was still attached to Ella's collar—just until we got underway. In a big burst of energy she hauled me up and over the first icy incline.

Hang on, I thought, half cringing and preparing for an impending crash that never came.

We made it past the roughest, ridgiest patch and then it felt like magic. I sidled over and found the edge of the trail to be softened somewhat. We peeled along the flat straightaway, Iditarod ambitions flashing through my head.

Gee, *haw*. I only needed to teach her a few new commands, in sled dog language—*gee* for right and *haw* for left.

I relaxed and Ella settled into a comfortable lope. What fun!

Little did I know my purebred Labrador also had sled dog genes. With lightning fast conditions, it didn't take much effort to pull me. When I started to slide past Ella on one slight downhill, she glanced over her shoulder and saw I was gaining on her. She dug in and picked up the pace—she wasn't going to be passed by Mom!

I hung on tight! What a ride—a new record for that first mile—less than ten minutes. The other folks chose to walk for good reason.

I packed the leash away when we veered off the well-groomed path. With a slight rise in temperature, the sun softened the crust to a perfect corny half inch.

No tracks, no sign of anyone, we had the entire wilderness area to ourselves.

"Whoopie, whoa..." I bellowed. Ella stopped in her tracks to see what all the commotion was about, as I skied a harrowing, narrow downhill around corners.

"Yes, El, it's not a pretty sight, is it?"

A few minutes later, I shouted, "Whoa! Open water ahead!"

Ella easily rock-hopped across the river then stopped for a drink. Not quite as easy for me, I unclipped my skis to navigate past two collapsed snow bridges.

"Now it's clear sailing, El," I said.

She busily followed a coyote track and sniffed its scat right in the middle of the trail. Fresh snowshoe hare tracks abounded at the height of land. Ella dashed off, hot on the scent of a rabbit but quickly returned when I called.

I imagined my dad standing there in his royal blue sweater and navy hat.

"How lucky we are to be out on a day like this," I could hear him say, eternally appreciative of these outings and in awe of the cloudless, rich blue sky.

We carried on. Ella loped, sprinted, jogged, sniffed, and chewed, while I skied, snacked, savored, climbed, and chugged.

We sled-dogged back to the car the last mile, finishing our seven-mile loop with gratitude.

Our birthday day ski tradition was alive and well, and Dad was clearly with us.

THIRTY-FIVE

WHEN DAD FINISHED his New England boiled dinner, he, Wally, and I burst out the front door with the two dogs, anxious to immerse ourselves in sun and fresh air. We wandered all the way to the neat white house with picket fence on the corner where blue flag and yellow iris bloomed in a tidy flower garden, flanked by several different kinds of hostas. Dad pointed to a lone robin hopping across the lush lawn while a little Chipping Sparrow flitted in a nearby azalea bush.

"There's a mockingbird, Dad. I thought I heard one singing its imitations," I said when a long-tailed bird with large white wing patches flew across our path. Ever so briefly, like the mockingbird in flight, we spread our wings and felt the freedom of gliding through wide open spaces with the wind against our faces, free of the confinement of rooms and buildings—for a precious hour.

On our way back up the hill, Gerda and Ella rushed to smell a signpost and Dad chuckled. "Must be something good," he said.

We settled under our mountain ash tree fully leafed-out. Gerda and Ella lay at Dad's feet, beside the bench on the grass—relaxed, content, supportive—soothing in their mere presence and simply being their wonderful dog selves.

"Here's a good picture of you at Chebeague, Dad. We had such a fun time playing tennis there, you and Wally against Mom and me, except for one wayward serve from your partner," I said.

Wally cringed.

"He almost killed me!" Dad said.

Wally did hit him hard and Dad crashed to the court, luckily uninjured.

Dad reached out for another piece of my perfectly ripe peach.

"So sweet and smooth, it melts in your mouth. I wish I had more," I said, as I shared my last pieces with Dad.

Wally smiled. "We loved meeting you and Doris at the Bellows Falls courts early in the morning and then eating breakfast at Father's Restaurant."

"That was fun," Dad said.

"It's Father's Day next Sunday," I said. "I always looked forward to giving you a Father's Day tennis lesson, Dad. You loved it."

"I did."

"I remember the first time I played tennis with you and Mom…"

AT FIFTEEN I HAD DISCOVERED TENNIS. That first evening I hit a few balls with my parents at Living Memorial Park I had so much fun I became hooked. I wanted to play every day, and my dad and mom obliged. If we found puddles on the court, we'd sweep them off—I just had to play.

We progressed to points, then games and sets. Before long, I could beat my mother, but my dad was another story. The better I played, the better he played—with his hard, flat serve, the backhand he sliced with a pronounced downward chop, and the blistering forehand he loved to wallop. He scampered to every ball with ease and played just well enough to beat me each time. I desperately wanted to get better. Sometimes I took the losses hard, after I worked so diligently to improve and would still lose, but Dad wouldn't relinquish the family tennis crown without a fight.

Dad and Mom patiently hit balls with me almost every day for the rest of that summer, commencing a love affair with the game that captivated me for many years.

The following spring in my sophomore year I tried out for and made my high school tennis team. Before long, I taught group and private lessons, played tournaments around New England, and competed on my college tennis team. I passionately pursued my tennis dreams out west for several years. Now I was glad to be back in New England, closer to my family. After the death of my sister, we needed more time together, including workouts on the tennis court once again.

"Time for our traditional Father's Day tennis lesson!" I said to Dad. He loved refining some aspect of his game and urged me to share any new tennis tips I'd gleaned in Arizona.

We warmed up slowly and eventually had our favorite forehand to forehand slugfest.

"What do you want to work on this time? Your serve?" I asked.

"Yes, I'd like my serve to be more consistent."

Dad had a good, strong serve, but there was room for improvement. Sometimes it came in "like gangbusters," as he would say. Other times it fell limply into the bottom of the net. Understandably, he wanted his serve to be more reliable.

We did some simple service motion warm-ups and then some very easy serves.

"Now, Dad, this time when you hit it, keep your head up," I instructed. "Keep your head up even well after you've hit the ball."

Fine-tuning tennis strokes at Living Memorial Park and the Outing Club in Brattleboro.

He accomplished that. The ball cleared the net nicely and landed deep in the service box. My compliant student repeated this time and again.

"Now—this time—watch the ball as you hit it and keep your eyes focused on that point of contact even long after you've hit the ball. I want you to exaggerate watching the ball. Try it."

Dad made a good toss and did exactly as I suggested with the first try. Impressive results—the best serve he had ever hit!

"Good job, Dad. That's exactly what I mean. Try it again."

"I can't believe it," he exclaimed, completely stunned at the realization that for the first time in his life—at age fifty-seven—he had actually seen the ball hit his strings during a serve. He assumed he had always watched the ball, for that's what tennis players did. That's what every coach and teacher says to do. After all, how could anyone hit a ball without watching it? But deeply watching it was another thing.

He diligently practiced this one specific assignment, wanting to recreate that exhilarating feeling that produced a superior, consistent serve.

"Head up, longer... loooooonger," I emphasized.

"Exaggerate it," I offered reminders and bits of encouragement. "Even more."

Dad desperately wanted to make it a habit—this brand new act of seeing the ball hit his strings on his serve. We focused intently on all of Dad's strokes during this Father's Day lesson until he had had a thorough workout.

"Thanks, Donna. That was amazing. And fun. It's so good to be on the tennis court together again."

Days later Dad was still in awe. Years later he still raved about that revelation.

He never forgot that day on the court and his game showed it!

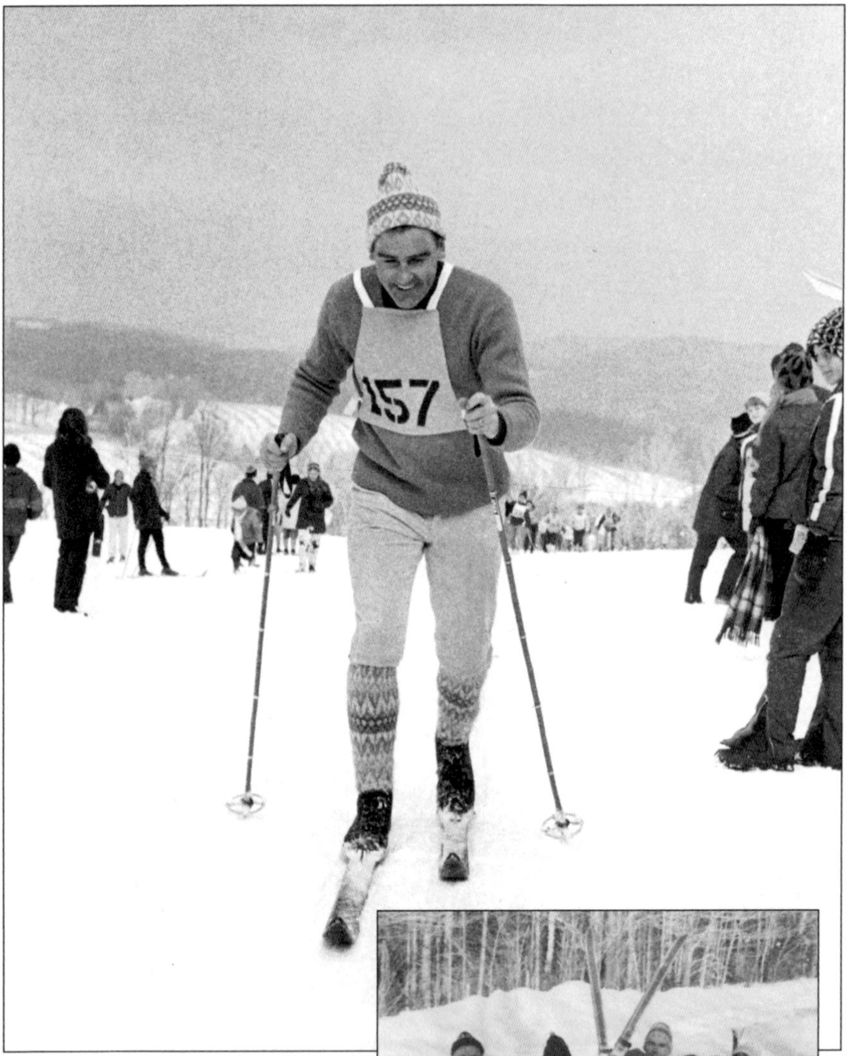

Finishing strong at the 1970 Washington's Birthday Race in Putney, Vermont.

Sunday afternoon family cross-country skiing in Readsboro.

THIRTY-SIX

A RED-EYED VIREO sang nonstop from a nearby branch as the roar of Hellgate Gorge echoed loudly up the hill to our cabin on a little knoll. On a girls' retreat, Gerda, Ella, and I settled into Hellgate Hilton in the Grant—a true haven—at a time I desperately needed a peaceful place for reflection—to slow down, be deliberate, and take stock.

We hiked steeply to Finneson's Cliff for unobstructed views of thick spruce forest and old logging clearings, an elusive pewee accompanying us with its shrill *pee-ah-wee* whistle. The sunny day lured us down to the gorge for swimming, stick-fetching, water romping, and sniffing—Labrador heaven.

Mosquitos swarmed in full attack mode soon after the hour-long torrential downpour with intense lightning ended and we gladly took refuge in our cabin—with screens. Rays of sunshine hit the lower half of the screen on the window over the sink, illuminating the green Palmolive dish soap, white bar soap, and ragged blue sponge. A raucous crow *caw* broke the silence.

It haunted me to think of Dad's life, so completely different from the rest of his life—his life so well-lived. Why this ending? Why this sharp contrast to his former life?

It was soothing to be with my two best buddies—longtime faithful Lab Gerda stretched out on the worn wooden cabin floor and young, energetic Ella with the silky coat snuggled up tight to me, content like a baby, as I wrote to Dad:

Dear, dear Dad,

What is it like to be you right now? When you cannot find words are you frustrated? Do you wonder why we aren't helping you more or why we aren't fixing things? Are you OK?

*Dad, it was always a pleasure to go on a trip with you. I envision you standing somewhere on a trail in the middle of nowhere, on a mountaintop, or on cross-country skis in deep snowy woods—you standing there with a look of deep contentment—*This is the life, *you'd say. You scored the highest level on the happiness index with your appreciation of the simplest things.* We're as happy as peas in a pod, *you'd laugh at the cliché, at the image. But it was true, we were happy and content . . . doing what we loved, being in nature, spending time together.*

You were an example to others—admired and looked to for feedback and solutions. You came through for so many. You embraced your role and took responsibility to help others, to guide and nurture them—your own kids, the kids of the town who became your kids. *When there was leadership needed, you did not hide or stay silent. You came forward and came through. You served, you gave, you loved.*

Why was all this taken from you? What reason? What lesson?

Every day you smiled, were kind to others, joyous, appreciative, fun-loving, making the best of whatever your situation. I look to you now, in my sadness, as I struggle mightily.

I try to live fully and well, as you would want me to. Sometimes I do. In truth, I'm heavily weighed down with sorrow—seeing you this way. I don't know how to say goodbye to you without feeling deep sadness. Is it possible?

How can I be different or handle it better? I want to enjoy the moments, the camaraderie, and being together, but our now *seems tinged with the sadness of the impending* goodbye *and the cold reality of this situation. Dad, you set the best example of living in the moment.*

You lived a life to be proud of—a model citizen—thoughtful, methodical, loving, mindful. Just as you ate, savoring every bite, sitting at the table taking your time, even when everyone was done, honoring the process and the food, appreciative of each detail of life. Every day was a success, a paying attention. Worship was not only on Sunday.

I wonder—what would you do? How would you handle this? I think of the ways you handled adversity—with fortitude, patience, and grace.

I recall your first Washington's Birthday Cross-Country Ski Race. You set out from Westminster West to cover seven miles on skis to Putney School on heavy, old ski jumping skis. You told me how you labored under the weight of your inappropriate skis and wore way too many clothes so you were soaking wet by the top of the first hill. You slipped and spun, having no traction to be able to push off, to kick and glide as others efficiently did, since you knew nothing about waxing. No wonder your quadriceps tired and slowed you to a plod!

Even though it must have been demoralizing to be passed by one skier after another, you completely dismissed the thought of dropping out. You persevered to the finish—for the reward of lingonberry juice— only to find not a drop of juice left! I still feel a pang recalling that moment—the crushing blow you experienced upon discovering the lingonberry juice was all gone—the injustice.

Even more important, what did you make of your adversity and suffering? You turned it into a positive outcome. You went right out and bought genuine cross-country touring skis for all of us and learned all you could about waxing and technique.

Thanks to you, our family had a new sport and cross-country skiing quickly became one of our favorite family activities. I remember the fun we had! Often four families headed out after church— the Crosbys, Davises, Maddens, and Dearborns—into the woods or on an old logging road. We skied in deep powder and through birch glades, past snow-laden balsam and orchards, roasted hotdogs over a fire . . . I remember one epic fall you took. Only your head and one pole were showing—you were buried. We took your picture before we helped you up.

Dad, we all benefitted from your courage to try something new and the way you turned a fiasco into something good. You were an inspiration then and so many times throughout my life. Thank you. I will summon the patience and resolve you modeled so well and try to keep a positive frame of mind. I will return home with renewed strength and replenished peacefulness…

While I accept that you usually cannot find words to express yourself and that I might never again have a conversation with you, I never give up hope that someday you will talk to me again.

I will continue to do all I know to do—to go and be with you—with hugs and kisses, stories and photos and hold your hand to transfer love, warmth, and support.

Dad, oh, Dad, I miss you in our daily life. We all do.

Love, Donna

THIRTY-SEVEN

I LOVED ICE CREAM sundae day at the nursing home! Every Thursday during the summer, two cheery senior volunteers wheeled the sundae cart through the hallways.

"What kind of ice cream do you want? Your usual vanilla?" I asked Dad.

"Yes."

"How about hot fudge?"

He nodded his head to indicate "yes."

Each Thursday revealed different flavors and a special topping, served with a smile, and made to order. What a perfect way to put a smile on the faces of nursing home residents!

Dad had no trouble finishing every morsel of his hot fudge sundae, as usual. Gerda sat at full attention with her eyes riveted on the cart, remembering in the way that dogs do, that they always offered her a bowl of vanilla. And this day was no exception. She waited for my okay and then licked it slowly without a break.

"I'll try the butter pecan, please," I said.

Delicious summer air beckoned us outdoors for a stroll around the grounds. We paused in the beech tree's shade for a break, just in time to count the cars following two engines pulling the freight train that rumbled by.

"Fifty-six, Dad. Is that what you counted?"

He nodded in agreement.

"I brought your running trophy with me today. That was quite a race over in Saco, a fun time." He clutched his little trophy of a runner in stride.

"I remember it well," I added. "I was so proud of you..."

"In the 60–69 category, first place, Frank Dearborn," the announcer said.

"Dad, that's you—you won your age group!" I exclaimed. The announcement took me by surprise, too.

Dad remained frozen in place, too stunned to move. He was a middle-of-the-pack runner and had never before finished first in his age category in the ten years he had raced. Dad was still a great athlete, as he was in high school when he lettered in three sports. He didn't train exclusively for running, preferring to participate in a multitude of lifetime activities for the sheer joy of moving his body and the rewards of staying fit and healthy.

I had finished the race ahead of Dad, so I ran back to meet him, encourage him, and race the last stretch with him. He relaxed and even waved and smiled to Mom the camerawoman who took his photo as he approached the homestretch. Showing us his strong kick, he accelerated impressively across the finish line.

When he climbed the podium to accept his award we cheered loudly.

"Good job, Dad," I congratulated him.

"I must have been the only one in my category," he joked in his self-deprecating manner.

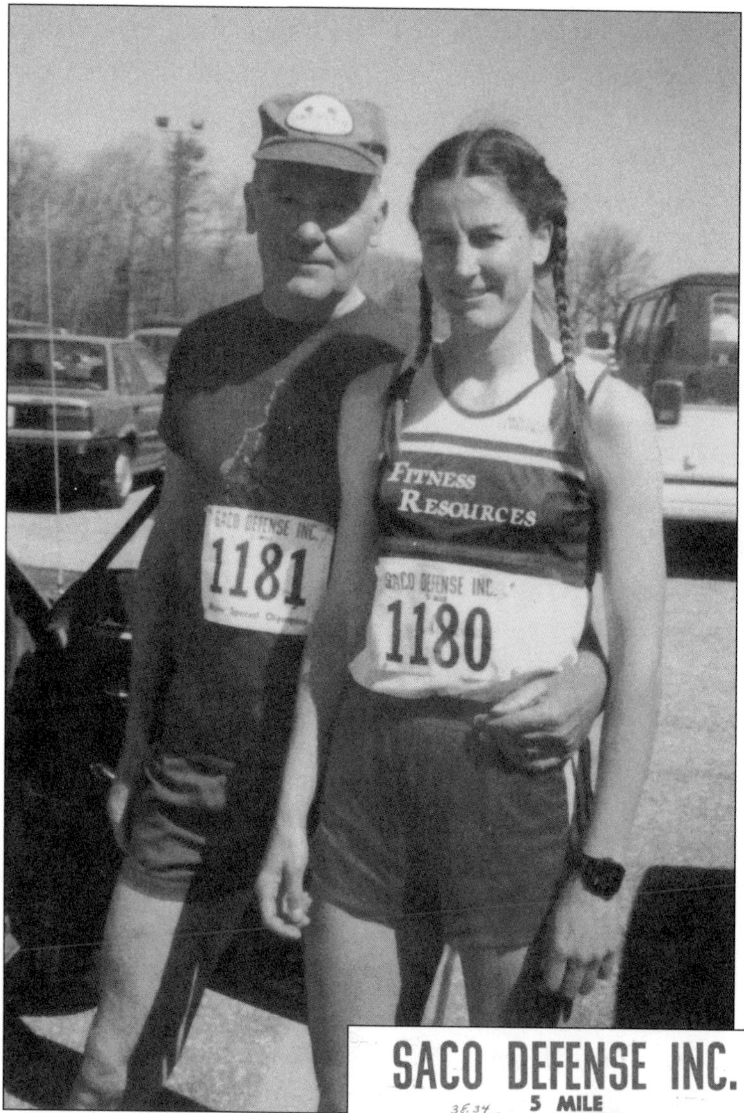

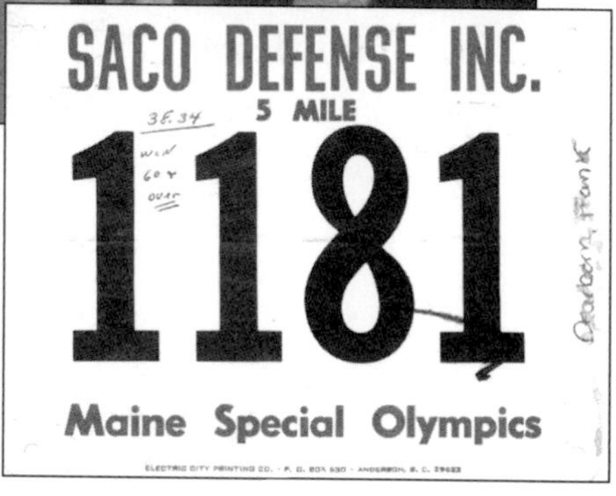

Saco 5-mile road race—first place in the 60-69 category—Frank Dearborn

That wasn't true. The race had more than three hundred runners and plenty of other competitors in Dad's new age category, the 60+ that he had just entered two months prior.

I felt proud of my dad who had trained hard and joined me at many road races that year. Just one month before the Saco five-miler, winds gusted to thirty miles per hour, delivering a stiff headwind to significantly challenge and slow us down in the Concord Turtle Trot. We surprised ourselves by winning hooded sweatshirts for finishing second at the Concord Couples five kilometer race in the 75-99-year-old bracket of the Father-Daughter division. Dad cheered me on first, as I raced the flat, fast course, then I encouraged him to his fastest time yet.

Prior to the start of the five-mile Jingle Bell Run for Arthritis, a large contingent of us huddled together to keep from freezing, then we all took off in a mad sprint that Dad remembered as the coldest race start ever. We sweated profusely in Brattleboro's annual Fourth of July race down Main Street, challenged to drink enough to remain hydrated. The Turkey Trot remained one of our favorites, our chance to exercise rigorously prior to the Thanksgiving meal and choose our food award from the table no matter which place you finished. Everyone won a prize.

THE LITTLE TROPHY from the Saco race reminds me of our races—the wind, heat, cold, and hills that all made Dad stronger—and especially our no-holes-barred talks during training runs when thoughts and emotions flowed freely and we solved all the problems of the world as our feet glided lightly over the pathways.

THIRTY-EIGHT

I WHEELED DAD OUTSIDE for some much-needed fresh air after I helped him into his blue fleece jacket.

"Hi, Frank," Birches residents Larry and Anna called out as we cruised past.

We waved back with a familiarity realized from doing it for nearly five years.

Maple leaves had turned slightly brownish—a tired, golden color—almost grown old in a matter of days.

Dad remained serious and speechless, his lips sealed shut. Something about it was unbelievable, so wrong and hard to comprehend—even after so many years. You'd think I would have been used to it. I was in a way and would never be in another sense.

The crisp air enticed us farther down Stebbins Road, to the small, old cemetery across from towering spruce trees. Weathered stones leaned and the earth buckled around them, justified rebellion after more than a hundred years.

I wanted to keep walking on this perfect fall day as if doing so could transport us to our glorious fall hikes before Dad suffered a stroke. I wanted to keep pushing him in his wheelchair, on and on, as if no nursing home existed, mile after mile... until he started talking again.

Since Dad talked very little these days, many spoke to him in a loud voice, assuming that since he didn't speak he also didn't hear well. He heard perfectly well. I knew he heard me, he just couldn't verbalize a response. Certainly he would talk if he could, talking one of his favorite things and interactions with people bringing him pleasure his whole life.

I thought of times we'd be hiking along a trail and all of a sudden Dad wasn't there behind me. He had stopped—once again—to chat with a passing hiker. I missed that. I missed Dad talking.

I took solace in recalling a time when Dad flourished as an articulate leader and entertaining public speaker, the day I wanted to stay home from school when I was in the fourth grade...

THAT'S WHAT I'D DO—stay home from school! At the thought, the churning in my stomach subsided a little bit.

I loved school. I liked Mrs. Storey, my strict fourth grade teacher at Academy School, even though she was the first teacher to ever give me a grade other than an "A" on my report card. Not only did I fail to achieve an "A," I received a "B minus" in Oral English, barely a "B."

I couldn't possibly stand up in front of the entire class again! I could only think about the other time I had given a report in front of the class and the embarrassment I felt. Nervously looking out at the sea of eyes staring at me, I completely froze and couldn't remember what I planned to say—complete paralysis.

My classmates weren't strangers. I had known almost all the kids in my class since kindergarten—we'd been together for more than four years. Most of my best friends sat in that class—Nancy, Gretchen, JoAnn, Peggy, and Priscilla. That didn't matter.

I excelled in math and did everything else well in school, but I would do anything to get out of presenting that oral book report.

Dad realized we had a problem if I didn't want to go to school, so he sat me down at the kitchen table. I poured it all out, including the all-important detail of how Gary Haskins, who sat behind me, pulled my braids and got away with it.

"Hmm," was all Dad said at first, as he sat there nodding and taking it in with a seriously furrowed brow, fully present and calm. I felt better already, knowing Dad listened carefully to my complete story. Certainly he'd feel my fear and completely agree that I needed to stay home from school.

His answer took me by surprise. He said that he had been extremely shy in the fourth grade, afraid to stand up in front of his class, just like me. Though hard to believe, he precisely described his lightheadedness and woozy stomach, exactly how I experienced it. He knew!

It was nearly impossible to imagine that my dad was ever shy by watching him at age thirty-four—an outstanding public speaker. Often invited to speak at local clubs—Rotary, Elks, American Legion, and others—he readily obliged and loved it. Dad directed staff meetings and trainings—relaxed, confident, and funny. He stood up in front of hundreds of people at Town Meetings when he gave his annual recreation report and calmly answered questions.

Always entertaining, Dad interspersed quips and anecdotes in his presentations. The Oak Grove Parent Teacher Club thanked him for coming to speak at their May meeting: "You were just great! Your talk was informative, interesting, and amusing, which is a perfect combination!"

He practiced his Old Vermonter stories and jokes on us. We never tired of his "Chicken Chow Mein" joke. "One day I got talking to a man. He told me he was a Kamikaze pilot during the war, how many missions he had flown, his code name was 'chow mein.' Then I asked him, 'weren't kamikaze pilots supposed to sacrifice their lives for their country? Why are you still alive?' He said, 'Me chicken chow mein.'" We delighted in Dad's animated rendition of the punch line.

Never lost for words, how did he always seem to know just what to say? I needed to know how my dad went from shy fourth grader to comfortable, highly-sought-after speaker.

The solution emerged, far simpler than I imagined—practice, practice, practice. Determined to overcome his nervousness, Dad forced himself to speak in front of groups until little by little he became more comfortable.

He told me about his plan. While in college Dad deliberately pursued jobs that would not only be adventurous but good experiences in leadership positions to help him move beyond his innate bashfulness. He vividly remembered how he forgot his lines in a skit one night at a council ring program at his first summer camp job on the shores of Lake Winnipesaukee. He felt embarrassed and hadn't learned how to ad-lib yet. Dad had evolved considerably since that night—into a quick-thinking, unrattled master of the extemporaneous.

Dad regaled me with stories about midnight snake dances at a coeducational adult camp near Philadelphia where he taught archery and organized social programs. His eyes sparkled when he talked about the dream job of his college days. After sailing for five days to Aruba, he taught swimming at a glamorous beach and directed social events for 550 enthusiastic children of Standard Oil Refinery workers from all over the world.

Dad kept immersing himself in new and different situations as a leader—and it worked. All it took was bravery, perseverance, and practice?

I would go to school the following day, staying home obviously not the solution. Though still nervous when I presented the book report, at least I didn't feel alone. After all, my dad had once been a shy fourth grader just like me! I aspired to become comfortable speaking in front of a group, just like Dad.

THIRTY-NINE

WE INTERRUPT THIS PROGRAM to bring you breaking news: Frank is talking—non-stop—bursting—words bubbling out. You have to see it to believe it.

"You won't believe how much Dad talked today," Mom exclaimed, when she arrived home from the nursing home one day in January 2009. "He never stopped talking."

"What? You're kidding?" I said.

"No, he said to tell you we had a good visit."

"I hope he's still talking tomorrow!"

"I hope so, too."

MY DAD SPEAKING? Speaking beyond a one-word answer? Even one word was rare enough those days, more than five years after his stroke.

"Is my dad still talking?" I asked, when I called the nursing home the next morning.

"Oh, yes, he's joking with the nurses right now," Wanda said.

I rushed to him as fast as I could. I wanted to experience this window of opportunity. When I arrived, the difference was striking.

"Hi, Donna," Dad said clearly and enthusiastically.

"Hi, Dad."

"It's good to see you," Dad continued. "I'm glad you're here."

I held his hand and looked into his bright eyes which were livelier than usual.

I made it in time! I certainly didn't want to miss any opportunity to talk with Dad. Who knew how long it would last? Now and then he was more alert for a day or two and we wanted to be there for those openings since they didn't last long. We became accustomed to the window abruptly slamming shut.

"I've been gone a long time, but now I'm back," Dad said. That was the truth. What had it been like? How long would it last?

"Five years ago you had a stroke, Dad."

"A sad day. I tried to forget it."

"We were snowshoeing, you fell and couldn't get up."

"That was a traumatic thing. Little things were big."

"What was it like, not to be able to talk?"

"I was really mystified."

"It's amazing."

"Let's take stock—see where we are."

After his severe stroke and subsequent seizures, Dad was put on a variety of anti-seizure medications to protect against further seizures. When he developed a rash over much of his body, Dad's doctor surmised that he was allergic to carbatrol, even after several years of taking that particular drug. To everyone's complete amazement, including his doctor, four days after the carbatrol was stopped, not only did the rash disappear but Dad started talking and hadn't stopped. Even more miraculous, it was not only words but sentences. He was carrying on conversations with us. Conversations!

"Dad, you never smoked, did you?" I asked.

"No," he said.

"Mom did, a long time ago."

"She smoked everything."

"She did?"

"Marijuana, cigars..." he said, then laughed.

I couldn't believe he said that. "Really, Dad?"

"No, I'm kidding."

"You've always been a kidder and embellisher."

"I've been known to do that."

"What does *embellish* mean?" I wanted to test his clarity.

"To add to."

"How do you spell *embellish*?"

"E-M-B-E-L-L-I-S-H."

"You're pretty sharp."

"Once in a while I get something pretty right."

"DAD, YOU USED TO THROW a knuckleball pretty well. It would really wobble unpredictably. You tried to teach me," I said, as we played catch for the first time in a long while.

"Hoyt Wilhelm's knuckleball. This is how you hold it," Dad said, as he curled up his fingers. "You try to take all the spin off the ball."

"We used to have fun playing catch."

"We sure did—all the time."

I opened one of his first photo booklets. "Dad, here you are in your baseball uniform. Was that in high school?"

"Yes, I was a pitcher, a good athlete."

"We were both such baseball fans. My notebook had all kinds of statistics. You taught me how to keep score, all the symbols and notations on an official score sheet."

"I wanted to be a baseball announcer! I listened to all the games on the radio, kept a score sheet, and then announced the game again into my microphone."

"Remember the time we had a flat tire on Storrow Drive on the way to Fenway Park?"

"Yes—and we made it to the game in time."

Dad and I drove to Fenway Park once or twice a year to cheer on our Red Sox who were firmly entrenched in the bottom half of the American League for my first six years as a fan. No wonder I was drawn to the Yankees, American League Champions for four straight seasons from 1961 to 1964, World Series Champions with exciting Hall of Fame players. Going to New York City to their home ballpark was completely beyond comprehension.

"Dad, I remember when you surprised me with tickets to a twilight doubleheader at Yankee Stadium."

"Wasn't that something?"

"And then I couldn't believe when you turned off the highway in Hartford."

"That was a good surprise—flying to New York City."

"The first time I ever flew—my eyes were big. And then the taxi to Yankee Stadium. I held on for dear life. That was another first. I was hoping Whitey Ford would be pitching, but Mel Stottlemyre was on the mound," I said.

We'd sat in regal, red seats in the huge stadium. American League pennants and World Series Championship banners hung from the rafters, evidence of their long history of excellence. Babe Ruth, Lou Gehrig, and Joe DiMaggio came alive. I was in heaven. Even though it was one of the worst seasons in Yankees' history, nothing could diminish my delight at being in Yankee Stadium.

"What players do you remember, Dad?"

"Mickey Mantle, Roger Maris, and Joe Pepitone."

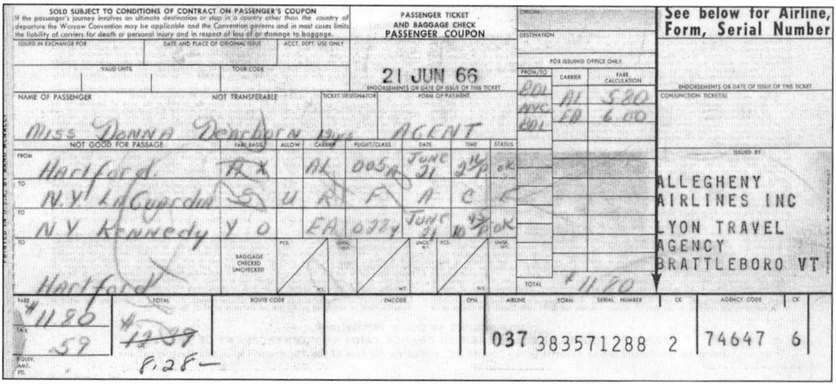

SOLD SUBJECT TO CONDITIONS OF CONTRACT ON PASSENGER'S COUPON

PASSENGER TICKET AND BAGGAGE CHECK
PASSENGER COUPON

See below for Airline, Form, Serial Number

21 JUN 66

NAME OF PASSENGER: Miss Donna Dearborn

NOT TRANSFERABLE

FORM OF PAYMENT: AGENT

FROM / TO	FARE BASIS	ALLOW	CARRIER	FLIGHT/CLASS	DATE	TIME	STATUS
Hartford	TX		AL	005	June 21	2	ok
N.Y. LaGuardia							
N.Y. Kennedy	YO		EA	0924	June 21	10	ok
Hartford							

FROM/TO	CARRIER	FARE CALCULATION
BDL	AL	580
NYC	EA	600
BDL		
TOTAL		$11.80

ISSUED BY
ALLEGHENY AIRLINES INC
LYON TRAVEL AGENCY
BRATTLEBORO VT

FARE $11.80
TAX .59
TOTAL $12.39

037 383571288 2 74647 6

Plane ticket from Bradley to La Guardia on June 21, 1966.

Ace pitcher on his junior high and high school baseball teams in Franklin, New Hampshire.

"Elston Howard was the catcher and Clete Boyer at third base. We had great box seats on the first baseline. Mel Stottlemyre was not at his best. The Yankees got behind early, but what an ending! Do you remember?"

"How could I forget."

"We thought for sure Roy White hit a home run to win the game. Frank Robinson fell into the right field stands as he was trying to catch the ball. When he got up, he had the ball in his glove! We couldn't believe it," I said.

"That was some catch! Ralph Houk stormed out of the dugout. That was something. Remember how he stood face to face with the umpire and kicked dirt on the umpire's shoes?"

"I know. He followed the umpire nose to nose and spit tobacco between his teeth. The stadium went silent. Fans threw food and cups onto the field. What an ending!" I said.

"That was some day for a thirteen-year-old kid. I'll never forget it, Dad. Thanks again."

"I'll never forget it either."

Details from our trip to Yankee Stadium remained vivid, since Dad and I periodically evoked the memorable events of June 21, 1966, but to relive that momentous day with Dad after he had barely spoken for four years was extraordinary.

FORTY

"ROLL OUT THE BARREL, *we'll have a barrel of fun. Roll out the barrel, we've got the blues on the run,*" the hearty tenor voice sang out in the nursing home dining room.

It was Dad! Dad singing! Out of the blue—for the first time in over four years.

I joined in, "*Zing, boom, tararrel, sing out a song of good cheer. Now's the time to roll the barrel, for the gang's all here.*"

Dad sang every word clearly and with gusto.

Wow—what a joyful moment. What fun to sing with Dad, to feel his spirit, to see him participating in one of his favorite activities that had been absent for so long. One more part of Dad was back. Gerda wagged her tail, sensing our excitement.

"It's good to be with you, Dad," I said. "Let's go down the hall." We found an empty room and turned off its blaring television set.

"We have a lot to catch up on. What did you do this morning?" Dad said.

"I took Ella for a long walk," I said.

"That's peaceful. That's good," he said.

"Look at Gerda. She's so content... basking in the sun," he said.

"Frank," Wally said, "do you understand the Latin in the Catholic services?"

"No, I don't understand that. Gerda does though, she understands it," Dad said and laughed.

"Dad, did you know that Wally turned sixty-four? Does he look sixty-four?" I asked.

"At least that," Dad joked.

Conversations continued, both serious and lighthearted. Words that had been locked away burst forth. Dad was almost like a modern-day Rip Van Winkle, except that Dad didn't fall asleep to escape a nagging wife, nor was he gone for twenty years.

"You don't miss anything," I said.

"I try not to."

"You're a good man."

"There aren't many of us left," he said. After a pause, he asked, "How's mother's attitude? Is it good?"

"She's doing the best she can, Dad," I said.

"She's bright. She keeps up her standard of what she wants to do and her friendships. She's a good gal. I wish I could do more—to keep up with her."

"You married well," I said.

"It's a good thing. It's been an important part of my life... Doris' consistent backing."

I opened his newest booklet of photos. Certain photos captured Dad's attention, especially one of him with his tennis racket that he pointed to.

"You look professional, Dad."

"You're right, I do. I look good in my white tennis shirt."

"Remember the time you and I played in the Outing Club mixed doubles tournament? I wrote a story about one of our matches. I think we should read it aloud. Do you want to start?"

"I'll try." Dad read:

WHAT ARE YOU DOING?

I lay in a disheveled heap on the tennis court in the middle of a hot August day, my freshly-washed white skirt smeared with greenish clay. Gritty clay clung to my sweaty arms and legs. I took a breath as I surveyed the damage.

"WHAT are you DOING?" I yelled and refused Dad's hand to help boost me back onto my feet. A large crowd had gathered at the fence near our court to view the spectacle.

In the heat of the moment during a crucial point in our mixed doubles match, my dad had shoved me out of the way so we wouldn't collide and he could make the overhead shot. I'm sure he didn't intend to send me crashing to the court so hard that my racket went flying.

"Are you okay?" he asked. "I'm so sorry. I saw the lob go up and all I could think of was hitting it."

We hadn't properly communicated and both of us had moved to hit the ball. My larger and stronger dad won out.

"At least we won the point!" he said later, after I had toweled off and regained my composure. What a big point as we battled neck and neck in the extremely close second set…

He paused. "I can't even talk—that drink paralyzes me," Dad said. "You did a good job. Do you want me to read now?"

"Yes, that would be good."

I continued with the story:

Surprisingly, we had reached the semifinals of the highly competitive Brattleboro Outing Club mixed doubles championship. With my mother recovering from routine surgery, I had gladly filled in and teamed up with my dad for the club tournament. What fun we had on the tennis court over the years. When I was in high school Dad especially loved hitting the ball as hard as he could to test me while I stood at the net. He would be doubled over with laughter at the end of those slugfests, amazed that I returned every ball. Now I was twenty-nine, had taught tennis for several years, and had come a long way since those days.

Having never played in a tennis tournament together was an advantage—we were neither seeded nor favored. Relaxed and uninhibited, we had breezed through the first few rounds, until this semifinal match. We found ourselves among the final four teams, pitted against the number two seeds, the ever-steady, experienced Dunham team. Fans lined up along the fences, taking notice of this dark-horse team.

Phil, the Flying Dentist, and his wife, Mary, had won the first set in resounding fashion, crushing us 6-1. That trouncing not only embarrassed Dad and me, more importantly, it lit our competitive fires to a high intensity. Dad had passed his fierce competitiveness along to me.

After the first set, Dad had turned to me and said, "What are we going to do?"

"Quick conference at the baseline," I whispered to him. I put my arm around him and told him my plan as we walked to the back of the court. Losing that first set inspired me to completely change our strategy. "We're going to lob more and make them move, anything to run them around. We've been feeding the ball right to them. We can do a lot better than this. We're more fit...we can win this." We had been implementing this new strategy of changing the tempo and trying to disrupt Phil and Mary's rhythm. Finally it had started to pay off against this crafty couple. Then we collided, putting a temporary halt to our comeback.

Though dirtier, at least I hadn't been injured in the fall. I composed myself, forgave Dad, and returned to the task at hand. Vowing to communicate better, we continued our comeback, and won the close second set. We kept up our momentum and concentration to score a big upset by also winning the close third set, thus the match.

"Way to go, Dad, you were great," I said.

"Thanks, partner. That was fun. I'm so glad we could play together. It's amazing what our change in strategy did. Good job, coach."

Dad proudly told Mom the details of our come-from-behind, upset victory. In the finals the next day we beat Reeve and Essie Cantus in an anticlimactic match after our hard-fought semifinal battle. Big underdogs, Dad and I had won the club tournament.

"That's a good story. It's fun to remember it."

"I heard Phil and Mary stopped in to see you this week, Dad."

"Yes."

"They're great folks, aren't they?"

"Yes, I've known them a long time."

We had the blessing of this quiet space to ourselves, a rare occurrence in the nursing home. No distractions or television noise. No beepers proclaiming that someone was trying to stand who shouldn't have been. No interruptions.

I treasured the gift of my father speaking and interacting with us—even singing.

"It's important to retain the relationship with your daughter. You're a wonderful girl who has kept your ties to your mother and your father," Dad said, when it was time to leave. "It's good to have you here."

Freshman year at Springfield College, Springfield, Massachusetts.

Springfield College motto: Spirit-Mind-Body.

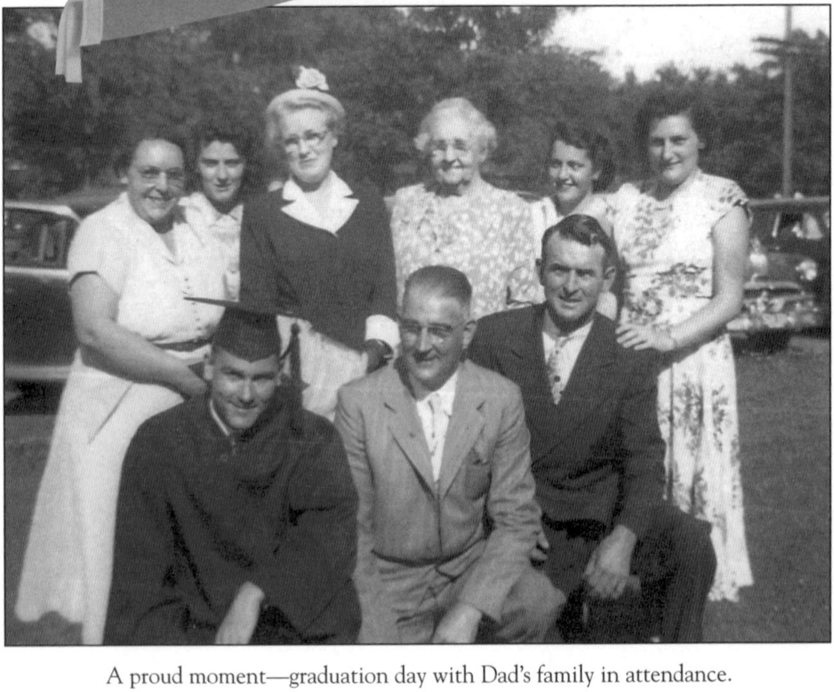

A proud moment—graduation day with Dad's family in attendance.

FORTY-ONE

"I DON'T CARE FOR THIS," Dad said, after we had listened to an older fellow play country music on his electric guitar for a few minutes.

"You don't?" I was surprised, as Dad loved most of the wide variety of music concerts at the nursing home.

"No, I'd rather go outside for a walk with you."

Outside on a mild, early March day, Dad was curious about everything. He watched a rather portly yellow Labrador walk by with its owner.

"A yellow moose," Dad said, and he was accurate, as the dog must have weighed at least 120 pounds, about twice as much as our Labradors.

"I'm glad we're outside. Good idea, Dad," I said. "Look at the icicles."

"Beautiful. It's fortuitous that you and I should meet."

"Yes, this is more fun than tomorrow. I have to go to the dentist and have a crown put in," I said.

"That's a nuisance," Dad said. "But you can't worry about the things you can't control."

Back inside, I handed Dad a little present. "I brought you a new Springfield College banner for the wall in your room."

"Thank you," he said.

"Springfield was a great place for both of us, wasn't it, Dad?"

"Yes, it was. I graduated in 1952. 'Spirit, Mind, Body,'" Dad said, as he read the Springfield College emblem on his banner and traced the words on the three edges of a maroon equilateral triangle which surrounded the lamp of learning.

Dad had embraced the "spirit, mind, and body" philosophy of his alma mater and devoted attention to all three in establishing his well-rounded, balanced approach to life.

"I remember seeing your transcript. You must have worked hard to get such good grades." Dad hadn't applied himself to his studies in high school—sports were everything—but he certainly did in college.

"I did. I loved it."

"Except boxing. Did you really get an 'F'?"

"Yes, that class nearly killed me."

"Let's read an excerpt from a letter you sent to me when I was a freshman at Springfield. I love the story about you ending up at the wrong college."

Dear Donna,

Times were a little different when I was at S.C. Panty raids? We never knew about panty raids, in fact, I've never ever heard of that term. There were only men until fall of my senior year. Sept. 1951 was the first time women were admitted. They lived in Abbey hall, your dorm, which I think was brand new that year. Your room situation sounds exasperating, to have the three of you in that small room—and with the late-night phone calls, too. There must be a solution.

When I was a freshman we had to wear caps too, though I do not remember them being called beanies, and ours were white.

Since we lost the rope pull to the sophomores, we had to continue to wear our caps—like the campus badge of identification. The sophomores beat us easily and we quickly ended up in the Massasoit.

I was two years older than you are when I started college, since I joined the Navy right out of high school. Probably I've told you before, Eddie Gregg and I went down to the recruiters, seeking adventure or a new experience. Boy, were we naïve! We signed up at the same time, thinking we'd be together, but our paths never crossed after that day.

I was so lonely being away from home for the first time. Boot camp was an awakening. I felt beat up and homesick at the beginning and mail call was a big moment. Other young men envied the amount of mail I got.

After about twenty-two months in the Navy, I was discharged in April, 1948. The service was a very positive aspect of my life. I matured as a lad and became aware of the world beyond little Franklin. As a result of my naval service, I was entitled to the G.I. Bill of Rights which created a dramatic and marvelous opportunity for me that I never had even thought about.

I checked with my high school guidance counselor to find out how I could apply to a college. My ambition was to be a coach, physical education teacher, or a teacher related to sports. When I was very young I dreamed I would become a baseball announcer. My advisor listened to my ambitions and suggested that I apply to American International College in Springfield, Mass.

To my surprise and disbelief, I got a letter indicating that I was accepted to attend there and to come for an interview. Meanwhile, I had just been accepted to be a counselor at Camp Belknap, a YMCA camp on Lake Winnipesaukee. So I went to Springfield for the interview. The counselor in the Admissions Office listened carefully and then said, Young man, you have the

An active member of the Hosaga Tribe at Springfield College which performed shows to portray the lives of the American Plains Indians.

wrong college. You should be applying to Springfield College across town. Youth workers, P.E. men, and Y men attend that college. We're a business college. *This is the truth, even though it is hard to believe that this mistake could occur.*

So I went across town to Springfield College and saw the Admissions Officer. I applied and was told it was too late to attend S.C. in September, but they did have a special six-week class in the summer for those who applied late or had other special reasons not to apply when they should. He said it was competitive and only a small number would be accepted. Those who got good grades and showed what he called a S.C. aptitude would be selected for fall classes. I immediately applied for that class and told the Director at Camp Belknap that I was not available (he made me promise to come the following summer).

I loved the classes, students, school, and teachers and I never worked so hard in my life. I took academic, skills, and orientation classes and I was thrilled to be accepted at S.C. at the conclusion of the summer. It was one of the top moments of my life.

As a freshman, I lived in Alumni Hall, a real beehive of noise and activity. Needless to say I did my studying at the library. My roommate was Harry Dotson from Portland, Oregon, and we became good friends.

Starting college two years later was probably a good thing for me. I was ready to do the studying necessary to succeed in college. I was the first one in my family to go to college. Later, my youngest sister, Glenice, was the only other one of us five kids to graduate from college.

I was a star *baseball pitcher for Franklin H.S. but I failed to make the S.C. freshman baseball team. During the tryouts, Coach Ed Steitz asked me to show him my curveball. I didn't have one—nuff said. That was one of the biggest disappointments of my freshman year.*

So I went out for the soccer team. I made the team though I question why. I played in each of the seven games and enjoyed it. Vern Cox was our coach—a great guy.

I enjoyed my academic courses such as Public Speaking, Educational Psychology, Great Books, Sociology, Economics, History of Western Civilization, etc. I tried to relate everything to my future work with people. It was challenging, fun, and worthwhile.

I liked my professors. As a recreation and camping major I will always remember the members of the S.C. faculty in that department—Chic Weckwerth, Don Bridgeman, and Gerry Harrison. I got to know them and their families and they were a great influence to me in my resolve to be a recreation professional. Those were good days for me at Springfield. I was so happy there.

Glad to hear that field hockey is going well and you're the starting center halfback on the varsity. We'll see you at the game on Saturday—bearing gifts.

I guess I got carried away. You probably didn't expect such a long-winded discourse, but I know you can handle it. Look forward to seeing you soon. Sending lots of love and support, Dad

"It's fun to recall some of these memories," Dad said.

"That must have been tough, Dad, not making the baseball team."

"Yes, it was."

"You sang in the glee club, didn't you?"

"Yes, I sang second tenor all four years. Gil Vickers was the director. I enjoyed it so much."

"Did I ever tell you I went streaking when I was a junior at Springfield?"

"No." He laughed.

"It was crazy. I guess Spring Fever hit me. Students were doing it on college campuses all across the country then. A police officer walked by and asked if everything was okay just as we were getting ready. I don't think I ever told you."

"You ate at the Lido, too, when you were at Springfield, didn't you?" I said.

"Yes, the best Italian food."

"Dad, if you think of something you want, let me know."

"Do you want me to put it in writing and mail it to you?" He laughed.

"Great to be with you, Dad."

"It makes my day and my week."

"Love you, Dad."

"Love you, Donna."

FORTY-TWO

ON MONDAY, MARCH 16TH, I wedged myself into the small space in the back of the Ford van between my dad's wheelchair and the side panel. Although uncomfortable, I sat on a tiny plastic ledge with the metal extension from the footrest poking into my leg. I wanted to be close to Dad in order to hear every word he said. Gems popped out all the time. Sometimes they were quiet and quick. I didn't want to miss one word, now that he'd been talking again for two months.

"Dad, Wally and I are taking you on a birthday tour," I said.

"That's good, thank you."

"Are you ready, Frank?" our driver Harvey called out. He'd known my dad for fifty years. Harvey lowered the back of the wheelchair-accessible van and we were on our way.

Dad and I had a good view out the rear window on this perfectly clear, sunny day.

"Who's that?" he asked as he pointed to the car traveling behind us. He was curious about everything and overflowed with questions.

Dad's birthday card.

Leaving the Recreation Center.

He read each word on the front of his birthday card I placed on the tray of his wheelchair: "'Happy Birthday to the Best Dad, Frank Holt Dearborn, March 16, 2009.'" It was one of my traditional homemade cards, this one with a photo of our family in 1958, the five of us.

"Look," he said, "I have on a starched white shirt and a necktie." And then he laughed.

"That's right, Dad, you do." I thought to myself, this is so worthwhile—already—and we've just barely started.

"*Happy Birthday to you*," I started to sing. On the second line, my dad joined in, "*Happy Birthday to you . . .*" To hear his sweet singing voice completely melted my heart.

We finished the "Happy Birthday" song together and laughed.

"What's it like to sing 'Happy Birthday' to yourself, Dad?"

"It's unusual," he said with laughter in his voice. It was still inconceivable that he was talking, let alone singing.

Harvey drove us north on route 142 to Main Street, around to the back of the recreation center where Dad had worked for thirty-three years as Superintendent of Parks and Recreation. The current recreation director came out to greet us.

"Hi, Frank, good to see you," said Carol.

"Good to see you, too, Carol."

She was floored and overjoyed when he responded. Last time she saw him he hadn't spoken, he had just stared into space. Carol gave him a card and a staff T-shirt in his favorite blue.

"Thank you," he said.

I urged her, "Tell Dad about everything that's going on."

Carol obliged. She told Dad they had just closed the skating rink for the season. They talked about Nelson Withington whom the rink is named after. Dad lauded Nelson as one of the best supporters of recreation. Carol told him about the new park she was planning along the West River.

"Where are you getting the money?" Dad asked. That question was right-on; Dad knew how much work went into funding projects like that. He listened, answered, and asked just the right questions, thoroughly enjoying the interaction with his former program director. It was hard to leave, yet we needed to continue with the rest of our tour.

"I'll pass the word—Frank's back!" she said in disbelief.

We turned on Cedar Street and drove to the Harris Hill ski jump.

"It's been completely renovated, Dad, doesn't it look good?"

"Yes, it does. I walked up all those stairs."

"That's right, you did, lots of times. That was a good workout, wasn't it?"

"The best." He looked back at the 1958 family photo on my card. "There's you and Debra and David and mother. Doris always looks good."

He kept looking at that photo from more than fifty years ago and kept reading his card.

We drove to West Brattleboro and pulled into Melrose Terrace to see my brother at work. He had Dad's favorite Dunkin' Donuts coffee waiting for him.

"Hi, Dad," said David, a big smile on his face.

"Hi, David."

"See this picture of you, Dave, you're not even a year old," I said as I showed him the card.

"That's Big Dave," Dad joked. "I'd call him Little Dave, but I might get in trouble."

We had missed Dad's sense of humor. Never in our wildest dreams could we have imagined he'd be joking and kidding with us again, after a five-year absence.

The time went way too fast at Melrose.

"There's no rush," said Harvey, our patient driver, as he saw me checking my watch.

"Thanks, Harvey, but Mom is expecting us for lunch and birthday cake back at the nursing home. They have a room all ready for us."

We stopped at Living Memorial Park for a tour. This was a deeply familiar place, where Dad had invested a lot of time and energy in developing the facilities and programs starting in 1957.

We drove past the T-bar ski lift for which he had campaigned to replace the old rope tow.

"Remember that old rope tow, Dad? When I was little you'd hang on to me and up we'd go together."

"It would almost pull your arms off," he laughed. And indeed that was true!

"The T-bar sure was an improvement," I agreed. "There's the swimming pool buried under three feet of snow, the playground, the old pond. Dad, I remember one Saturday you were plowing the pond with the Jeep and you fell through the ice. You had to be pulled out by two wreckers. The next day in the *Reformer*, there you were. Remember that?"

He nodded. "That was crazy."

Back at the nursing home, Mom welcomed us and Dad devoured his beef stroganoff.

"Wally's taking big bites," Dad carefully observed. It was true—Wally was ravenous and made short work of the bulging roast beef grinder that Mom bought for him.

He kept a close eye on Wally. I think that roast beef grinder looked pretty good to Dad, especially since his stroke left him unable to swallow many of his favorite foods.

Dad sang "Happy Birthday" to himself again, singing along with us for the entire song, with gusto and completely enjoying the experience.

After blowing out the candles, he savored his piece of chocolate éclair cake that Mom had made. I just watched him in awe and gratitude.

The Dearborn family at Howard Street in 1964.

FORTY-THREE

"I'M GOING TO GIVE YOU a bear hug," I said, when I greeted Dad near the front door of the nursing home.

"Okay, but be careful not to damage the merchandise," Dad said, still bubbling over with words and witty answers.

"Good to see you, Dad!"

"I'm glad you came. Your visits mean a lot to me."

I felt drawn to visit Dad, pure joy to sit there and listen to him. I asked questions and delighted in his bright answers. How rewarding to take him places and watch him interact with others.

"What do you want to do?" Dad asked.

"We should sing. What do you think?" I said.

"They'll think we're drunk," he joked. Later we did sing "Onward Christian Soldiers," one of Dad's favorites.

"Those books over there . . . See if there's a good one," Dad said.

"There's one on trainwrecks—that should be good."

"As long as I'm not in it."

I had my dad, as my dad, more so than I'd had him with me for years. I didn't really know how or why, but he'd come back to us. We didn't know for how long, but that didn't matter either.

I went to be in his presence and appreciate the miracle for the moment.

"I enjoy talking with you, Dad."

"I do too. We have a good time just talking."

Gerda barked.

"She needs attention," he said.

"Do you bark when you need attention?" I asked.

"Arf, arf," he said, then laughed.

We looked at an old family picture of the five of us from 1964.

"You're the best," I said.

"I try to be. I loved you children."

"We sure still miss our Debbie."

"That was a tragedy, losing her so young. She was such a lovely girl...She was so pretty. I'd give my arm and a leg to see her again."

"I know you would. So would I."

"Dad, you taught me a lot."

"What did I teach you?"

"To do what you love, be good to others, never give up, think positive, enjoy the outdoors, be active..."

"How did I teach you that?"

"By example, spending time with us..."

"Here's a picture of our old umbrella tent. I can still smell that strong canvas smell. What a struggle to put up, but we had so much fun on our vacations. I loved the Smoky Mountains National Park," I said.

"A bear came to our campsite and Aunt Ella shined her flashlight in its eyes to scare it off," he said.

"You raced me along the dunes at White Sands. It reminded us of snow. And Luray Caverns was one of our favorite stops."

"The carillon concerts beside the lake and the caves. It's fun to talk about these things."

"We had so much fun cross-country skiing in the woods all over—there were no touring centers then. Remember the day you and I went out for a quick jaunt on skis and ended up lost in the woods of Marlboro?"

"Oh, boy, that was something."

I thought back to that day…

"Let's ski Ho Chi Minh today!" I suggested. It was our favorite Marlboro College trail.

"Sounds perfect," Dad said. "What are you waxing?"

"Swix blue," I said, for it was twenty degrees, an ideal Swix blue day.

Dad wore his trademark tan corduroy knickers over long blue wool stockings, a white turtleneck neatly layered under his striped sweater, and a royal blue hat. We knew we'd heat up quickly and took care not to overdress.

We cruised along through snow-draped spruce and fir groves where others had earlier packed out the deep powder. Now, there was no one. Blood rushed to warm my extremities as muscles cried out for more oxygen. Arms and legs moved in synchronous efficient movement, propelling my long, skinny cross-country skis on the narrow trail.

After a long uphill climb, we glided to a stop and listened. No birds, no voices, nothing except my strong, thumping heartbeat to break the silence. I loved that moment, stopping after prolonged exertion when all muscles have been recruited into action. Hands and arms tingling, face glowing, toes completely warm and wiggling. Standing completely still, I felt my heart booming—contracting, pumping, ready to bound out of my chest.

Our late start didn't concern us, as we had skied this route numerous times. We'd be home in plenty of time for dinner, we had assured Mom.

"Here's our turn, Dad," I pointed out, when we came to a side trail on the left.

"No one's been there," he noted.

No tracks on the Ho Chi Minh Trail. All the more exciting for us; we'd have untracked powder for the twisty, hair-raising downhill turns on our favorite section. Dad and I negotiated the first broad turns expertly. After that, Dad waited until I successfully maneuvered the next steep, narrow section with two sharp turns before he came whooping and hollering around the same challenging bends. Our turns were not always perfectly carved, the sight not always pretty. But who was watching and who cared?

This was in the heart of the Vietnam era, the Ho Chi Minh Trail in Marlboro taking its name from the elaborate web of jungle paths, tracks, and roads that enabled troops to travel from North Vietnam, through Laos and Cambodia, all the way to Saigon during the Vietnam War. Named after the North Vietnamese leader Ho Chi Minh, the Vietnam trail network traversed rugged mountains, primeval rainforests, and dense jungles for nearly ten thousand miles, while our abbreviated Vermont version coursed through steep, undulating terrain of spruce, fir, beech, and maple groves for less than ten miles. Unlike the six months it originally took a soldier to trek the entire trail in Southeast Asia, we figured we'd breeze around our loop in a couple of hours.

We felt exhilarated after surviving the technically difficult portions without a fall. Dad and I continued on our way, completely immersed in the challenge of the twisty, powdery trail on this perfect ski day. As we reconvened after the last of the harrowing sections, I suddenly sensed the drastically dwindling daylight.

"Do you have a flashlight?" I asked.

"No," he answered slowly.

It had been a silly question. After all, we were just out for a short Sunday afternoon ski on a familiar trail. "We can make it before dark," I said. "It's not that far."

Dad and I skied with renewed intensity and sense of urgency. With our quickened, purposeful tempo, we covered a lot of ground rapidly. After about twenty minutes of pushing the pace, we stopped to evaluate.

"Shouldn't we have reached the car by now?" he asked.

"Yes, we should have."

"Nothing looks familiar."

I nodded. Why weren't we at the car? Why didn't anything look familiar? Had we been so absorbed in our kicking and gliding that we raced past a turn? Clearly, we were lost.

I pushed out thoughts of spending the night in the woods. The temperature had already dropped to the teens and would likely plummet below zero later on.

"Your mother's going to be wondering why we're not home yet." Dad was far more concerned about worrying Mom than being lost.

The fleeting idea of anyone searching for us was so completely embarrassing that I focused all my energy toward solving our dilemma. Where had we gone wrong? How far had we skied the wrong way? Would we be able to find our way out in the dark? I knew not to panic, to make a plan, and stick together.

We skied slowly and deliberately back the way we'd come. We moved just fast enough to stay warm while paying attention to every detail and searching for any familiar landmark. Everything looked the same. My eyes eventually adjusted to the waning half-moon that created long, eerie shadows and provided a little light. Even though nothing looked familiar, we continued to intently scan both sides of the trail. No time for doubt or hesitancy, nervousness, or fear.

I thought I recognized a familiar form on the right side of the trail.

"Dad!" I shouted. "Look! Over there. Isn't that the old jalopy?"

"Oh, my. It sure is," he said and breathed a sigh of relief. "Thank goodness for the old jalopy."

The distinctive top of the old junk car poked out of the snow just enough so we could recognize our old landmark. We had skied and walked past the old jalopy for years, never imagining that one day it would become our savior. We knew exactly where we were—not far from the car.

Adrenaline propelled us to the car in record time. No phones nearby, no option to call home, and no time to relax. Our relief and gratitude for arriving safely back to the car were quickly tempered by the sobering fact that we were more than an hour late for supper already which would cause Mom undue stress. We hurriedly clamped skis and poles onto the roof rack and quickly sped home to Howard Street.

"Dad, we were in hot water when we got home."

"Yes, I felt bad. There was nothing we could do."

"This is fun, hanging out with my dad."

"We're putting things together... we're on the way up."

"See you soon, Dad. Love you."

"Love you, too."

FORTY-FOUR

"I LOVE MY DAD," I said, as I greeted Dad at the nursing home on May 13th.

"I love my Donna," he replied, then laughed.

I felt thrilled to find Dad still talking. Even four months after he had awakened, we still treasured every second with him sharp and talkative. We still didn't take it for granted and had no idea how long it would last.

I gave him a big bear hug, maneuvering my way in close, as I had done for over five years. Our visit obviously meant the world to him.

On this sunny spring day, I wheeled him outside to see Wally, Gerda, and Ella. Different from our usual routine, this time we walked past our favorite mountain ash tree and visited under a gnarly, old beech tree that guarded the paved entrance road to the nursing home. Wally and I sat on the park bench while Gerda and Ella lounged at our feet, sampling the first light green sprigs of grass.

"Here's a smoothie, Dad," I said, placing a straw into the strawberry yogurt drink.

"That hits the spot. You're smart—you think of everything."

"How old are you, Dad?" I asked.

"A hundred," he replied, as he laughed heartily.

"Mom is eighty," I reminded him.

"She is? She's well-preserved... like a pickle..." Dad kidded.

He was in good spirits. We talked and talked and just enjoyed each other's company.

"Big Game Hunter," Dad said, as he pointed to Wally's T-shirt with a buck on the front."

"What did you eat when you were away bow hunting in South Dakota?" I asked.

"Squash!" Dad said and laughed, before Wally could answer. He knew Wally hated squash and loved joking with him.

Wally regaled Dad with his latest hunting stories.

"I don't know whether to believe you or not, Wally," Dad said.

"Dad, remember when we were supposed to take Wally up Wantastiquet for a *starter* hike, except we hiked Shrewsbury Peak for his first one," I reminisced about meeting Wally in 1998.

"That's a terrible one to start on," he accurately replied. Indeed, the trail rose steeply over rocky, uneven terrain to the 3720-foot-high summit. Dad had kidded with Wally that he intended to take him on a starter hike, since he hadn't been hiking much.

The afternoon passed too quickly. We extended our stay—we couldn't bear to leave. We all savored every moment of this peaceful, mild spring day.

When Dad saw me jotting a word in my notebook, he asked, "What are you writing about?"

"I'm writing about you, Dad."

"That might be a dry subject," Dad said, then laughed.

We still didn't want to leave, but we needed to head home, tough to say goodbye. We couldn't have had a more tranquil, heartening visit.

"I love you, Frank," Wally said.

"Love you too, Wally," Dad said, as we wheeled him towards the front door.

Back inside the nursing home I stooped to hug Dad goodbye and felt his strong grip that didn't want to let go.

"You always come through every time, everywhere," he said.

"I love you, Dad."

"I love you, Donna," he replied, then he blew me a kiss.

"Just come down for no reason." Dad's last words to me that sunny spring afternoon.

AND THEY WERE HIS very last words to me—ever.

The next evening we received a phone call from the nursing home—Dad was having a seizure. They always informed us, but this was devastating news to hear. Dad had talked and interacted with us as he hadn't for several years precisely because he had been free of seizure medication for four months. The thought of him being back on seizure medication distressed me.

A short while later, another call—they couldn't stop the seizure so they were taking him to the hospital.

We rushed to the hospital where my brother was already waiting. David was subdued. We hadn't located Mom—she was at a concert.

Dad breathed heavily, rapidly, laboriously—unconscious. Frightening. It was fortunate that my mom wasn't there. As difficult as it was to witness this, we held his hand and talked to him. Surely he was soothed by our familiar voices, our touch, and our presence.

The CT scan revealed significant, widespread bleeding throughout his brain.

"He's had a massive stroke. We don't expect him to live long," the doctor on call informed us.

We told Dad we were with him no matter what.

"We love you, Dad," we kept repeating. "We're with you, Dad, we're here. We love you."

Standing there in the emergency room, I felt numb.

"We're so lucky we had yesterday," Wally said, as he embraced me.

I nodded. "It was a great visit—couldn't have been better."

Yes! I could almost hear Dad saying: live each day, each moment fully. Indeed, I'd felt the urgency to pay attention to the important things, above all—to love and cherish our special ones. We had all taken the time to shower Dad with love. We treated each of our times with Dad as if they were our last. We had no regrets.

DAD DIED THREE DAYS LATER on May 17, 2009, after more than five years in the nursing home.

Amidst the enormous sense of loss and sadness was the blessing of knowing he was now liberated from paralysis, the nursing home, and the limitations of his earthly body. Dad's spirit soared free and strong, and we rose above nursing home sadness and our continual reminder of loss. We could once again feel Dad's true essence.

FORTY-FIVE

NO SIGNS. This must be it—a small, nondescript building at the end of a short driveway off a quiet country road.

Soft-spoken and reverent, Ellen greeted me. "In here."

Dad looked serene and peaceful, as if he were sleeping and would wake up any second and talk to me.

I placed one of his baseball caps on his head. "World's Best Dad," it read.

"Dear, dear, dear, dear dad. I love you," I whispered.

I wheeled his body closer to the giant furnace, pushed it into the compartment, and pressed a button to lower the door.

Breathe. Breathe. I pressed the button to start the retort.

I sat down. My pen never left the page as I tried to keep up with the flood of thoughts and emotions:

May 20.
Bye, Dad. I love you.

Goodbye to your earthly shell, your handsome, beautiful body. How fit and strong you always kept yourself. You paid attention. You did all the right things oriented toward the goal of good health to stay vibrant and able, capable and healthy till a hundred. You did all the right things in so many ways.

My brain is fuzzy and tired so I may not find the proper words to say anything in the eloquent way you deserve.

You deserve high praise and a tribute as big as the universe. Yours is a life well-lived! The stories could fill a book, there is so much to say. I will do my best to convey the essence of Frank Holt Dearborn, my precious, dear dad, and also the story of a father and a daughter who had an unbelievable bond—sharing, depth of understanding, and being there for each other.

Dad—I know you are already watching over me and all of us, looking down, smiling and talking, free of pain, discomfort, disability. I am here for you, with you, for our final earthly moments together—until your body is no more.

Who else would want to do this—to be here? No one. It's something I want to do, to go to the very end with you, Dad, in faithful service and love.

I am glad you have moved on from this earth, though I am sad to never see you again. I am sad I no longer can hold your right hand with the good strong grip. Yet I am glad you are now in a better place. You are now pure love—glowing, shining, spreading happiness, love, good cheer even further afield.

I am sad I can no longer wiggle my way in to give you a giant bear hug with your right arm squeezing me tight, your gentle kiss on my cheek. I will miss our conversations. I will never forget your voice or your words.

I will not miss going to the nursing home. Today is Wednesday, one of our usual days together. I am here at the crematory instead. The retort roars with hot fire. Hot enough—1750 degrees—to turn your body to ashes, your World's Best Dad *hat on your head for your final earthly journey.*

Hot enough to burn the faulty blood vessels in your brain, those cursed vessels that leaked and bled, that failed you over five years ago. Betrayed you when you put so much energy and effort into health—excellent health. The utmost care you took so all body parts were finely tuned to last and keep you on this earth till ninety or a hundred. To be able to continue your mission that you were so good at . . . to live and to be—love, kindness, caring, compassion. Be a role model and example of tenderness, listening, hearing people. A huge and available, loving heart that anyone who came into contact with you would feel, experience, and benefit from. You were pure love. By example you taught.

And I am the luckiest of all. The luckiest, most fortunate, triply blessed to have had you as my dad. How did I get to be so lucky?

My dearest dad, I love you forever. You are within me and around me. I will carry you with me in so many ways. You will help me, I know, to put our story into words that do justice to the amazing person that you were—the greatest I have ever known.

I thank you for always listening to me, for providing wise counsel, or just going hmmm *when that was the right thing to do. You knew just what to do.*

How grateful I am for all the adventures we talked about, pursued, and put into action. We didn't just talk and dream, we acted. We lived our dreams. We climbed to the top of so many rugged mountains. We savored each step along the way, each trillium or snow-covered fir branch, each other with the utmost appreciation and gratefulness. We felt blessed. We still are blessed for all that we have had and that we have.

Dad, I will carry on your legacy. I feel you within me strong and sure, to carry on the Dearborn tradition, with laughter, fun, and caring. Most of all love and being kind to each other, everyone.

Laughter. I will miss your laugh. You who loved to kid others and enjoy getting needled back. You knew how to entertain people with anecdotes and old Vermonter stories, how to keep them laughing and from being bored in a talk.

Yes, it's hitting me as I sit here in the crematory, listen to the roar, and see the temperature gauge at 1750 degrees. Yes, this is final. You are here no more. You are no longer with us in bodily form to touch, hear, and laugh with. I will miss you so much.

I am glad I am here for the final journey of your body. You still looked good, amazing. You looked peaceful, resting, calm. Peaceful as if you were just sleeping, resting, and would wake up any minute.

Even though you looked as if you could wake up any second, I do not wish that for you now. You have suffered enough in this earthly body. We have suffered enough with you.

Now—be gone from it—leave it behind and be free of it. Released. Be free to be pure love. Check in on me often, Dad. I love you. I will be open, listening, feeling, and waiting.

FORTY-SIX

DAD LOVED HIS first full metal-edged backcountry skis and stiffer boots that helped him carve expert turns and improve his control on difficult downhill runs. The red Karhu Pavo skis that he received for Christmas one year were just getting broken in when he had his stroke. I was glad that Dad skied on them for one full winter, sad that he didn't have the chance to clip into them for many years.

As they'd started to collect dust, Mom encouraged me to fit them to my boots and is happy they're being used. Now I ski on them and Dad travels with me on each adventure as the red skis plunge through deep, fluffy, virgin powder and glide swiftly over hard-packed, corny, spring-like snow. He would want to be along, my favorite cross-country ski partner, appreciative of striding and gliding through silent, deep woods and ever in search of a good workout and new exploration.

ELLA AND I BOUNDED out the door for a morning ski, thermometer registering a mere one degree. I pulled on my old, blue balaclava and my warmest mittens along with the usual layers.

Chickadee-dee-dee. Chickadee-dee-dee. A lone, diminutive black-capped bird greeted us. Its call faded in the distance as Ella followed Ruffed Grouse tracks in a convoluted trail—here, there, and over there.

Staccato Labrador footsteps didn't touch down on the frozen ground for long. Ella's snout burrowed deep into a deer track. What information did she gather? When did they wander by? Where were they heading?

Brrr. I pulled the balaclava up farther over my chin, inspired to move faster. The waxless red Karhus nimbly navigated the narrow path.

A dusting of snow on top of crust was all we needed to glide through cold, crackly woods in fresh morning light before the sun poked up.

Who cooks for you? Who cooks for you tooooooo?

Ella stood in classic pose—at attention—still—listening.

"Ella, it's only the silly, old Barred Owl. I don't know what he's doing out now," I told her. She relaxed.

I flew over an unintended ski jump, a little more exciting than I imagined. Skis smacked down hard on the crust beneath just as we reached the snowmobile trail. The sun's first rays glinted off Ella's shiny coffee and cream coat as she broke into full greyhound-like strides. We were just getting warmed up, bringing Dad with us.

DAD'S RED SKIS have traversed more than twenty different sections of Catamount Trail since I dusted them off.

As soon as Dad heard about the trail in 1985 he bought the first guidebook published. Together we searched for trailheads which were often hard to find. If he was leading others, he'd drive there the day before, to be sure to find it, an adventure in itself. The brand new Catamount Trail held appeal for Dad, with his love of discovering different ski trails and exploring fresh woods.

In the late 1980s the trail seemed poorly marked and not yet established in many places, in sharp contrast to today. Dad and I weren't successful in following much of the trail, abandoned our Catamount quest and stuck with our long-standing trails. How Dad would love and appreciate the Catamount as it is today!

Another morning, I skied north on section twenty-seven of the Catamount Trail and entered the trails of Craftsbury Outdoor Center, one of a motley group of twenty-six skiers out on a sunny, mild Tuesday. Conditions were marginal, grass showing through in places.

Suddenly I felt Dad's strong presence—a kind of *déjà vu*. He was vividly standing there at that intersection in the same outfit—tan knickers, blue windbreaker and navy hat—he wore twenty-one years earlier when Dad, Mom, and I had lingered at that exact spot while skiing at Craftsbury. Broad smile on his face, Dad stood there surrounded by bountiful fresh powder.

I remembered skiing ahead down a hill with a sharp turn at the bottom. I stopped and took out my camera—staged for an action shot—and waited for them to ski by. I captured them one at a time flying around the bend, wild-eyed, ski tails spread in a wide, strong snowplow—no dramatic wipeouts.

"Hang on, good job," I encouraged them as I snapped their photos. They were strong, enthusiastic cross-country skiers who never turned down an opportunity to glide through woods and across fields.

As I skied along in my quest to ski all thirty-one of the Catamount Trail sections, I felt Dad right there with me—his red Karhu skis pointing the way on section twenty-seven.

As THE RED SKIS glided along another section of the Catamount Trail, I couldn't help smile at the familiarity, even though I had never traversed this particular piece. A sizeable group of enthusiastic skiers chatted while striding along having a relaxed, fun time. I flashed back to the late 60s to one of our Sunday afternoon family cross-country ski outings when we visited and laughed, snacked often, and were just happy to be outdoors on a beautiful day. My gregarious dad would say it was a winning combination—skiing, outdoors, woods, camaraderie, conversation, snacks, exercise, and fresh air. Dad's red skis seem to seek out these gatherings.

Dad must be smiling, heartened his red skis have ventured far and wide, even hut-to-hut in Norway, weathering a blizzard, rock gardens, and river crossings. Their metal edges gripped the crusty slope tenaciously during interminable sidestepping when vertigo plagued us.

At least fifty times each winter they have journeyed through peaceful woods on voyages of exploration past rounded porcupine troughs, distinct fisher tracks, rabbit scuffles, and moose rubs. They are scratched and chipped, well-used and cherished—not collecting dust.

Dad would have strongly identified with my goal of becoming a Catamount Trail End-to-Ender and was surely with me last winter as the red skis glided and led the way on my final five sections.

FORTY-SEVEN

LONG, WOODEN PUNCHEONS carried us over some of the wettest, boggiest sections of the Long Trail into Little Rock Pond.

"Meka, do you know what this is?" I asked my niece, in the middle of a long span of logs.

"No," she replied.

"This is a *puncheon*," I said. "Your Grampa Dearborn loved these."

"A what?" she asked, perplexed.

"A puncheon! It's a bog bridge or a walkway across a muddy area. Grampa would spell the word out to someone who had never heard of it: P-U-N-C-H-E-O-N. It was one of his favorite words."

Dad loved the sound of the word and the fact that most people didn't know the word or what it meant. He quizzed hikers when he came across a puncheon—"who knows what this is?" seizing a teachable moment.

"Grampa loved puncheons so he could keep his boots dry and clean," I told her. Meka could appreciate that too.

Our happy pups, Vanella and Ella, energetically retrieved sticks and played in the icy waters of Little Black Brook. Four bubbly southbound hikers passed us, very impressed with ten-year-old Meka embarking on her first backpacking trip.

We stared, then smiled, when a young fellow breezed by wearing a skirt. A well-toned couple on their way to the Appalachian Trail's northern terminus of Mount Katahdin had already hiked for four months from Georgia. An older, bearded man hiking south stopped to talk. He told us his name—*Captain Bly*, his trail name, of course. Meka laughed.

"Meka, what's your trail name?" I said. "Everyone should have a trail name."

"What's yours?" she asked.

"*Antelope*. It started when I was leading an Outward Bound trip. Sometimes they called me *Prantelope*, short for Prancing Antelope. Ella's trail name is *Lightning*, Grammie's is *Turtle*. Grampa's was *Holt*. He just loved being called by his middle name."

After discussing all the possibilities, Meka declared her trail name—*Meaty*.

"Are you sure?" I asked.

"Yes," she was sure.

Meka expertly made her way around the mud by stepping on stones, occasionally slipping into the slimy muck where no puncheons existed.

"I hope those aren't your Sunday-best sneakers," I exclaimed.

"No, they're not."

"Have you ever tasted Indian cucumber, Meka?" I asked.

"No." She sounded skeptical.

I found a large stand of the tall, distinctive plant well off the trail, carefully dug one up, and cleaned off the pure white root.

"What do you think?" I said, handing it to her.

She took a bite. "It's good!"

"Grampa was surprised how tasty they were too!"

The sky was turning black. We looked at each other, sensed the imminent rain, and picked up our pace.

Just past the Lula Tye Shelter, sprinkles started. We raced to claim a tent platform at the Little Rock Pond Tenting Area where some archeologists were just finishing lunch. An aggressive dog snarled at Vanella and Ella.

"Dog, come here," its owner called. The dog didn't obey. We weren't impressed and veered off the trail, giving the snarly mutt named Sausage a wide berth.

We were on a mission to get our tent set up before it rained any harder. I set up the green tarp above our tent platform while Meka quickly assembled the poles. Together we pushed the poles through their sleeves and into the correct grommets, flung the fly over the top, and secured it in place. *Voila*—our home for the night.

"Meka, you go in first, just leave your sneakers in the vestibule. I'll hand the sleeping bags in to you and you can get our beds set up."

I quickly inflated sleeping pads, threw warm clothes into the tent, and dried the dogs off as the rain intensified—much more than sprinkles.

"I'm sending the dogs in now," I warned Meka.

Our two-year-old dogs dashed into the tent, immediately curled up, fast asleep in seconds.

"I'm coming in. I found the cards," I said.

We counted the seconds between lightning and thunder as the storm raged over us. It circled away, only to return multiple times. We all snuggled close together on our sleeping pads, dogs oblivious to the storm. When the storm moved more than five miles away, we played the card game, War, for two and a half hours which helped divert our attention from the pouring rain.

When the skies cleared, we and the dogs floated and paddled in the picturesque pond.

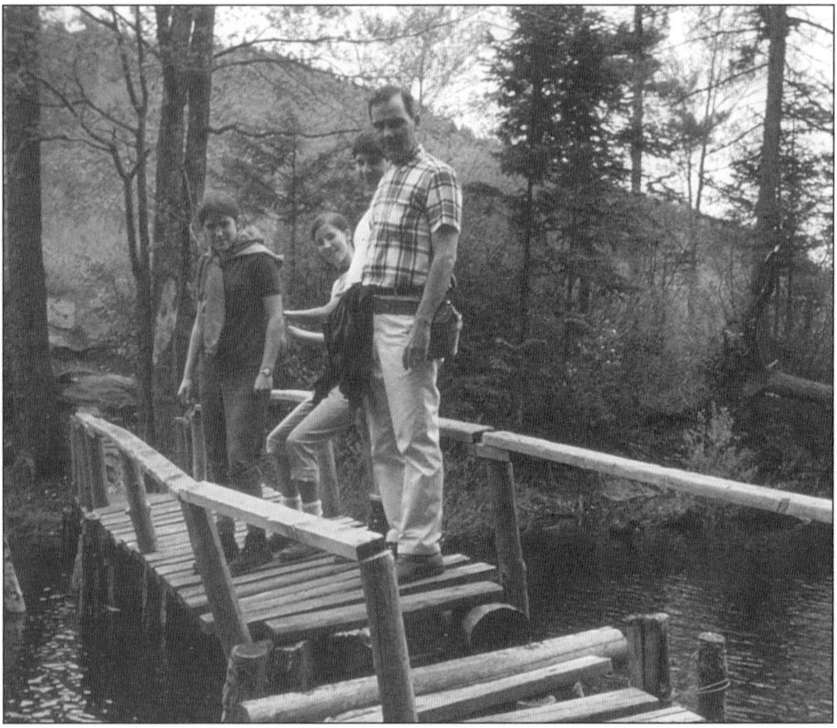

Crossing the old bridge to the island in Little Rock Pond.

"There used to be a shelter on that little island over there," I said and pointed across the pond. "I went there when I was your age. I loved it."

"Can we go there?" Meka asked.

"No, the bridge is gone. We'd have to swim there."

Though this was Meka's first time, it was familiar territory for me—almost fifty years of history. In the 1960s our family hiked the two miles into Little Rock Pond on Sunday afternoon outings after church with other families. Dad expertly led the way to the west side of the pond across a bridge to Little Rock Pond Shelter on the small island. What a perfect place to catch polliwogs and skip rocks across the pond. Sometimes we made a fire in the fire pit next to the small lean-to and

A banner day on the summit of Green Mountain near Danby, Vermont.

roasted hot dogs. We had a ball! Though the shelter is long gone, first relocated off the island to a spot just north of the pond in 1972 and now absent, vivid memories remain.

I gazed up at the cliffs that overlook the pond and envisioned Dad sitting down at the dramatic viewpoint eating his sandwich. Dad and Mom joined Wally and me many times on the seven-mile loop past the pond, up and over Green Mountain, sometimes with chainsaw and loppers on our way to perform trailwork on our adopted trail—the Green Mountain Trail.

Meka and I had macaroni and cheese for supper. It hit the spot. Rare pieces of dry wood and some crucial birch bark enabled us to have just enough fire to roast marshmallows for s'mores.

No one around on a peaceful midweek Tuesday evening in early July, I sprinkled some of Dad's ashes next to his favorite puncheons around Little Rock Pond.

ON OUR NEXT BACKPACKING TRIP, Meka and I hiked to Griffith Lake—the perfect place for a kid. After we set up our tent, Meka raced with Vanella and Ella over a long string of puncheons near the lake. Ninety-five, she counted. The next series was a record-breaking 130 in a row. Dad had counted those same ones, with identical results, just like he counted the cars in trains.

No matter where I'm hiking, whenever I traverse puncheons I can't help think, "Dad would love this." He was curious how workers transported materials into particularly remote locations. He'd appreciate the craftsmanship—the sill and stringers fit just so—and wonder who constructed the handy log walkway. Was it level or sloping, dilapidated or new? He'd warn of slippery footing and steer clear of dangerously-protruding spikes.

I thought of Dad as I hiked the Stratton Pond Trail across an elevated wooden pathway in the middle of nowhere . . . over extensive, expertly-crafted puncheons that kept my boots clean and dry. No wonder Dad had a penchant for puncheons.

FORTY-EIGHT

COLD, CRISP AIR greeted Ella, me, and my hiking buddies, Diane and Dagny, as we hoisted our packs at the Stony Brook trailhead. With hard rain all night, it was no surprise there was a dusting of snow and it felt like mid-winter even in early December. What a sharp contrast to the previous day when we had hiked in the clouds with temperatures in the 40s and not a trace of snow, even at Cabot's 4167-foot summit. The weather had changed almost hourly since we'd left home, far more unsettled than we anticipated. Winds howled from the west, unusually strong at the trailhead.

We had our sights on the 4049-foot summit of Mount Moriah, in our quest to help Dagny reach the top of all forty-eight White Mountain four thousand footers. This would be number forty-two for her, our ninth as a team in two months. I had my doubts about reaching the summit, almost from the start. Since we had stayed overnight in Gorham after our hike up Cabot the day before, we were already in the heart of the White Mountains. Why not at least give it a shot?

Looking regal in her striking red coat, Ella reveled in the fresh powder that grew deeper as we hiked higher.

"Are your feet warm?" I asked Diane. Did we have boots warm enough for these conditions?

"They're okay so far," she answered.

"How are your fingers?" I asked Dagny. Dagny's hands seemed susceptible to the cold. The temperature registered almost thirty degrees colder than the previous day.

"They're fine," she replied.

We had enough extra layers, plenty of snacks, lunch, and hot tea. Since we hadn't anticipated this much snow and wind, goggles had not yet made it onto our radar or into our packs.

As we hiked higher, winds predictably grew stronger, even in the protection of the hardwoods which transitioned to spruce and fir. Snow piled up— four inches deep, then six. I anticipated the exposed ledges to come, remembering them from a winter hike two years prior. We'd get blown flat! Yet as long as some trees sheltered us, why not continue to trudge up the mountain and enjoy the journey.

Red berries skittered across the snow and landed at my feet. Mountain ash berries—I quickly identified.

Instantly I thought of Dad and our mountain ash tree in front of the nursing home, our dear friend that had shaded us in summer and rained down orange-red berries in the fall. Wally and I, with our two Labradors, sat beneath our mountain ash tree when we had visited Dad in all seasons for more than five years. Showy, white flowers blossomed in the spring. Dull, dark green leaves turned orange, purple, and fiery red in autumn, while clusters of berries hung on through the winter. We felt a special kinship with that tree, and when Dad died we planted our own mountain ash tree in our front yard in memory of him. Wally calls the tree "Frank."

I picked up a cluster of berries and felt Dad's strong presence. There was no doubt he was watching over me, looking out for us. Ahhh... Thank you, Dad.

I felt calm and reassured. I knew for certain we'd make smart decisions with safety foremost and could ascend a little higher, one step at a time.

We reached the Carter-Moriah Trail junction, intersecting the spectacular ridge trail at three thousand feet of elevation—a thousand yet to climb.

We hiked across the first ledge and had a tough time remaining upright in winds I estimated at fifty to sixty miles per hour. Branches swayed violently in the stronger winds, much more challenging conditions than we'd imagined.

As we struggled, Ella trotted along in her typical fashion, sniffing and exploring as usual, generally unaffected by the wind due to her lower, compact stance.

Microspikes on! We needed traction. Snow piled up deeper and winds gusted higher. We crouched down to withstand the blasts and quickly rushed back into the cover of trees. Whew, this is something!

Diane's microspikes fit poorly, triggering words of frustration.

"Everybody okay?" I checked in with our team. "Go a little farther? To the next point?" They nodded.

Drink, snack, plug along. Deep drifts slowed us down, as we reached the five-hour mark of ascending. We'd soon need to turn around, summit or not.

Then we saw a sign—"Mt. Moriah 0.1 mile." We made it—nothing short of a miracle.

We crouched low and managed a couple of summit photos.

"Let's get out of here!" I shouted to be heard above the roar.

Howling wind and cold temperatures hurried us along. What a relief to get past all the exposed ledges to lower elevations and back to mountain ash berries. No doubt, Dad was with us in spirit.

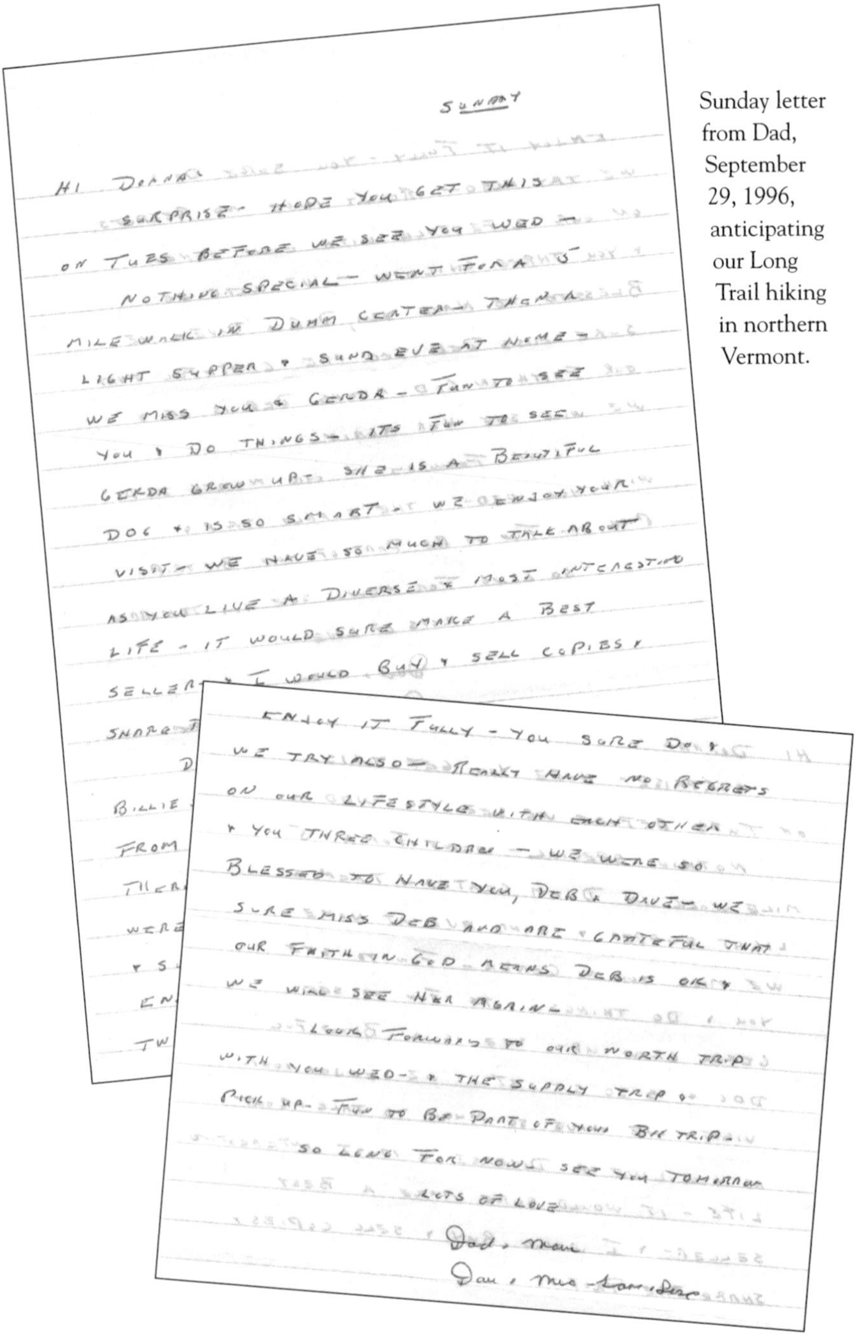

Sunday letter from Dad, September 29, 1996, anticipating our Long Trail hiking in northern Vermont.

FORTY-NINE

SIXTEEN STRONG backcountry skiers toured south on the Catamount Trail from Jay Pass on a cold, blustery February day in over forty inches of fresh powder. Our snow prayers had been more than answered with a monster storm that dumped prodigious amounts of snow throughout northern New England. Trail breaking was tediously slow, even with many of us trading off in the lead. We struggled to stay warm in the ten-degree air.

Not long after leaving the pass I glanced over my right shoulder to see majestic Jay Peak cloaked in white, flanked by Big Jay and Little Jay.

A vivid memory brought a smile to my face…

MY ONE-YEAR-OLD YELLOW LAB, Gerda, and I hiked south toward Shooting Star Shelter on the Long Trail in northern Vermont on the first day of our six-day backpacking trip.

My parents, Gerda, and I had driven four hours from Brattleboro so my dad could hike his final section of the Long Trail up and over Carleton Mountain to the Canadian border. After twenty-five years of section hikes and day trips, Dad couldn't have had a better day to complete the 272-mile-long path—clear, sunny, sixty degrees. We had celebrated amidst the brilliant reds and yellows of peak foliage surrounding border markers that dotted the international boundary swath, retraced our route to their car, and then my parents drove to the Brick House B&B to spend the night in Irasburg. The following day they would hike north from Jay Pass to meet Gerda and me at the summit of Jay Peak as we hiked south.

We hadn't counted on the storm that blew in that night. By morning the temperature was thirty degrees and falling, stretching the limits of my old goose down sleeping bag. Gerda—my sixty pound white beauty—snuggled in as close as she could get.

Snow, hail, and high winds replaced rain in the night. The next day Gerda and I sped along to stay warm and after almost four hours reached the ski trails of Jay. Only October 3rd, it felt like the dead of winter! Snow obscured white trail markers; rime ice coated signs and branches. Thank goodness for Gerda's blue pack, otherwise she would have blended right into the wintry scene.

"Gerda, find the trail," I instructed her. And she did. I was relieved to see the few white markers I could discern.

Poor Gerda's eyelids iced over, her whiskers froze solid. The wind blew stronger and snow piled higher as we reached the tram house.

We found the summit completely socked in—brutal. Gerda and I had little choice, so we made our way across the exposed, icy, rocky top. No views, no need to linger in this inhospitable spot. There's no way Dad and Mom are going to hike up here in these conditions, I thought. I hoped they had lingered longer at their B&B.

The trail dropped steeply off the summit. When I looked ahead I saw something out of place—a piece of paper on the end of a twig wavering in the wind. A note for me—written on an envelope—in my mom's handwriting!

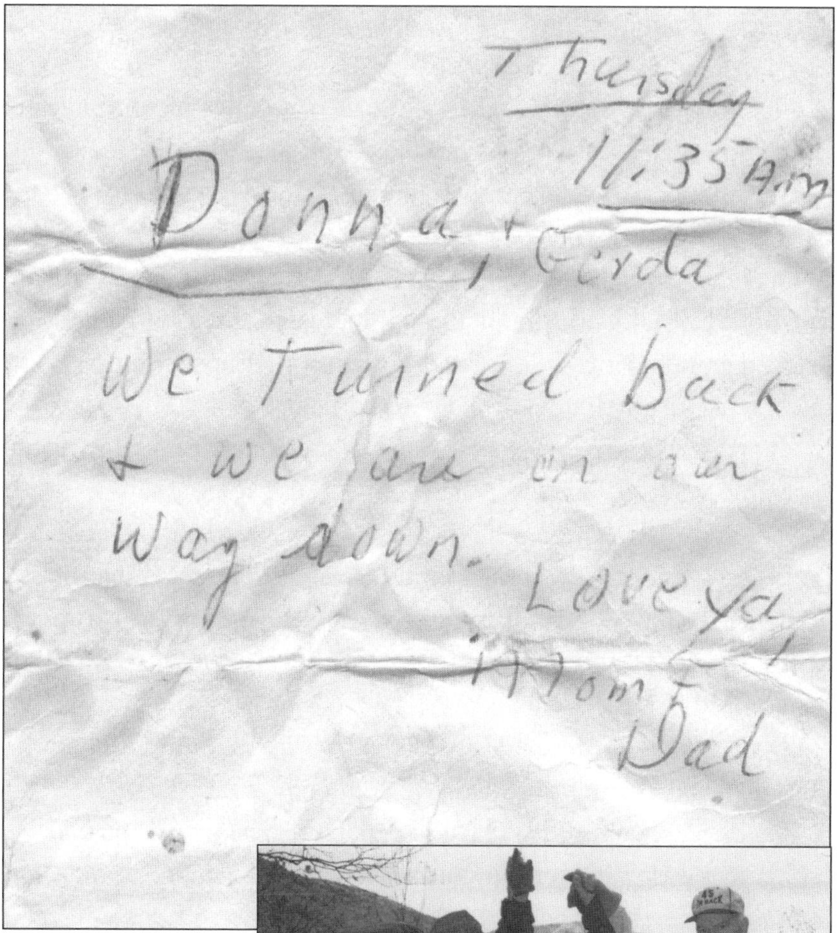

Thursday
11:35 A.m.
Donna, + Gerda
We Turned back
+ we are on our
way down. Love ya!
Mom + Dad

A piece of paper on the end of a twig, wavering in the wind…a note for me!

Good to see you! Happy reunion south of Jay Peak on the Long Trail.

It said: "Donna, Thursday 11:35 am, we turned back and are on our way down. Love ya, Mom & Dad."

I looked at my watch—11:48—thirteen minutes after Mom had written the note. How far away would they be?

"Woo hooooo," I yelled in their direction, the wind muting my message. How would anyone be able to hear my call?

"Woo hoooooo," came the reply I knew was my mother's distinctive two-note call. Not wasting a second, Gerda sprinted off to find her beloved grandparents. I descended slowly on the slippery rocks, eventually reuniting with my worried parents.

"Wow! Can you believe these conditions? Are you warm enough?" I asked.

"That's why we turned around! We're not prepared for winter conditions yet—it's only the first week in October!" They had improvised with an extra layer and gloves that they kept stashed in their trunk.

"I love your note! I saw a piece of paper hanging on a branch—and it was for me!" I exclaimed.

"I can't believe I found a little envelope in my fanny pack and a pen…so cold I could barely write," Mom said.

"We didn't know if you would see it or if it would blow off," Dad told me.

"Wow, I wasn't expecting you to make it up this high," I said. "I'm impressed."

"We brought you a muffin from the B&B, but let's get down at least a little bit out of this wind before we take a break," Dad said. "We are sooooo glad to see you."

We shared our harrowing morning stories as we steadily descended to Jay Pass.

FOR FIVE HOURS as I skied south on the Catamount Trail, I looked back at the Jays profiled against the deep blue February sky, warmed by the memories of that October day.

FIFTY

March 7, 2011

Dad,

I can see why Mount Abraham remained one of your favorite peaks, why you reluctantly left the top last time you were there. I can see us—Gerda, you, and me—lingering on the open, flat summit, appreciating the 360-degree panorama in the heart of Vermont for a few extra moments, before descending to catch Mom on that mid-October day.

You and Mom both remarked that the mountain had gotten steeper since the previous time you summited. After we stopped at Battell Shelter for a snack, we scaled the steep, rocky pitches over ledges that did seem vertical at times.

As I ascended the very same pitch on snowshoes, I could hear your words, accompanied by laughter. Even though ten years had passed since our hike, I felt you climbing with me to the snowy mountaintop.

What a perfect day for your ashes to fly north, just windy enough to carry them over nearby Mount Ellen, all the way to distinctive, white-capped Camel's Hump and other familiar places along the Long Trail. Dad, you've walked every inch of it—nearly 120 miles to the Canadian border and more than 150 miles that extend to the Massachusetts border. Standing on Abe, I couldn't help recall our rigorous dayhikes and overnight adventures, how we helped each other become End-to-Enders—you, Mom, and I.

You, too, would have savored the outstanding views on this early March day: to the east, Mount Washington and the Presidentials where we braved white-out conditions, savored anniversary dinners, and were entranced by Northern Lights; to the west, Lake Champlain and the Adirondacks; to the south, the ski trails of Killington. More memories surged—climbing the Bucklin Trail up the steep, rock gully past Cooper Lodge to the summit ledges of Vermont's second highest peak—flies and all.

I opened the container. Your ashes soared as you once soared over this mountain in a glider—suspended in the air with a bird's eye view, free and quiet.

Miss you, Dad.

Love you, Donna

FIFTY-ONE

April 21, 2012

Dear Dad,

Some of your ashes just took flight in the rarified Himalayan air, carried across stark glacial moraine toward the sharp-topped peak of Ama Dablam that dominates the eastern sky. They're soaring to the flanks and summits of surrounding peaks and integrating into the soil of this rugged landscape.

Your ashes have hitched a ride in my pack for seventeen days as I trekked through remote Sherpa villages, alongside neatly-terraced fields, now beneath the Himalayan giants.

It's day eighteen and I'm happily alone, well off the beaten path in a majestic spot. My steps are slow this day, a chance for solitude and reflection, so I merely gaze—no need to climb—the mere 17,200-foot "hill" of Awi Peak above.

I feel only gratitude in realizing this long-held dream of experiencing the mountains and culture of Nepal.

You'd be in awe, Dad, as I am, mouth agape at the ruggedly-chiseled peaks. Climbing, breathing, resting, gazing, ever-gazing. Move slowly, deliberately, walk like a yak, *my guide always says.*

At times I count to fifty or a hundred, adopting your strategy to manage a certain incline, as a distraction from fatigue or breathlessness, more often simply to feel your presence.

What would you think if you were here? No Dunkin' Donuts coffee to start your day! Of course you'd make do, though not without some eyebrow-raising and smiles. What's this? *you might ask. Water buffalo? Yak? I know you'd sample everything at least once. Never a fussy eater, you always ate everything! True to form, you'd clean your plate as you stocked up on the traditional dal bhat. You'd rejoice at the apple pie and apple pancakes. I'd certainly share my stash of chocolates with you.*

Most of all, you'd love visiting with the Nepali people, appreciate their welcoming nature and generous hospitality. You'd adore the curious children, some shy about practicing their English, others busy at play, content with simple toys.

Sometimes Namaste *might be the only word spoken, as you'd bow with palms together in greeting. Even so, communication would be rich. They'd be drawn to your kind face and open heart.*

You'd notice the vast differences in resources and opportunities as our disparate worlds intersected, yet you'd focus on our similarities and feel a strong kinship with these happy, fun-loving people.

Dad, you'd savor all the moments.

Why have I bothered to carry your ashes all this way, since you're with me anyway—every day? I talk to you, seek your guidance, and feel your strong presence, but I like knowing there is a tangible piece of you here for eternity amidst not only some of the world's highest mountains but also the kind and generous Sherpa people—that your travel horizons have expanded to the awe-inspiring Khumbu region of Nepal.

Love, Donna

FIFTY-TWO

IN LOVING MEMORY OF
FRANK HOLT DEARBORN
1928–2009
"THERE IS ONLY ONE SUCCESS—
TO BE ABLE TO SPEND YOUR LIFE IN YOUR OWN WAY"
C. MORLEY

THIS QUOTE is engraved on a granite bench along the Winnipesaukee River Trail in Dad's hometown of Franklin, New Hampshire. Dad's bench sits on a picturesque promontory amongst giant oaks at a bend overlooking the churning river.

The spot is ideal, appropriate for many reasons—elements of history, trains, recreation, and nature—in the town where Dad grew up.

As I sat on Dad's bench I imagined life in the 1800s and early 1900s, sheep farmers settling the area, woolen mills springing up along the banks of the river powered by water, the railroad line bringing

Dad's bench beneath stately oaks on the Winnipesaukee River Trail
in Franklin, New Hampshire.

raw materials to the mills and transporting the manufactured goods to markets in Boston and New York—how different the scene back then.

Trains used to pass within inches of where Dad's bench sits. Remnants of the old railroad tracks can be found nearby—spikes, rails, and pieces of old ties. Only a few miles from where Dad grew up, I imagine some of the same trains chugged past his house on the Boston and Maine Line, the trains that fascinated him as a boy. Sulphite Bridge, with its unique upside-down design, "the only deck-covered railroad bridge in the country," still stands not far from Dad's bench.

The Winnipesaukee River now freely races over rocks through the narrow valley near downtown Franklin, the woolen mills long since closed. The rail line became defunct in 1973. But the end of the mill industry provided an opening for a different use of the old railroad bed.

Dad would certainly appreciate and applaud Franklin residents who had the foresight to not only envision the creation of this recreational path from an old rail bed, but also the drive and perseverance to apply for grants, raise the necessary funds, and see this impressive project to fruition. The river and the old rail bed are once more the scene of activity in Franklin, tying communities together through this path.

How perfect that Dad's bench sits beside a well-used recreation path. Walkers, bikers, runners, and cross-country skiers pass by, enjoying lifetime sports, staying active, and breathing fresh air in a beautiful setting. Down below, whitewater kayakers maneuver through Class III rapids on their way to Zippy's Final Plunge, a Class IV challenge just downstream. Kingfishers flit and wood ducks float. Nearby cattail wetlands and a beaver pond attract Red-winged Blackbirds and Song Sparrows. Purple flowering raspberry and touch-me-not proliferate at trail's edge. It's a tranquil, peaceful spot, a place we can go to sit, reflect, and remember Dad. We're comforted just knowing it's there.

The Winnipesaukee River Trail is now 5.1 miles long. Dad would endorse the long-term vision for this trail to reach all the way from Lebanon to Meredith, connecting with other existing trails to cover approximately eighty-five miles—many regional spurs also in the works. I envision how excited he'd be as he found trailheads and explored the path on foot and by bicycle.

"There is only one success—to be able to spend your life in your own way." Dad loved this quotation by the American poet Christopher Morley and felt grateful he had been able to do just that—spend his life in his own way.

Every year, thousands of recreators amble past Dad's bench. No doubt, some pause alongside, others take a break and sit on it. Maybe they ponder this favorite quote of Dad's and perhaps wonder who was this Frank Holt Dearborn.

to be frank and earnest . . .

By Frank Dearborn and Ernie Hoffman, Co-Sports Editors

A whole week has gone by since the birth of our column and as yet there hasn't been any burning of its writers in effigy nor any throwing of rotten eggs and tomatoes. As neophytes to this game of sports writing, we hope these signs mean somewhat the same as the old saying, "No news is good news." And so we feel brave enough to warm up the typewriter for a second trip. But just a bit of repetition from last week's column . . . . we do welcome and encourage comments, material, and suggestions you fellows may have to offer. And if you are one of the few Massasoit tribe members who can afford to buy rotten eggs and tomatoes, we even welcome those too if they're legitimately aimed.

Station WSRB is planning to broadcast all of the Springfield College varsity baseball games played here on our own Berry Field, and is also hoping to broadcast a few of the big "away" games. It looks as though this year's version of the Allenmen is really going to get the backing of the student body, and this announcement by Station WSRB is a great step toward promoting more interest in the team.

Without a doubt, the boys over in the radio station are giving this campus that certain twentieth century touch. Might even make us a bit lazy after awhile. Just think of it . . . don't even have to rise from our usual horizontal positions anymore. Just flick on the radio, tune in on the game, relax with a copy of *Don Quixote* in one hand and a bottle of Coca-Cola in the other (see ad on page 6) and listen to the radio announcer go through the excruciating task of filling up the usual lags in a baseball game. It'll probably sound something like this:

"Springfield's pitcher Bert Beebump picks up the resin bag. He rubs it up. Wipes his forehead with his sleeve. Bert sure looks as though he's working up a good sweat out there today. Yep, there's no doubt he's working up a good sweat today. I can actually see the beads of perspiration falling from his forehead. By golly, it's hot out here this afternoon. Weatherman says it's around 90. The people in the stands here at Berry Field are hot too . . . attendance is good today. About 20 students, 1 reporter from THE STUDENT and 10 stray dogs. But Bert isn't letting this tense crowd bother him. He's played before big crowds many times in the past. Bert stands a good 6-3, weighs 210, dates a girl from Bay Path and has a mole on his left shoulder. Bert looks over his shoulder now. Brushes his ear. Scratches his ribs. Burps twice and here comes his first pitch . . . ball one! Springfield's pitcher Bert Beebump picks up the resin . . . ."

"To Be Frank and Earnest"—Dad and Ernie's second sports column in the Springfield College *Student*, April 13, 1951.

FIFTY-THREE

"TO BE FRANK AND EARNEST." I loved the name of the sports column Dad wrote with his co-worker for his college newspaper.

"Really, Dad? Your co-sports editor was named Ernest?" I kidded him.

"Yes, Ernie Hoffman."

It intrigued me, yet for a long time I knew very little—except that Dad loved covering the sports beat, traveled overnight to many of the away games, and enjoyed sitting in the press box at UNH where he ate fried chicken at halftime and wrote up the game later.

Finally one day I took the time to find out more about "To Be Frank and Earnest," having no idea how many columns Dad and Ernie had written—only determination to find out.

I contacted Jeff Monseau at Springfield College Archives and soon after I sat in a comfortable basement room at a large table piled high with volumes of old S.C. *Student* newspapers. I started with Dad's senior year. Bingo—I found one! And then another. I had struck gold. The columns captured my attention and I soaked up every word of all fourteen entertaining pieces that Dad and Ernie wrote between April 1951 and March 1952.

> Wouldn't it be wonderful to be able to approach the equipment room window down in the West Gym basement without being made to feel that you are a concentration camp prisoner begging for rations or a lowly army private pleading with a cranky supply sergeant for clothes that fit?
>
> We all know that Andy is an institution here at Springfield and well he should be for all his years of service. But just because someone is an institution doesn't make him impeccable and beyond all reproach. How about a little smile down there once in a while, Andy? All we ask for are clean towels and equipment, not the Hope diamond or other precious minerals which you evidently feel you possess in the equipment room (The *Student*, May 11, 1951).

> Old Man Field House certainly witnessed a dichotomy in basketball talent during the past week's activities on the Arena hoopgrounds. A week ago Thursday, Holy Cross and the Maroons performed in the style befitting a royal performance before a queen. And then just two nights later the Tufts Jumbos and the Maroons displayed a brand of basketball befitting a lunchtime pickup game at the Fulton Fish Market... Oh, never mind, let's just pass it off as being a bad dream or something. The evening's one bright spot, however, Al Schutts' perfectly executed over the shoulder passoff in the bucket to Larry McClements breaking off the post. The play was so exceptional that it even woke up some of the spectators (The *Student*, February 22, 1952).

I felt Dad's presence, his humor, and his voice. I had found another piece of Dad—something tangible from sixty years ago.

Disappointed that I couldn't share my find with Dad, as he had been gone for more than three years by then, I wondered about Ernie Hoffman. Was he still alive? Could I find him? My initial search revealed hundreds of Ernest Hoffmans. I decided to call the Springfield College Alumni Office the next morning, but one last attempt led me to the class page for the S.C. Class of 1952 which had been updated with twenty-nine names and six e-mail addresses because of their recent 60th reunion. The e-mail address for Ernie Hoffman caught my eye and I sent a message right away, late that night:

> *Hello—I'm trying to reach* Mr. *Ernie Hoffman, class of '52 Springfield College, who was co-sports editor for the Springfield Student in 1951-52 with Frank Dearborn.*
>
> *I'm Frank's daughter, Donna Dearborn. I just read fourteen of your sports columns,* To Be Frank and Earnest. *If you are the right one, I'd love to hear from you! Thanks so much!*

In the morning I received a wonderful e-mail back!

> *Dear Donna—I was thrilled to get your e-mail. Yes, I am the Ernie Hoffman who was co-sports editor with your Dad. I've attended four alumni reunions (35th, 40th, 45th, and 60th in June 2012) and had always hoped that I'd see Frank. I was saddened to see his class photo on a poster board with 156+ classmates who have departed our thinning ranks. Frank and I created the column title way before the Frank and Ernest cartoon. I would like to visit with you over the phone and learn more about Frank's life and family. Wow—you've made this a wonderful*

evening as I checked my e-mails one more time before retiring!
Warmest regards, Ernie Hoffman

I HAD FOUND THE OTHER HALF of "To Be Frank and Earnest," alive and well. I felt surprised and elated to connect with a special Springfield College classmate of Dad's, a collaborator, a friend.

We had a phone conversation soon after, and I found Ernie to be a delightful man who reminded me of Dad—with similar values, style, interests, a *company man* who stuck with the same job for over thirty years as Dad had—the same vintage, same age. He told me he had been part of a writing group for fifteen years and had published a book of reminiscences for family and friends—*All My Pinup Girls Are Dying*. When I read the loaner copy he sent me, I realized even more from his well-told stories how he and Dad would have had a grand time reconnecting later in their careers or in retirement, as they had so much in common and would have had a lot to talk about. It's a shame that Dad had attended the two reunions (their 25th and 50th) that Ernie hadn't, all the more precious that I had connected with Ernie.

FINDING THE SPORTS COLUMNS and Dad's co-editor was part of a larger endeavor to remember Dad—his qualities and how he lived—inspired in part by the sadness and despair I felt visiting him in the nursing home.

Writing about Dad raised my spirits, shifting the focus from despair to gratitude. Remembering and telling stories of our Long Trail hiking adventures, birthday ski trips, and memorable train rides helped keep those memories alive, as his strokes and seizures began to erase the man I'd known. Consistent with Dad's philosophy, I attempted to accentuate the positive and reflect on the blessings of our family. The stories transported me back to simple times of laughter, fun, appreciation, and love.

Frank Holt Dearborn was truly a busy man with a demanding job as recreation director, but we three kids always felt we were the most important thing in the world to him. He unwaveringly gave us the gift of himself: his time, attention, support, and unconditional love. Kids flocked to Dad and wished they had him as their father. Not many fathers were like him. We knew we had won the jackpot!

Every Sunday I was the lucky recipient of a weekly epistle and reminder—"you are loved." How fortunate I was to have his kind, wise, guiding hand throughout my life—truly blessed to be his daughter. While I will never stop missing Dad, I am comforted by these memories of a great man who lives on in smiles, hugs, and laughter—puncheons, train whistles, and mountain ash berries red against the snow.

Frank Holt Dearborn in his Brattleboro Recreation Department office in 1977.

TRIBUTES TO FRANK HOLT DEARBORN

"Frank was an exceptional human being...an approachable man of vigor and integrity, a wonderful role model for the youth and adults of our community, a generous volunteer, and an objective group moderator...a man of peace for certain."

—Karen Davis, Letter Box, *Brattleboro Reformer* (October 2, 2010)

"Frank was truly an outstanding Superintendent of Parks and Recreation and a role model for me as a professional. I can honestly say that during his era he was one of the best there was."

—George Plumb, Letter Box, *Brattleboro Reformer* (October 2, 2010)

"Thousands of Brattleboro residents remember Dearborn fondly for the way he cared about everyone he came into contact with. Brattleboro is a better place to live, thanks to the spirit and foresight that helped create Living Memorial Park and the Gibson-Aiken Center. Frank Dearborn forged that spirit and foresight into a priceless community resource. As someone who truly loved life and living, he more than lived up to the words on the plaque at the park he helped shape and that townspeople will enjoy for years to come."

—Editorial, *Brattleboro Reformer* (May 20, 2009)

"Frank Dearborn is the 'Dean of Recreation of Vermont,' one who is truly a giant in the leisure services profession. Frank has a record of service to his profession that is difficult to match. He is the 'professional's professional.' There are few like him."

—Vermont Recreation and Parks Association newsletter (1989)

"Your record of achievement in Brattleboro is well documented, but few people recognize the contributions you have made to improved recreation throughout your state, the New England District and across the country. You have faithfully attended educational meetings, conferences, and workshops and contributed solid, down-to-earth usable information at each. You have the ability to analyze a problem, study its pros and cons and offer suggestions for its solution. You do this with dignity, unswayed by emotion, so that listeners respect your words. Frank, you lead by example. All those young people who have worked under you and gone on to successful careers can attest to that.

—Wink Tapply, retired, Community Recreation Services,
State of New Hampshire (May 12, 1990)

"It seems just like yesterday that two young men came to Vermont to pursue their careers. It's been a pleasure for me to have known you all this time. You have been nothing but inspirational to your fellow recreators. You have lived a good Christian life, giving much of yourself."

—Jeff Cioffredi, Superintendent of Recreation and Parks,
City of Rutland, Vermont (May 8, 1990)

"You will surely be missed by both the Town of Brattleboro and your colleagues, as you have inspired us to strive for the professional excellence that you have achieved. I have always, personally and professionally, looked up to you with the utmost respect and have enjoyed learning from you. You have been one of the few great professionals who has truly been an inspiration to me."

—Gwen Kermode, Natick Recreation and Human Services,
Natick, Massachusetts (April 25, 1990)

"There is one word that briefly best describes Frank Dearborn. That word is 'great,' and we mean great in the best and complete sense of the word."

—John Madden, former pastor of First Baptist Church,
Brattleboro (May 31, 2009)

ABOUT THE AUTHOR

DONNA DEARBORN grew up in an active family in Brattleboro, Vermont, where her adventurous spirit and love of the outdoors emerged at an early age. She received a Bachelor's Degree in Math and Environmental Science from Springfield College, and Master's Degrees in Exercise Physiology and Biochemistry from Montana State University and Dartmouth College.

Donna has been an English teacher in Korea, Outward Bound wilderness instructor, fitness director, algebra and trigonometry teacher, hut warden in New Zealand, ski instructor, director of a Human Performance Lab, tennis pro, tax preparer, and field hockey coach. Her story "A Well-Guarded Fort—Escape Not Guaranteed" was recently published in *Peak Experiences—Danger, Death, and Daring in the Northeast*, edited by Carol Stone White.

She continues to hike, canoe, ski, kayak, and carry on the legacy of her father who was eternally curious to discover what was around the next bend. She has trekked the hill tribe country of northern Thailand, hiked and skied hut-to-hut in Norway, built trails and backpacked in Alaska, sea kayaked in Newfoundland, gone scuba diving on the Great Barrier Reef in Australia, and explored southern Patagonia. While still a vagabond at heart, she's happily settled in the familiar, rolling green hills of Vermont with her husband, Wally, and yellow Labs, Ella and Eva.